D1578290

Weymouth College
Learning for Life

Library
Tel: 208820
This item to be returned on or bef
date stamped b

Tory Wars

Tory Wars

Conservatives in Crisis

Simon Walters

Politico's
PUBLISHING

First published in Great Britain 2001
by Politico's Publishing
8 Artillery Row
Westminster
London
SW1P 1RZ

www.politicos.co.uk/publishing

Copyright © Simon Walters 2001

A catalogue record of this book is available from the British Library.

ISBN 1 84275 026 7

Printed and bound in Great Britain by Creative Print and Design

Contents

To Kay and Arthur

Preface

It is the constitutional duty of Her Majesty's Loyal Opposition to oppose the Government of the day. But long before polling day in June 2001, William Hague's divided and disloyal Conservative army knew they had little chance of defeating Tony Blair's rampant New Model Labour Party.

Unable to beat the enemy, the Tories turned their fire on each other. The result was a second successive landslide victory for Labour which forced Hague to resign and led to a bitterly fought leadership election eventually won by Iain Duncan Smith.

Before the former Scots Guards Captain can think of vanquishing Tony Blair, he must bring peace to his own party's warring factions. Only then will it become clear whether the Conservative party is in terminal decline or whether it can regroup and relive past glories. This book examines the policies and personalities, the tensions and tantrums that condemned William Hague to becoming the first Conservative leader for nearly a century not to become Prime Minister. It attempts to explain what went wrong and why.

I am indebted to the many people great and small in the Conservative Party who have helped shed light on some of the extraordinary events that went on behind the scenes.

I would like to thank Iain Dale, Sean Magee and John Berry at Politico's for their support; Martin Northrop, Scott Fannen, Liz Cocks, Tom Bernard and John Rubinstein for their help; and my wife and family for their forbearance.

Simon Walters
September 2001

1   Endgame

'Where was Jeb Bush when I needed him?'
William Hague, 8 June 2001

William Hague and wife Ffion arrived at Conservative Central Office in Smith Square, Westminster, shortly before 7 a.m. on 8 June 2001, to be greeted by party chairman Michael Ancram and more than fifty Tory party workers.

There was also an uninvited welcoming party. On one side was a William Hague lookalike posing for pictures, and a bookie with a chalk-board marking up odds on the next Conservative leader; on the other, an autograph hunter and two weirdo protesters; and behind Hague sounded the hooting of a Labour battle bus on a victorious drive past.

Ignoring reporters' shouts of 'Will you resign?', Hague bounded up the stairs to his first floor office to deliver his reply to the men and women with whom he had fought – and lost – the general election . . .

The moment the scale of Labour's second successive landslide victory had become clear in the early hours of that Friday morning, urgent messages were sent to a group of Shadow Cabinet loyalists to get back to Central Office in time for the defeated leader's return. Shadow Home Secretary Ann Widdecombe, Shadow Defence Secretary Iain Duncan Smith, Ulster spokesman Andrew Mackay and Michael Ancram raced from all corners of the southern counties to be there. The party leader in the House of Lords, Tom Strathclyde, spared the inconvenience of having to win his own Parliamentary seat, had stayed in Central Office all night. He got home at 6 a.m. to catch up on some sleep, only to be woken up at 6.15 and told: 'Get back, William is on his way.'

Strathclyde had phoned Hague in Yorkshire at 3 a.m. and urged him: 'Don't resign too hastily, William, you must think very carefully before doing anything' – a conversation identical to the one which had taken place in the early hours of 2 May 1997. Hours after John Major was swept away by Blair's first landslide, a senior Conservative got through to him on the phone and pleaded with him to carry on as leader for the sake of party unity and stability. Major rejected the advice out of hand and told his loyal supporter he had no choice but to quit: his leadership was too badly damaged to continue. Major resigned immediately and went to the Oval to lick his wounds and watch cricket.

The senior Conservative who begged him to stay was William Hague.

Now it was Hague whose leadership had been fatally undermined and, like Major, he knew he had only one option.

Major was blamed by some for not allowing the party enough time to give proper consideration to choosing a new leader. It had chosen Hague, and now Hague had had enough. It was no longer a question of whether, but when. 'He was half minded to resign in Yorkshire, straight after his count,' said a Conservative source, 'and only delayed because people like Duncan Smith and Strathclyde said they wanted to talk to him first.'[1]

As Hague and Ffion made their way to Smith Square, Widdecombe, Mackay, Strathclyde and Duncan Smith met in Central Office and hastily agreed their tactics to persuade him to stay. While waiting for Hague to arrive, Widdecombe went to sleep on a sofa in Ancram's office. Mackay volunteered to see Hague alone and act as spokesman, but when the leader arrived he insisted on seeing them all together, and told them straight away: 'I am going to resign and I am going to do so in about twenty minutes. To be frank, my mind is made up, but I will hear what you have to say.'

Duncan Smith led the appeal to him to reconsider: 'You should let the dust settle and not make a hasty move. The party needs time to reflect on what has happened and the best way to achieve that is for you to continue, at least for the time being. Is there any way you would agree to delay it? In my view, you should do nothing until after the weekend.'

Hague responded: 'No, I'm not prepared to do that and I will explain why. Whatever I do, the leadership election is going to start now. I can't stop it, and if I'm not careful the focus will all be on me and I don't want that to happen. The party will tear itself apart if I stay on. It must start talking about what it must do to put things right, not agonise over whether I should remain. It won't be able to do that if we spend weeks discussing whether I am good enough to lead. I have looked at all the options. I said I would carry the can and the only solution is for me to go.'

Strathclyde said: 'I'm not trying to persuade you to stay on for ever, William, but nobody is calling for your resignation. If you leave, the chairman will want to leave too. Why don't you leave it for a couple of months? We are in no great hurry. Why not let the party settle down and see what broad direction it is going in before leaving?'

Widdecombe was more outspoken: 'You have a duty to the party to stay on, William. We need this like a hole in the head. Think of all the volunteers who have worked their guts out up and down the country. They will all feel let down if you just walk away. There should be a pause for due reflection. The party needs stability.'

But Hague was adamant. 'Perhaps, but I'm not staying. I have made up my mind. I'm sorry but you haven't convinced me otherwise. I have thought long and hard about this.' Nor was he the only one in the room who believed he should go straight away. Michael Ancram came straight to the point: 'I think you are right, you should go now.' His brutally short advice shocked some of those present, but came as no surprise to Hague, as Ancram and Chief Whip James Arbuthnot had spoken to him just before the meeting, and all three had agreed that the leader had no choice but to resign – Arbuthnot observing enigmatically 'You have always been right on these things in the past, and you are right now, William.'

Hague produced his resignation speech and told the meeting: 'This is what I am going to say.' He briefly ran through its contents and, after the front benchers had departed, called in his closest Central Office advisers, including head of media Amanda Platell (whose eyes were red raw from crying all night), deputy head of media Nick Wood and deputy private secretary Tina Stowell. Hague told them: 'I am really proud of what you have all done. You have organised a great campaign for me and you are not responsible for the result.' He paused mid-sentence and grabbed Ffion's hand, before continuing: 'You could not have given me a better platform for fighting the fight, but I have decided to step down.'

Ffion said, 'William and I have had a great time during the election. Never forget that, or what a great job you have done for us both', to which Hague added: 'None of you should believe you have failed. In life, the only failure is not to try.'

Stowell, who had served in Downing Street with John Major, responded: 'I would just like to say on behalf of everyone here William, how very proud we all are of you.'

At 7.28 a.m. Hague went to the media room where the Tory press conferences had been held during the campaign. This time the press were kept out: his words were addressed to the entire Central Office staff.

'You have all run an incredible election campaign, I have never known such a slick operation. None of you have failed and it is important that young people like you carry on the fight. The only thing you must not do is to lose heart. The battle for the things we believe in goes on and it goes on through you.' He even summoned the courage to joke about the result: 'We got everything right: we had the right tone, we went to the right places and had the right tactics: the only thing we didn't get right was the result! Where was Jeb Bush when I needed him?' – a reference to George W. Bush's brother Jeb, Governor of Florida, whom Hague had met and knew well, and who Democrats will always believe was responsible for handing victory to the Republicans in the 2000 Presidential election following the hotly contested count in Florida.

In contrast with his candour with his senior advisers, Hague omitted one fact in his speech to the assembled staff. He did not say he was about to resign. As a result, when minutes later he went outside and made his resignation statement, some of them watching inside on television gasped with shock. They couldn't understand why he had not told them, but one source explained: 'William omitted it deliberately when he spoke to the staff because many of them were so young and so emotional that he thought they might all burst into tears, and he wouldn't have wanted that.'

In theory, William Hague's fate in the 2001 general election was not known until 2.58 a.m. on Friday 8 June – the moment that the Labour

Party passed the winning post by notching up its 330th seat, enough to guarantee an overall majority in the 659-seat House of Commons of at least one.

A few minutes later, as Hague waited at Northallerton Leisure Centre in Richmond, Yorkshire, for his own constituency result to be announced, the Conservative leader spoke to Tony Blair on the telephone and conceded defeat. By the time the last votes were counted, Labour's majority over the other parties had fallen to 167, only a dozen short of its record-breaking 179-seat victory achieved in the 1997 landslide.

Theory was one thing, but reality was very different, and the delegation of Shadow Cabinet loyalists who met their leader in Central Office three hours later, hoping to persuade him to stay on, were wasting their time. Hague had made up his mind more than a year earlier and had confided only in Ffion and in his Chief of Staff, adviser, judo partner and soulmate, Sebastian Coe.

Labour's lead in the opinion polls had remained stubbornly fixed at around 25 points for eight long years. Hague knew that, barring a miracle, he had little chance of winning, and his main objective was not victory but survival. He had lost none of the passion for politics that he had displayed in front of Margaret Thatcher as a precocious sixteen-year-old at the 1977 Conservative conference in Blackpool and, at only forty years of age on polling day 2001, was still prodigiously young for a political leader. There was every likelihood that Blair's prolonged honeymoon with the British electorate and memories of Tory sleaze and 'Black Wednesday' back in 1992 might fade, and who could know what 'events' might knock New Labour off course in its second term?

A second Conservative defeat had looked on the cards the moment Tony Blair stepped over the threshold of Number 10 in 1997, but there was no reason why the Tories – and Hague – should not mount a serious challenge next time round if he could claw back enough seats this time to claim he had won a 'moral victory' – if not a real one.

So Hague set himself a target. If he reached it, he would stay. If he fell short, he would walk away.

There was endless speculation among MPs and pundits as to the magic figure Hague needed to hang on, and by the New Year of 2001 the consensus was that if he could whittle down the Labour overall majority to 100, he could keep his job. That meant gaining some forty-five seats, depending on regional variations.

But what no one knew, including the friends and colleagues waiting for him in Central Office on 8 June, was that the threshold for survival Hague had set himself was far higher than anyone had imagined, and was based not on cutting Labour's majority but on increasing the number of Tories in the House of Commons. He had pinned his hopes on winning between 240 and 260 Conservative seats.

If he had achieved it, Blair's majority would have plummeted to about 50: Hague could rightly have claimed that he had inflicted a major blow on Labour, that the Tories were on the way back and that, given five more years, he could turf Blair out of Downing Street. But as the months went by, Hague's target disappeared into the blue yonder, and by the time polling day arrived, expectations of the Tory performance had been lowered further, with most experts predicting another landslide. Some Conservatives believed that even if Hague achieved only a modest reduction in Labour's majority – cutting it to, say, 120 or 130 – he might yet live to fight another day.

On election night Hague was with Coe and Nicholas Gleave – a friend and aide – at home in his flat in Brough Hall, a converted manor house in Catterick Bridge, sitting down to a curry cooked by Ffion and a bottle of red wine when at 10 p.m. he heard news of the gloomy exit polls. The declaration of the very first result, Sunderland South at 10.41 p.m., confirmed his worst fears: there was a 3 per cent swing to the Conservatives, a trend repeated throughout the night in other Labour heartlands, but it was nowhere near enough for him to survive.

Within two minutes of that first result the Tory sharks were circling.

John Maples, still bitter at being sacked as Shadow Foreign Secretary by Hague, told a television interviewer: 'People were interested in police, health and education – and we didn't talk about those things nearly enough.'

By ten minutes after midnight Hague's last hopes were gone, as Labour's

Gisela Stuart retained Birmingham Edgbaston, a key marginal. Even New Labour hate figures were romping home. Keith Vaz, the former Europe Minister vilified for his controversial business interests and links with the Hinduja brothers, registered a huge majority in Leicester East; Peter Mandelson, twice forced to resign from the Cabinet, won easily in Hartlepool; and millionaire Tory turncoat Shaun Woodward, parachuted into working-class St Helen's South at the last minute, celebrated his victory with a pint of bitter.

At 4.25 a.m., after receiving the scant consolation of a massively increased majority in his own Richmond constituency, Hague addressed his supporters from the stage of Northallerton Leisure Centre: 'There is no doubt that the results tonight across the country are deeply disappointing for my party. I feel for the candidates and activists who have worked so hard for so little reward. The Labour Party will continue to form the government and I congratulate them on that and I have already spoken to Mr Blair to congratulate him in person. We must accept the verdict of voters and listen to what they have said. Clearly, we in our party must review, redouble and intensify our efforts to provide alternative government in the future. I will set out my views later this morning on how that process should begin.'

That last sentence gave the first hint of what was to follow in a few hours.

James Arbuthnot had travelled with Hague to Richmond in order that they could discuss an instant reshuffle: they had long given up pretending they would be handing out government portfolios, but were clinging to the hope that they might yet be in a position to rearrange shadows.

It was the night of the Tory long knives that never was. Out would go Shadow Chancellor Michael Portillo, who Hague believed had deliberately undermined him and who had performed poorly in the Commons against Gordon Brown. Out also would go Portillo's main ally, Shadow Foreign Secretary Francis Maude, whom Hague had planned to sack sixteen months earlier, only to be talked out of it at the last minute, a change of heart which he regretted.

Following the reshuffle Hague would challenge his critics to put up or shut up – in the hope that they would lack the nerve (as Portillo had done in 1995 when John Major used the same tactic to beat off his rivals) and thereby seal his continued leadership for the next five years.

But by the time he and Ffion walked up the steps of their private jet shortly after 5 a.m. to return to London, they realised there was only one resignation to be announced that night: Hague's.

He was not the only Tory who had seen the defeat coming, and who had made plans.

Hague's suspicions over Portillo, his movements and motivations, had increased to fever pitch in the run-up to polling day. The Conservative leader's aides had told him of rumours that Portillo planned to 'disappear' soon after the polls closed at 10 p.m. to avoid being tarred with the stigma of failure. This intelligence had led to a bizarre exchange at one of the last 'Leader's Meetings' – the daily gatherings where Hague and his senior Shadow Ministers and advisers would discuss election tactics. Hague had gone round the table asking each of his front bench spokesmen and women where they planned to be on election night, and turned finally to Portillo, who remarked that he would be available for interviews until around 10 p.m.

'And after that?' Hague had asked.

'Oh, I will have to get back to my constituency' – at which Hague had shot a knowing glance at his advisers watching from the sidelines. Told of reports about Portillo's intentions, Widdecombe, who had volunteered for media duty, had muttered a rare expletive: 'Bastard.'

If the result was as bad as they feared, someone had to face the media and put on a brave face as the Labour gains were chalked up. As with every other political situation, there would be 'lines to take' to which everyone would have to keep. If Hague was to have any chance of survival, the defeat had to be managed, and Shadow Ministers were under orders not to concede defeat until Hague had done so after the count in his Richmond constituency.

There was a row when Tory officials were told that Portillo and Maude wanted to go further than the agreed 'line' and admit Hague had lost. Shortly after midnight, Portillo said on television: 'It appears the

Conservatives have not been successful tonight' – causing one aide to emit an emotional outburst that 'They can't wait to dance on his grave', as the atmosphere of treachery gave way to paranoia and anger.

But other senior party figures defended Portillo: 'It was madness to pretend things were going to improve,' said one: 'There was no point whatsoever trying to put some kind of spin on it. It was too late for all that.'[2]

Portillo left Central Office late on Thursday night to attend his count in Kensington, returning briefly at around 1 a.m. to thank officials in the Tory HQ 'war room' from where he and Maude had masterminded the campaign. 'The least said and the least done the better; we should let the dust settle,' he told one young activist.

Pressed on television to say if Hague should stay on to fight the next election, he pointedly avoided giving a direct answer, saying the party needed time for 'reflection' and adding: 'I very much hope that whatever happens, he continues as our leader.'

By 2 a.m. Portillo had left Smith Square to return to his Belgravia home, where he prepared for another journey later that morning, while Shadow Cabinet troops raced back to London to rally round their defeated general in his hour of defeat, Portillo was heading in another direction. Shortly after Hague's private jet arrived in London from Yorkshire, Portillo boarded a different plane at Stansted airport and flew to Morocco for a holiday with his wife Carolyn. The couple had paid £2,000 each to take part in a special visit to the Roman ruins at Volubilis and help raise funds for the excavation of Arab remains at the site. The trip had been organised by the London based socialite Rita Bennis, who runs the Gazelle d'Or Hotel at the foot of the Atlas mountains in Morocco, a favourite sanctuary of the Portillos. Arab horses and chauffeurs are freely available to guests; children are not allowed. Portillo's departure appeared to be timed to perfection.

'When I started to organise it, the election was thought to be on May 1st,' said Ms Bennis, 'so Michael said yes immediately. His cheque was the first to arrive. Later he cancelled. Then at the last minute, he decided to come.'[3]

Portillo's 'last minute' decision meant that he was not among the Tories who gathered outside Central Office to observe another set of ruins: the shattered remnants of William Hague's leadership. He would not be among those who stood there, their eyes welling with tears, to provide a guard of honour for their leader in one last defiant public show of loyalty. And he would not be inside, among the small group of Shadow Ministers who consoled Hague and begged him to carry on.

Only weeks earlier, when the press was full of reports of plots against Hague by the Portillo camp, the leader had lectured his Shadow Cabinet on the need to make sure their 'body language' was right – that they looked loyal, united and confident and supported each other, especially in public. The Shadow Chancellor's body language could not have been more eloquent. He was on his way to Africa – without waiting for the dust to settle.

Francis Maude, too, was absent.

As Hague prepared to face the world and deliver his resignation speech on the steps of Central Office, the final corrections were being made to another Conservative analysis of the result: a savage attack on Hague by Michael Heseltine was about to roll off the presses of the London *Evening Standard*. Heseltine had been no more supportive of William Hague than he had been of another Tory who had held the post that had eluded him – Margaret Thatcher – and it was only a second untimely heart problem after the 1997 election that put paid to his hopes of succeeding John Major as Tory leader, forcing him to stand aside yet again as someone else took the prize. Hague had been deeply hurt by Heseltine's withering attacks on his policies, and in particular his decision to share a platform – along with Kenneth Clarke – with Tony Blair to promote the case for joining the single European currency.

'The focus on hard faced Little Englander rhetoric created a disastrous image at odds with the real nature of Conservatism,' declared Heseltine in his *Standard* article: 'It created a party as unelectable in 2001 as Labour was in the 1980s.'

If this broadside was meant as one final push to get Hague out of Central Office, Heseltine needn't have bothered. Standing just inside the double set of wooden doors at the Central Office entrance, waiting to face the media, he turned to Ffion and Coe on either side of him and told them: 'I want you to stand with me when we go outside.' He stood for a minute or two as he re-read his handwritten resignation speech, running his fingers over the text. He shut his eyes as he pondered what he was about to do, kissed Ffion and walked out into the bright morning sunshine.

'We have not been able to persuade a majority, or anything approaching a majority, that we are yet the alternative government that they need,' he said, squinting in the sunlight. 'Nor have I been able to persuade sufficient numbers that I am their alternative Prime Minister. I wish I could have led us to victory but we must all work for our victories in the future. No man or woman is indispensable and no individual is more important than the party. I have therefore decided to step down as leader of the Conservative Party when a successor can be elected in the coming months.'

At 7.39 a.m., it was – for William Hague at least – all over.

2 The Spaniard's Return

'I have made my decision. I am bringing Michael Portillo and Archie Norman into the Shadow Cabinet and getting rid of Redwood and Maude.'

William Hague, January 2000

Ever since the return of Michael Portillo to the House of Commons in November 1999, the central question facing William Hague was: what to do with him? He was far too talented to ignore, but would it be more dangerous to embrace him than to keep him at arm's length? For months the Conservative leader wrestled with the dilemma. But the first hint that he gave to his advisers of his intentions was over lunch in Warsaw, Poland, in the last weekend of January.

Hague was attending a conference of European centre-right parties in the last weekend of January 2000, but his mind was elsewhere as he sipped a glass of mineral water and picked at a meagre salad. The surprise Shadow Cabinet reshuffle that ignited a series of bitter personal and political feuds which continued right up until the day of the general election and finally killed off any chance of Hague beating Blair, was three days away.

'I have made my decision,' the Tory leader told Seb Coe and Amanda Platell: 'I am bringing Michael Portillo and Archie Norman into the Shadow Cabinet and getting rid of Redwood and Maude.'

It was not his final decision. Over the next forty-eight hours there was intensive wrangling as Hague and his aides argued over where the axe should fall, and in the end he decided to axe John Maples instead of Maude.

Since Portillo's victory in the Kensington by-election two months earlier following the death of Alan Clark, the only question was when, not if, he would return to the front bench – and what job he would get. Hague had far too little talent available to him on the Tory benches to ignore someone of Portillo's stature. As for being a threat to Hague's leadership, the threat would be no greater – and arguably less – inside the tent than outside, and Hague regarded Portillo as a personal and political ally. He told one friend: 'I am closer to Michael than any member of the Shadow Cabinet. He and I agree on most things.'[1]

It was a view that changed rapidly once Portillo was facing him at the Shadow Cabinet table.

Some observers were surprised at how quickly Hague brought Portillo into his team and questioned why. The answer was twofold: desperation and fear.

Hague had been deeply depressed by a series of Tory scandals and controversies over the previous couple of months. His poll ratings were as low as ever at a time when the Government had suffered setbacks of its own including one of the worst ever NHS winter beds crises. Hague knew that he had to do something to revive his party fortunes – so he turned to Portillo.

Relations between the two men were cordial, but no more. When Hague entered the 1997 leadership contest, Portillo reportedly described him at a Westminster garden party as 'no more than another Major', and it was only at the last minute, when John Redwood lined up behind Kenneth Clarke in an attempt to defeat Hague in the final ballot, that Portillo swung in behind him. Like Margaret Thatcher, Portillo was horrified that the party might fall into the hands of a pro-European, while his long standing personal antipathy towards Redwood was an equally powerful motivating force.

Three years later, Hague was still grateful that Portillo, who they both knew would have been leader had he not lost his Commons seat in the 1997 election, had rallied behind him, and believed he could trust him. Hague knew that he had to build a dialogue with Portillo – even while he was exiled from the Commons – and the two had met regularly, Hague agreeing with Portillo that the party must broaden its appeal.

When Portillo came out of the Shadow Cabinet room on Tuesday 1 February 2000, having been made Shadow Chancellor, he looked more dumbfounded than delighted. 'It's not what I expected, not that job,' he told one colleague.[2]

The job he had expected to be offered was party chairman, a double-edged sword traditionally used by Tory leaders to keep rivals at bay during an election campaign: the post was sufficiently senior to use their abilities to the full, but it also tied them in, since the party chairman ran the election campaign, and if the party lost the election, the chairman would suffer as much damage as the leader. Therefore the chairman had to be loyal – or so the logic went.

The job that Portillo wanted, as opposed to expected, was Health or Education spokesman: either would allow him to display more of his new caring compassionate side, his social liberalism and his new found faith in the NHS and state education. He had spent a few days working as a hospital porter to show how much he had changed since his days as chief defender of the poll tax. His supporters had been accused of undermining Health spokesman Liam Fox and Education spokeswoman Theresa May to make it more likely for Portillo to be given one of the portfolios.

Portillo was far less shocked at being promoted than Redwood and Maples were at being sacked.

Hague called Redwood in at 4.30 p.m. and told him he was being replaced.

When Redwood asked what he had done wrong, Hague replied: 'Nothing. I know it's unfair, but I need to make room for other people' – and Redwood said afterwards that he did not believe Hague's heart was in it: 'William didn't look as though he really wanted to do it.'[3]

He was wrong, and within days there was a pro-Redwood backlash from activists and MPs, furious that one of the few Shadow Cabinet Ministers able to get his message across had been tossed aside. Hague promptly did a U-turn and promised to find a special role for Redwood, and in July 2000 he was duly appointed head of a new Tory Parliamentary Campaigns Unit with orders to expose Labour spin. As added compensation, he was allowed to keep his highly prized Shadow Cabinet room in Speaker's Court.[4]

Redwood believed he was the victim of a prolonged campaign to get rid of him by his enemies in Central Office, conducted mainly on Portillo's behalf. 'Getting rid of me and making a vacancy for Portillo and Norman was a necessary part of their strategy. It was a successful coup,' he said.[5] 'I couldn't be smeared over my private life because I wasn't sleeping around with anyone, so they went for the Vulcan thing. My family were very upset.'

Redwood discovered that Hague had been told that research from Tory focus groups showed that Redwood was a liability and a 'reminder of the past' – information leaked to the press. 'When I demanded to see this research they refused. I found out that the research showed that I was seen as the most honest and hard working member of the Shadow Cabinet, but they deliberately withheld that information from William,' said Redwood, whose anger at being sacked was intensified by the feeling that he had been sacrificed to make way for Portillo.[6]

The deep enmity between the two men dated back to the morning of Monday 26 June 1995, when they met alone in Portillo's Commons office. It was days after John Major had resigned his leadership and challenged his Tory critics to put up or shut up, and the meeting prompted frenzied speculation that Portillo – then Defence Secretary, and hot favourite to succeed Major – would challenge the Prime Minister. Portillo was on the brink of doing just that when Redwood knocked on his door that Monday.

'I have resigned from the Cabinet, but I have not yet declared that I am going to fight for the leadership,' he told Portillo. 'Will you join me? I don't mind if I run as the number one or as your number two.'

Portillo replied: 'No, I will not, but if you run in the first round and succeed in knocking out Major, I will come in for round two.'

'Life is not like that, Michael. If I run in round one and get through to round two then obviously I will continue. I am not going to stand aside, having been the one to take all the risk and do all the hard work.'

'I will only do it if you are prepared to step aside.'

'No, Michael. You must decide now. If you stand I will back you. Without you, we may not get to the second round.'[7]

Redwood left the room and announced his own challenge to Major. It narrowly failed, but the biggest loser was Portillo, who went as far as installing phone lines in a campaign HQ in 11 Lord North Street, Westminster, before backing out. His reputation suffered lasting damage. 'Redwood knew he had little chance of beating Major, but was jealous of Michael and wanted to replace him as the flag bearer of the right wing,' said one Conservative MP, and Redwood himself said later: 'He thought I should run for him and then bow out. Michael and his supporters had a grudge against me. They thought I stood to embarrass Michael. I stood because I thought if we didn't change the PM we were finished. I didn't care too much who replaced him, as long as it was someone who gave us a chance of winning. If he had come with me, we would have done it easily between us. He spoke for at least twenty votes.'8

Redwood attempted to heal relations four years later when Portillo admitted to gay experiences before entering public life. He phoned Portillo and the two met at a London hotel, where Redwood offered tea and sympathy and urged his rival to 'let bygones be bygones'. But the two were uncomfortable in each other's company and had little more contact.

Redwood's allies believed that his sacking by Hague was Portillo's revenge. They claim Portillo made it a condition of his return that his right-wing enemy Redwood must go. It has also been suggested that Portillo secured a written undertaking from Hague to this effect and at the same time guaranteeing him a free hand in economic policy, though there is no evidence to prove this, and when in February 2001 Hague was challenged on BBC Radio about claims of an agreement, he said: 'There is no such deal.'9

Hague knew of the tension between Portillo and Redwood, and in addition felt that he owed no special loyalty to Redwood, having been deeply hurt at the time of the 1997 leadership contest by rumours spread by Redwood's team that Hague was gay. Hague owed his Cabinet promotion in 1995 to Redwood's resignation as Welsh Secretary when he challenged John Major, and made it clear that he did not approve of his predecessor's style, reportedly observing: 'Redwood has left this department bankrupt in terms of political capital. I am having to begin again. I barely regard him as a politician – I have zero regard for his supposed political skills.'[10]

The choice of Archie Norman as his successor was equally hard for Redwood to swallow. He had never had a high regard for the former Asda supermarket boss, and Redwood's former aide Hywel Williams described how Norman refused to back Redwood in the 1997 leadership contest on the grounds that the party needed 'exciting leadership': 'Norman remained uncommitted – and would have been even more of a Redwood-sceptic had he known of the Wokingham One's resolve to keep the ASDA chief on the backbenches for a very long time. Redwoodian jokes that 'Archie Norman' had replaced 'Gordon Bennett' to express bewilderment at conduct of baffling peculiarity may not have helped matters.'[11]

Norman's appointment was as fraught as Portillo's.

Amanda Platell, who regarded most of the Tory front bench as dreary second-raters, had long urged Hague to promote Norman, who had joined the Commons as MP for Tunbridge Wells in 1997. To Platell, Norman was a go-getting entrepreneur, the nearest thing the Tories had to their own Richard Branson. Were it not for the fact that he shared the failing of most businessmen-turned-politicians, a lack of charisma and oratorical skills, Norman would have been ideal leadership material – his undoubted aim when he turned his back on business for the backbenches.

But when Hague asked Norman to take on Redwood's job as Shadow Secretary of State for the Environment, Transport and the Regions, opposing John Prescott, Norman said no. He complained that he knew nothing about the subject and told Hague he wanted the Trade and Industry slot, his special subject. Otherwise he was not prepared to join the Shadow Cabinet. Hague was worried about a possible conflict of interests caused by Norman's business activities and insisted he take the DETR appointment. Norman refused, and Hague, who rarely vents his anger and meditates daily, was furious. His reshuffle was in ruins: if Norman would not take the job, he would have to go back to square one. He had hoped to announce the changes in an hour or so.

'I just don't believe it,' he exploded in his Commons office. 'We will have to call the whole thing off.'

Amanda Platell, Norman's main sponsor, offered to intercede: 'Give me half an hour and I will try and persuade him to take the job.'

Hague snapped: 'You've got ten minutes.'

As Platell left to find Norman, Arbuthnot said dismissively: 'What makes you think you can make a difference?'

Platell spat: 'At least I'm going to bloody well try.'

She had known Norman before she got involved in politics, and he had recommended her to Hague. Platell didn't care which job he was given; she was convinced he would be an asset, and possibly, a future leader – and she marched into Norman's room and told him that unless he took the job, Hague's entire reshuffle would be wrecked and the Tory leader humiliated. When she returned to Hague's office and announced that Norman had caved in, Hague threw his arms round her in relief. The reshuffle went ahead as planned.

But in its wake it left a trail of battered egos, none more battered than that of Francis Maude, who was rudely pushed aside as Shadow Chancellor to make way for Portillo's return. Portillo shrewdly suggested to Hague that Maude retain his unofficial status as number two to salvage his pride, and also persuaded him to let Maude keep his Shadow Cabinet room, next door to Hague's own office. (It was Maude's lucky charm – it had once been Tony Blair's office.) In so doing, Portillo laid the foundations of the alliance that went on to challenge the entire direction of Hague's leadership.

Any hope Hague may have had of retaining Maude's trust was shattered when Maude found out he had been within an inch of being sacked.

When Hague dined with Coe and Platell in the capital of Poland on the Saturday, three days before the reshuffle, he was in no doubt: Maude was for the chop. But when the Conservative leader arrived back at his office on Monday, Maude's allies fought to save him.

They were led by Hague's Parliamentary Private Secretary John Whittingdale, who had been head of Margaret Thatcher's private office in Number 10 and was an experienced political wheeler-dealer. There was another reason why Hague made Whittingdale his PPS: few MPs were closer to Portillo, and Whittingdale had been one of the first to urge Thatcher to promote him to her Cabinet.

Redwood believed that Whittingdale had also had a hand in his fate, a charge Whittingdale has always rejected, though he later told friends he regretted not having defended Redwood: 'It was a miscalculation: we should have found a way of keeping him,' he said.[12]

But Whittingdale urged Hague to promote Portillo – 'He is too strong a performer not to use him' – and he was quick to defend Maude when Hague told him he intended to dump the Shadow Chancellor. Hague met Whittingdale, Ancram, Coe and Arbuthnot in his office on the morning of the reshuffle. Whittingdale urged the leader to keep Maude and sack Shadow Foreign Secretary John Maples. 'Maples doesn't believe in anything,' he said: 'Francis believes in what we believe in – Europe, the pound.'

Maples had the same credibility problem as Maude, but could be sacrificed without any great risk. Hague told him bluntly: 'Someone has to make way for Michael. It's either you or Francis, and I'm afraid it's you.'

Two weeks later, Maples was among the first to complain of Hague's drift to the right. The Tories had to look 'competent, sensible and responsible,' he said. Most of the major departments were shadowed by right-wingers. 'Perception is reality . . . Our policies and tone must be mainstream and speak to the whole nation. We have to convince them on the issues of basic concern to them – health, education, crime and the economy. We cannot win the election through private health insurance and being tough on asylum seekers.'[13]

Maude had good reason to be worried about the implications of Portillo's return.

He had long since been eclipsed by Widdecombe as the second most powerful member of the Shadow Cabinet, offering nothing to compare with her barnstorming speeches, strong opinions, colourful language and powerful personality. Yet for a brief moment, when Hague faltered in 1998, Maude had been spoken of as a successor. He was highly intelligent, likeable, had sleek if unconventional looks, was a strong family man (one of the few politicians with more children than Tony Blair – five) and was a Tory with a semblance of independent means, having used his defeat in the 1992 election as an opportunity to make serious money in the City. He came from a Tory dynasty which had proved its skill in political plotting, if not political leadership. His father Angus Maude was one of the small group of Tory MPs who toppled Edward Heath and replaced him with Margaret Thatcher.

But talk of Maude as a future leader faded after he failed to make an impact against Chancellor of the Exchequer Gordon Brown. Brown was one of the most powerful and able Chancellors of modern times and a master of oratory, a skill that eluded Maude. 'Every time there was an economic announcement, Francis would get into a tremendous state of nerves,' said one Hague aide: 'He was being hammered relentlessly by Brown.'14

Maude also made a fatal error early on as Shadow Chancellor when he overreacted to gloomy economic forecasts and predicted Britain was heading for a 'downturn made in Downing Street'. The words came back to haunt him when the economy continued to grow and unemployment fell. In private, Maude acknowledged his miscalculation with good humour, joking about his 'false dusk' prediction. Gordon Brown teased him that 'You only get one chance to predict a recession' – and one week later Maude lost his job.

Maude learned, just as former Chancellor Norman Lamont had done when he talked of the jobless total as 'a price worth paying' and said of his policies during the recession *'je ne regrette rien'*, how damaging a discordant soundbite can be.

'Francis was scared of Brown,' said Widdecombe. 'He wasn't able to handle him in the Commons. When Portillo came back into the Shadow Cabinet, Francis was nervous. He knew it would affect his standing.'15

Further evidence of Maude's unease is provided by former Tory MP turned parliamentary sketchwriter Michael Brown. A few weeks before the reshuffle, Brown forecast that Portillo's comeback spelled the demise of Maude, and shortly afterwards Brown received a phone call from a worried Maude asking him to come for a drink to discuss his views.

Until the reshuffle, Maude was a Hague loyalist. His views were at least as right-wing as Hague's. Indeed, it was Maude who had devised the controversial 'tax guarantee' policy that was to cause the biggest single political dispute between Portillo and Hague.

So why did Maude switch to Portillo? 'Francis knew that any hope he had of becoming leader was gone,' said a Shadow Minister: 'If Ann had overtaken him, Michael was going to leave him trailing. His best hope of surviving Hague's downfall was not by trying to be his successor but by hitching his coat tails to whoever would be. And from the moment it was clear that Portillo was coming back, that person was obviously Portillo.'[16]

Another Conservative source said: 'The greatest irony of all is that while it was Portillo who took Maude's job, Maude resented Hague, not Portillo.'[17]

Hague felt let down by Maude. His failure to get to grips with Gordon Brown put all the more pressure on the Conservative leader. Hague also believed that at crucial times, Maude had not provided him with the kind of support he expected from the Shadow Chancellor.'[18]

Some of Hague's colleagues say that the party leader was disappointed by Maude's lack of support in 1999 when former deputy leader Peter Lilley provoked a furore by making a speech which was a clumsy attempt to make a break with Thatcherism: Maude was said to have been less than enthusiastic about doing media interviews to try and sort out the mess. 'At one meeting William turned to Francis and said, "I have done two or three interviews, the chairman has done one, and I would like you to do one, Francis." It was William's way of telling him to pull his finger out,' said one senior party source.[19]

At the very time that Hague had drifted apart from Maude, Portillo moved closer. Until the reshuffle, Maude and Portillo had not been close, but Portillo's consideration for Maude's feelings in insisting that he and not Portillo be made number two, and that Maude kept his treasured room, paid rich dividends. The seeds had been sown for Maude's conversion from the Hague camp to the Portillo camp.

Maude was not the only Hague ally on the move.

At the time of his appointment to the Shadow Cabinet, Archie Norman was seen as one of Hague's strongest supporters. The two had been friends for more than a decade since Norman recruited Hague from Shell to McKinsey and Co management consultants, and Norman had supported Hague in the 1997 leadership contest. But within months of his own arrival in the Shadow Cabinet, Norman too found himself increasingly at odds with Hague, and in sympathy with Portillo. He was surprised to see the outward-looking, go-ahead, modern young businessman he knew in the 1980s turn into the anti-asylum, anti-liberal, anti-euro, little Englander figure Hague seemed to become as election day loomed.

The reshuffle of February 2000 was meant to provide Hague with a powerful and united team to spearhead his assault on Blair in the run up to the election. Instead it heralded a period of dissent which saw him lurch from one initiative to the next, with no agreed strategy. Far from uniting under Hague's flag, a powerful section of the reformed Shadow Cabinet appeared to rally behind Portillo. Furthermore, they started to challenge some of Hague's most basic beliefs in what the Conservative Party stood for. 'When William brought Michael and Archie into the Shadow Cabinet, he thought he was strengthening his position,' said Tory senior vice chairman Tim Collins. 'But all he did was weaken it. Michael had been an ally in the Major Cabinet and Archie had been a friend. But William did not know that Michael had gone cold on tax cuts and thought there was no real difference between Labour and Tories on the management of the economy. Michael had been the champion of the Tory right, but was now to the left of Ken Clarke.'[20]

Maude was even drier on economics than Hague, yet he had good reason to feel disenchanted, particularly since Hague had been only hours away from sacking him altogether. Maude's right-wing economic instincts, like Portillo's, were tempered by a more liberal attitude to social matters. He had been profoundly affected by the harrowing experience of watching his brother Charles die of AIDS.

The first hint of the changing allegiances in the Tory high command appeared seven days before the reshuffle, before anyone knew that Hague was planning to change his team.

Portillo and Maude were said to have hatched a plot in the secretive basement alcoves of the Goya tapas bar – a favourite meeting place of the so called 'Pimlico Portillistas' – whereby Maude would not run against Portillo in any leadership contest, thereby clearing the path for Portillo to succeed Hague.[21] Maude denounced the story as 'fantasy', but its prediction of a Portillo–Maude axis proved to be deadly accurate.

When Hague announced the reshuffle, the movement in the shifting Tory sands was not clear – even to Hague himself. What was clear was that he had gambled. He had brought Portillo – the most able and charismatic Tory of his generation – back into the fold right at the moment that the long march towards D-Day, the 2001 election, was about to begin. If it worked, and Hague and Portillo were able to harness their combined individual talents, Labour might be given a run for its money after all. Man for man, on the right day and right territory, Hague and Portillo were a match for Blair and Brown. But if it failed, Hague's prospects would be destroyed.

3   Taxing Times

'If Michael does not get a concession on the tax guarantee, he will resign in ten days.'
William Hague, 3 July 2000

It was Hague's flagship manifesto policy. A return to the tried and tested formula that had won the Conservatives four election victories in a row. Tax cuts.

Three years on from his general election victory, Blair's promise that Labour was no longer the party that put up taxes was looking tarnished, and the Conservative attack on Labour's so-called 'stealth taxes', a clever term coined by Maude, was one of the few that had hurt Blair and Brown.

The Tories' private polls showed that Labour was vulnerable on this issue. On the other hand, they also indicated that the Tories' reputation as the party that cut taxes was equally tainted, so if Hague was to convince voters they would really benefit, it would take more than words and be more binding than 'Read my lips: no new taxes.' George Bush senior had used and abused that one already.

This then, was the background to Hague's much vaunted 'tax guarantee'. The policy, also devised by Maude in consultation with spin doctor Nick Wood, was unveiled by Hague amid a great fanfare on Tuesday 4 October 1999, the opening day of the Conservative conference in Blackpool, as part of sixty proposals in a new policy document, 'The Common Sense Revolution', with the 'tax guarantee' the cornerstone of five 'guarantees' – an idea blatantly stolen from Blair's five pledges in 1997 – on key issues, including a patients' guarantee, a parents' guarantee, a work guarantee and a sterling guarantee.

Hague held a news conference to explain how it would work. If he became Prime Minister, taxes would 'fall as a share of the nation's income over the term of the next Parliament'. He continued: 'A tax guarantee in this form has never been given by any party before. It means an open and honest and transparent approach to tax. It means no increasing tax by stealth. No stealth taxes. Guaranteed. These proposals show the clarity, conviction and courage of a Conservative Party that is listening, learning and ready to lead once more.'

He could not have tied his flag more closely to the mast.

Critics were quick to identify potential flaws. *The Times* said:

> The Tories have this week imposed on themselves a financial straitjacket. The tax guarantee and the linked tough spending and borrowing limits are intended to have "no escape clauses, no fudging". But there is a snag. Previous governments have tried to set policy by similar predetermined targets and they have invariably come unstuck.[1]

Maude proposed 'a stability fund' to meet such concerns, and there were no complaints from the delegates in Blackpool's Winter Gardens, who were thrilled by the return to a Thatcherite agenda of lower taxes, less government and more freedom.

In his main conference speech on the Friday, Hague gave his most confident performance as Conservative leader. For once, he had trumped Blair, who had made a serious miscalculation in his own 'forces of conservatism' speech to the Labour conference the previous week.

Hague was convinced that at last, he had come up with a winner.

Apart from sporadic Labour attacks, there was no serious challenge to the 'tax guarantee' until 1 February 2000, the day that Michael Portillo became Shadow Chancellor. Within two days of his appointment, Portillo performed the two biggest Tory U-turns since the general election, abandoning the party's opposition to the minimum wage and to the independence for the Bank of England.

He had signalled his intentions at the first 'Leader's Meeting' held after the reshuffle. 'I have Treasury questions [in the House of Commons] coming up,' said Portillo. 'I am bound to be asked about our position on the Bank of England and the minimum wage. I don't think it is sustainable to stick to our existing policy on the Bank when we are in the midst of changing our policy. I think we should announce it here and now and end our opposition to the minimum wage too.'[2]

Maude had set up a 'commission' to investigate the party's line on the Bank of England independence, though in reality it was a vehicle for making a dignified retreat. But there was no such inevitability about changing the party's stance on the minimum wage. As recently as 20 January, Tory Trade and Industry spokeswoman Angela Browning had talked of the 'horrors' the minimum wage had imposed on small business.[3]

Portillo had struck with lethal speed. After hearing him call for both policies to be dropped, Hague looked up at the leaders' meeting and said: 'Agreed?'

No one dissented.

Two days after the reshuffle, Portillo announced during Treasury questions on Thursday 3 February: 'I want to tell the House today that the next Conservative government will respect the independence of the Bank of England' and 'the next Conservative government will not repeal the national minimum wage.'

Labour MPs cheered. Gordon Brown hailed 'the conversion of the Conservative Party to Labour Party policy' – which is how it looked to some Tory MPs. It also prompted further speculation that Portillo had a written pledge that he had full control of economic policy. The claims were denied, though from that day, Portillo acted as though he were in possession of such a document.

Despite all the claims that Hague was master of the party, the reality was different: his position in the polls had been weak for three years, and now his position in the Shadow Cabinet was weak. Hague failed to understand just how radically Portillo's approach to politics had changed since his days as a diehard Thatcherite. Nor had he ever had to face anyone on the Shadow Cabinet as powerful as Portillo.

And Portillo rapidly found allies, notably Maude and Norman.

If Hague thought the two U-turns would satisfy Portillo, he was wrong.

On Sunday 6 February, three days after the Bank and minimum wage

U-turns, Portillo was interviewed on BBC Radio 4's *The World This Weekend*, and was asked three times to state he would keep the tax guarantee. Three times he avoided the question. It was a direct challenge to Hague's authority.

Portillo discussed the issue privately with the party leader, telling him it was 'untenable', leaving Hague no choice but to confront the issue, which he did at the following day's weekly Monday morning 'Strategy Group' meeting at Central Office. 'I have had discussions with the Shadow Chancellor about the tax guarantee,' he said. 'He has reservations about it, but is not saying at this stage that we should ditch it. We need to discuss the matter.'[4]

Maude, who had formulated the policy said: 'We should stick with it.' And Hague's two most trusted policy advisers, Shadow Cabinet Office Minister Andrew Lansley and Tory vice chairman Tim Collins, were adamant. 'If we start to unpick this policy which we have set so much store by, what is going to happen to all the others?' asked Collins. 'If the Conservative Party does not stand for tax cuts, then what does it stand for?'[5]

Portillo countered: 'It is difficult to argue you should cut taxes in all circumstances. What happens if there is a global recession or war?'

Widdecombe, whose feud with Portillo was yet to come, supported him: 'People do not feel overtaxed: tax cuts only work when they do.' She said going into an election with a policy that could make spending cuts inevitable would be 'electoral suicide', a view supported by Education spokeswoman Theresa May.

Widdecombe did not always conform to her right-wing stereotype. In her previous post as Health spokeswoman she had clashed with Maude over his preoccupation with Labour's 'aggregate spending levels', telling him that it was 'inconceivable' that the Tories would go into an election promising to cut spending on areas like health and education. She was one of the first Tories to argue they should say openly that they would match Labour's spending levels on vital services – just as Labour had done with the Tory government's spending plans before the 1997 election – and move on.

'I will tell you this, Francis,' she said during one heated exchange: 'down at the Pig and Whistle they do not talk about aggregate expenditure levels.'

'You are being very silly,' he replied.[6]

Both Michael Ancram and James Arbuthnot said that if Portillo was unhappy with the policy, he had a right to change it.

One Shadow Minister said: 'Portillo was being disingenuous. We had always said there would be caveats. We had never said we would cut taxes if in the event of a plague or famine or if aliens landed in Parliament Square.'

But the battle was on, and the next day, seven days after the reshuffle, at a Central Office press conference to discuss the drugs problem, Hague appeared to run up the white flag. Asked about the tax guarantee, he said: 'A country that wants to compete in the future has got to bring down the burden of taxation over time – and that is the aspiration expressed in the tax guarantee.' Reporters seized on the 'A' word. Aspiration, as every political student knows, is a million miles from a commitment.

Hague denied it was a U-turn: 'The guarantee to reduce taxation is still a guarantee but, of course, there are further details to be added to that and there is a lot to discuss with the new Shadow Chancellor.'

The writing was on the wall.

Portillo's argument that the 'tax guarantee' was a liability was not supported by all economic commentators.

Times columnist Anatole Kaletsky wrote:

> 'Thus far Conservative economic proposals have managed to avoid universal derision for only one reason: nobody took Francis Maude seriously enough to bother picking his policies apart. The Tories dominated British politics for twenty years, largely because they were perceived as better managers of the economy and the party of lower taxes. In principle, the idea that a government should promise to reduce the share of national income absorbed by taxes is perfectly reasonable and realistic. Such a promise would not, as is widely believed, be exploded by an unexpected recession. On the contrary, a recession would actually make it easier to fulfil its tax guarantee, since tax revenues automatically fall in relation to national income in recessions.'[7]

Stung by claims that he was diluting the pledge, Hague hit back in the Commons the next day: 'The tax guarantee stands and the tax guarantee will continue to stand.'

The fight to control the heart and soul of the party between Hague and Portillo had begun.

Portillo kept chipping away at the guarantee. He and Hague had a series of face to face showdowns. Hague dug in his heels, but every time Portillo tugged, the Conservative leader's feet slipped a little further on the mud.

On 28 June, Portillo challenged his leader head-on at the Shadow Cabinet. He told the other Shadow Cabinet members what he had been saying to Hague in private for four months: 'The tax guarantee is not tenable in its present form and must be changed. There must be a fine print clause in the manifesto making it clear that we will not cut vital services to achieve tax cuts.'[8]

Hague was horrified: it would render his tax guarantee meaningless. According to some, Maude, who had devised the tax guarantee, started to back away from the policy he had invented, arguing that the Tories could fight the election 'on a pledge not to raise taxes'.

'You could almost see Francis moving from William's side of the table to Michael's. It was a symbolic moment,' said one Hague adviser.[9]

Maude's allies dispute this version of events and say he regarded it as a 'mistake' to drop the guarantee because 'it sent the wrong signal to voters'.

'Francis never intended the tax guarantee to be a banner headline policy. It was intended to be more a backstop, a signal that in spite of what happened under Major, we were the tax cutting party,' said one source. 'It was supposed to be our equivalent to Labour's statement before the 1997 election that they would match our spending levels, a reassuring gesture.'[10]

Hague's advisers told him he must not give any further ground – or he would be humiliated. 'I told William that if he gave another inch, people would say Portillo was running the show and not him. Portillo was trying to destabilise him,' said one. Hague replied: 'Michael insists the tax guarantee would not withstand the election campaign. He is determined.'[11]

Portillo showed how determined he was a week later on Tuesday 3 July, when he and Hague met alone again. The policy must be buried once and for all, he said Portillo; he would accept nothing less.[12]

A shaken Hague left the meeting and told colleagues: 'If Michael does not get a concession on the tax guarantee, he will resign in ten days.' The deadline: 13 July.13

Either Hague ditched it and was humiliated: or he kept it and Portillo walked out, provoking a Tory bloodbath and the near certainty of a leadership challenge.

It had happened before in the Tory party when Michael Heseltine walked out of Margaret Thatcher's Cabinet over what seemed like a trifling issue, the future of Westland helicopters. Thatcher stood her ground, Heseltine returned to the back benches, bided his time, and brought her down – but never became leader.

Heseltine once confided in Portillo that the Westland affair had taught him the most important lesson in politics: never resign. But it didn't stop Portillo making the threat.

Hague's inner circle – Lansley, Coe, private secretary George Osborne, Platell, policy director Danny Finkelstein and Whittingdale – all urged him to tough it out. Whittingdale told him that 'Michael Portillo is the only person with no faith in the policy and who believes it is economically illiterate', while another warned: 'Give in on this and Portillo will try and bring you down before the election.'

Then Hague came up with a new idea to buy off the Shadow Chancellor off. To reassure worries about cutting vital services, he would agree that the tax guarantee would not apply in the event of a severe recession. This was little more than the 'stability fund' planned by Maude at the outset, but it would be bolstered with a promise of specific tax cuts.

Hague used a novel parallel to explain his idea to the Shadow Cabinet: 'When you buy a washing machine, you get a guarantee that it won't go wrong, but the guarantee no longer applies if the power is turned off. Every product has conditions attached to the guarantee.'14

What he meant was that if the power driving the economy was switched off, it was perfectly reasonable to say the guaranteed tax cuts would not be paid. Osborne told him: 'The politics of this are hideous. We are undermining our commitment to tax cuts and at the same time we are embarking on spending cuts. It's all pain and no gain.'15

Hague considered two options. Plan A was to 'redefine' the policy – agree to water down the guarantee as Portillo wanted, but present it as 'reinforcing' the pledge by unveiling specific tax reductions. Plan B was the nuclear option: stick with the policy and lose Portillo.

Hague considered plan B but was terrified of the consequences and opted for plan A.

On the morning of Wednesday 6 July, Hague told colleagues he planned to change the tax guarantee – a course most of his advisers opposed – and Hague and Portillo met in the leader's office that afternoon.

Since Hague had discussed it with Portillo and was giving him most of what he had asked for, he assumed the Shadow Chancellor would accept the offer. He was wrong.

Portillo threw it back in Hague's face and told him: 'I am not prepared to say we still have a tax guarantee. I will not do it.'[16]

Hague accused him. 'You are reneging on the deal we have already reached, whereby we say we are reinforcing the tax guarantee.'

Portillo refused to budge.

Hague pleaded: 'Michael, I want you to have another think about this.'

Eventually, they agreed the policy would be killed off, but it would be done slowly to spare Hague's blushes, or, in the words of one Shadow Cabinet Minister; 'by slow strangulation rather than summary execution'.

'There was no need to abandon the policy completely,' said a senior party official. 'We could see the limitations and could have included any kind of proviso and qualification to make it clear that it was not some kind of scorched earth tax policy, but Portillo wanted to remove it completely.'[17]

Detailed negotiations between Hague and Portillo took place during which they agreed a form of weasel words whereby they would announce the policy was being 'reinforced' – whereas in fact it was being weakened to the point that it was almost dead.

Each man would have his say in the *Daily Telegraph* on 11 July, forty-eight hours to go before Portillo's resignation deadline expired.

Hague gave a hurriedly arranged interview in which he announced the tax guarantee would not apply 'in the event of severe recession, unexpected acts of God or war', and to try and distract attention from the

U-turn, he also announced that the Tories would restore the married couple's tax allowance, abolished by Labour two months earlier. This was to back up the dubious claim that the Tories were 'reinforcing' their commitment to tax cuts.[18]

The ruse worked almost too well. The *Telegraph* concentrated on the married couple's tax cut,and Portillo's supporters boasted to anyone who would listen that 'the real story' had been overlooked.

They pointed to an article by Portillo buried on page 18 of the same day's *Telegraph*. This appeared to be a routine attack on Gordon Brown, but its real purpose was contained in three sentences near the end: 'Our critics attack the Conservative tax guarantee as meaning that we might take risks with the public finances; or that if we ever had to choose between cutting taxes and maintaining vital services, we would cut taxes. The guarantee was not intended to imply any such thing. Our policy will guarantee that we can increase spending on priority public services, and cut taxes in any normal circumstances.'

The following day's papers got the message and proclaimed the U-turn.

Hague was badly bruised, but he had kept his job, Portillo had not resigned, and the tax guarantee would be quietly dropped.

Further humiliation was yet to come. An eagle-eyed aide suddenly realised that Hague's new draft manifesto, *Believing In Britain*, was to be published on 5 September. The tax guarantee had been launched in a similar document, *The Common Sense Revolution* launched the previous summer.

If the words 'tax guarantee' appeared in black and white in the new version, Portillo would threaten to resign again. If they weren't, the press would say it was proof that far from 'reinforcing' the policy, Hague had torn it up.

Once again, Hague sat down with his advisers and agonised over what to do. He had come too far to resist at this late stage: the words 'tax guarantee' were excised. Yet another newspaper briefing had to be set up so he could put a favourable gloss on the final climbdown, instead of being caught red handed when the manifesto was published a week later.[19]

One year on, almost to the day, Hague had driven a stake through the heart of the policy he thought could win him the election.

A source close to Portillo said: 'The tax guarantee was thrown together ten days before the Blackpool conference to get a quick headline. No one had thought it through properly. The Shadow Treasury team were aware of its defects long before Michael arrived. We could not go into the election with a tax policy that was widely believed to be incredible because it would have made it impossible to restore our reputation for competence. One or two people like Kaletsy supported it, but mainly on the basis that we could afford it by privatising large parts of the health and education service. We could not possibly have done that.'[20]

Other Shadow Ministers like John Redwood had expressed doubts when the policy was first conceived, but thought the policy was 'do-able' if the wording was altered, and believed it was 'suicidal' to do a U-turn. But Redwood was not there to defend Hague when Portillo demanded the U-turn: Hague had sacked him to make way for Portillo.

Why did Hague give in? Why not keep the policy and let Portillo walk out? If the policy really was a vote winner, Portillo would be the loser, not Hague.

The answer is at the heart of the problem faced by Hague in dealing with Portillo. Portillo never fully accepted Hague's authority as leader. He regarded Hague's strategy as ill-judged and frequently little more than a knee-jerk reaction to daily events. Initially, when Hague became leader, Portillo genuinely believed they agreed on the scale of changes necessary for the Conservatives to win back the trust of voters. But in Portillo's view, by the time he joined Hague at the Shadow Cabinet table, he discovered they were travelling in opposite directions: Hague was going backwards.

Portillo had a choice: he could do what his leader wanted him to do. Or he could resist. He chose the latter.

The signs were there twenty-four hours after Hague had first unveiled the 'tax guarantee' policy at the previous year's party conference in Blackpool.

The day after the launch, Portillo addressed a Bow Group fringe meeting on the Wednesday evening. It was his first major speech since admitting to homosexual experiences in his past and since announcing he hoped to stand as Tory candidate in the forthcoming Kensington and Chelsea by-election.

It was the first time Portillo had set out on a public platform his new, softer, more caring political philosophy. His views on economics had changed as much as his views on social matters. Tax cuts were no longer the be all and end all of politics. 'There is more to life than making money and collecting consumer durables,' he declared.[21]

He might just as well have said: 'There is more to life than guaranteeing to cut taxes.'

4 Two Tribes

'These are lies put about by Amanda.'
Francis Maude, February 2000

'Michael and I should both have walked out,' said Francis Maude. 'It would have been better for us and better for the party.'[1] Maude's comment was made after the last election and reflected the deep frustration felt both by him and Portillo. Between them they threatened to resign seven times.

One week after the reshuffle in February 2000, Maude and Portillo went to see the Conservative leader to demand action: they wanted him to sack the three aides upon whom Hague relied more than anyone else in the party.

'We want you to replace Seb, Amanda and Nick,' said Maude. 'If you don't, then we will need to reconsider our own positions.' It was the moment the Conservative Party divided into two tribes.

Platell, appointed less than a year earlier to transform Hague's nerdy image, Coe and Nick Wood, recruited for his skill in turning complex policies into vote-winning headlines, were the Tory leader's most trusted aides. He was closer to them than to any member of his Shadow Cabinet, and as the attacks from without and within the party grew, so did Hague's reliance on the 'closed door set', so called for the way they protected Hague. Portillo and Maude wanted all three dismissed.

Hague knew his leadership could never survive such a massive blow to his already weakened authority, let alone the personal loss of such close allies.

'Why do you want them removed?' he asked.

'Because of what they have said about Robbie,' replied Portillo.

The 'Robbie' at the centre of the dispute which threatened to destroy

Hague's leadership was neither a member of the Shadow Cabinet nor an MP. He was a spin doctor – and, on the face of it, a low ranking one. But he was a pivotal figure in the Portillo tribe.

Robbie Gibb had built up a formidable reputation as a Tory student activist before becoming Maude's Chief of Staff. He was deputy chairman of the notorious Federation of Conservative Students, scrapped by Norman Tebbit in 1986 as a result of its rowdy and reckless right-wing antics.

But although Maude was Gibb's boss, his idol was Portillo. Gibb was said to have a life-size cardboard cut-out model of Portillo in his Pimlico flat, and was reputed to be the unofficial leader of the 'Portillistas' – the band of fanatical Portillo supporters who saw him as the Tory party's saviour, and Hague as little more than a caretaker leader.

Some of the Portillistas, many of whom, like Gibb, worked in Central Office, were suspected of using their positions to undermine Hague, and the tensions came to a violent head when Portillo was appointed Shadow Chancellor. He wanted to appoint Gibb as his chief spin doctor: Gibb knew the Treasury portfolio inside out and Maude was happy to release him.

But Hague, acting on the advice of Coe and Platell, refused.

They told him Gibb would be 'Portillo's Whelan' – a reference to Charlie Whelan, Gordon Brown's infamous spin doctor who was eventually forced to resign after Tony Blair became convinced that he was briefing against him on behalf of the Chancellor. 'Robbie will do just the same to you,' Platell told Hague.

Portillo and Maude hit back, claiming Platell was behind a newspaper leak that Gibb's posting with Portillo had been blocked because he was suspected of being disloyal to Hague. 'Robbie has not been briefing against anybody,' exploded Maude. 'He is a dedicated public servant and has been defamed.'

'I am told that he has,' said Hague.

'These are lies put about by Amanda,' said Maude.

'Can you provide any evidence?'

'No, but we are certain.'

'I am sorry, but I am not prepared to act unless you have proof.'[2]

It was not the last time the trio held such a conversation – and the outcome was always the same. Hague was prepared to change his policies, members of the Shadow Cabinet even, but his 'closed door set' would stay with him to the end.

Maude and Portillo backed down, but they made repeated resignation threats over the course of the year – usually, though not always, over the same unproved claims and counterclaims about who was whispering poison into whose ear.

The resignation ultimatum followed an extraordinary two-week tug of war over Gibb. Maude phoned him on the day of the reshuffle and asked him if he would like to continue to work for him in his new post as Shadow Foreign Secretary. Gibb, who was out house hunting, agreed. Later that day, Portillo went to see Maude in his Commons room to apologise for having taken his job. He raised the issue of staff and said he admired Gibb's work, but could not employ him even if he wanted to. When Maude asked why, Portillo told him Hague had banned him from doing so: it was a condition of his becoming Shadow Chancellor. Maude was outraged, and the two decided to challenge Hague's decision.

Maude phoned Gibb and asked: 'Have you decided what you are going to do?'

'I'm happy to stay with you,' said Gibb.

When Portillo and Gibb met at Smith Square next day to discuss the handover of the portfolio, Gibb's curiosity got the better of him. 'If I had not been working for Francis, would you have been interested in employing me?' he asked.

Portillo paused for what seemed like an age to nervous Gibb.

'I'm not allowed to,' said Portillo.

Gibb was stunned into silence and asked why. The pair went for a walk to Portillo's house in nearby Belgravia, where the Shadow Chancellor told him: 'The allegation against you is that if you work for me you will do the same as Charlie Whelan. You will brief against William and set up a rival court around me.'

Gibb insisted he was the victim of vicious and unfounded smear. Portillo decided to back him and to force Hague to climb down and let him employ Gibb, the first of several occasions he was to challenge the leader's authority. He had been Shadow Chancellor for less than forty-eight hours.

He immediately set about enlisting support to clear Gibb's name. At least two Shadow Ministers, including Maude's treasury team deputy David Heathcoat-Amory, went to Hague to plead Gibb's innocence. Then Gibb went to see Hague in person and demanded to know the charges against him.

'What the hell is going on?' demanded the spin doctor.

'People tell me that you have been saying things about me and the Shadow Cabinet,' said Hague.

'I promise you it is not true.'

'Well, that is what I am told by people I trust.'

'It isn't true. How can I prove it to you?'[3]

Gibb said later: 'That is the first stage at which all the things that had been going on involving the people around William started to unravel. Until that moment I was completely unaware there was any problem between me and anybody else at Central Office.'[4]

That claim is a surprise to those who had seen an extraordinary spat between Platell and Gibb on the House of Commons terrace a few months earlier, when she attacked Portillo for taking a sideswipe at Tory treasurer Michael Ashcroft at the height of the row over his controversial business activities. 'Robbie was almost hysterical, saying Amanda had no right to accuse Michael of betraying the party,' said one witness.[5]

The moment that Portillo announced he intended to become Tory MP for Kensington in the summer of 1999, tensions between the Portillista tribe in Central Office and the Hague tribe had quadrupled. Gibb bumped into Platell in a corridor. Each accused the other of leaking against their man.

Hague called in Tory Chief Executive David Prior to act as referee. Meanwhile Gibb launched his own investigation to clear his name and was informed that one of the allegations against him was that he had plotted against Ann Widdecombe. She had complained to Chief Whip James Arbuthnot that Gibb was responsible for telling the press that her round of speechmaking to local Tory associations on the so-called 'rubber chicken circuit' was part of a leadership campaign.

'I have never briefed against you Ann,' Gibb told her.

'I was told by a journalist that you had,' she replied.

'But I admire you,' protested Gibb and demanded to know the name of the journalist. Widdecombe refused to say. Her mistrust of Portillo and the Portillistas continued to grow.

After several days, Prior ruled in Gibb's favour. Maude, Portillo and Gibb were delighted. But Platell and Coe were not prepared to concede defeat. Platell told Hague that if Gibb was allowed to work for Portillo, it would be a 'disaster for party unity' and lead to constant infighting. If Hague ignored her advice on a key issue of media staffing, both she and Coe said they would leave.

In the end, Gibb agreed to go. His Tory friends helped him find a job as deputy director of a right-wing think tank, the Centre for Policy Studies.

'I had no choice because it would have been a self-fulfilling prophecy,' he said. 'Anything that appeared in print that was remotely unsupportive of William would have been blamed on me.'[6]

Hague was determined to stand by Platell, Coe and Wood – even at the massive risk of losing his two most senior spokesmen. He had little choice: it was a direct attack on his bunker. If he sacrificed them, there was no one left but himself. It was the equivalent of Gordon Brown demanding that Tony Blair fire Alastair Campbell, Number 10 'gatekeeper' Anji Hunter and Chief of Staff Jonathan Powell.

Gibb's reputation as a political wheeler-dealer dedicated to promoting Portillo was well established long before Hague arrived at Central Office. The Tory leader's biographer, Jo-Anne Nadler described how:

> The twice yearly parties of Robbie Gibb have become a fixed point in the calendars of the young movers and shakers of the right. A long time supporter of Michael Portillo, Gibb had sealed his reputation as a party fixer par excellence through his

party activism since student days. As a BBC political producer he had been well placed to build up his contacts book into a 'Who's Who' of the Eurosceptic right. The summer party in his Pimlico basement flat was always packed with political fellow travellers, including MPs, journalists and advisers.7

Once Portillo lost his seat in the 1997 general election, Gibb was a cheerleader with no one to cheer for. He switched his allegiance to Hague in the leadership contest, acting as a go-between for Hague and Portillo, and persuaded Hague's close friend and right-hand man Tory MP Alan Duncan to make sure that Hague attended Gibb's summer party that year. Hague accepted and was duly ushered into the presence of Portillo, where they chatted over white wine and canapés.

It was a classic piece of Gibb power politics: he had proved his worth to Hague and after Hague's leadership victory was given a key job working for Francis Maude. But it did not mean he had given up his loyalty to Portillo.

Gibb was among the most prominent of the Central Office 'Portillistas' – the all-male bunch of thirtysomething, right-wing hangers-on, spin doctors and political wannabes who referred to themselves reverentially as 'The Movement'. Some of them were still inside Central Office at the time of Portillo's arrival in the Shadow Cabinet. Others, such as former Tory directors Andrew Cooper, Michael Simmonds and Ceri Evans, had left, or been forced to leave after Platell's arrival amid claims (proven in the case of Simmonds) that they had leaked party secrets.

On the day Gibb's departure was leaked, Redwood, who had been sacked in the reshuffle and believed he too was a victim of briefings by Portillo's supporters wrote: 'Barely a day, never a week goes by without some briefing, often from paid officials, against the leader or a senior shadow minister. It is a steady drip drip to damage reputations. It is disconcerting to our party activists to read these comments. Many believe them. They have no reason to know that they are planted for a purpose by people who should know better. They would be horrified if they understood that paid party officials are out to play around with the reputations of those who put their names on the line every day for the sake of the party and cause that they love. Amanda Platell, who has come in from the outside, quickly understood the damage this was doing and knew it had to stop.'8

Maude and Portillo claimed they were the victims, not the perpetrators, of the backbiting, briefing and sniping.

The hostility between Platell and Maude and Platell and Portillo was ferocious. Platell was head of Hague's tribe in Central Office, accused by Maude of deliberately stirring up trouble to distract from Hague's own failings. 'Amanda decided her role was to be William's protectress and that since it was jolly difficult to land a blow on the Government, the simplest thing to do was to invent all these internal enemies and devote your energy to defeating them instead,' said Maude. 'As soon as any member of the Shadow Cabinet was seen to be doing well, they were a threat to be undermined. I had one good year as Shadow Chancellor so I too was regarded as a potential danger to Hague who had to be seen off.'9 (Seb Coe was criticised as a political lightweight, but his slight frame disguised a ruthless determination to protect Hague.)

Maude did enjoy a brief spell when he was seen as Hague's most likely successor, but poor performances against Brown were frequently discussed by MPs in the tea rooms, and it was hardly surprising that such talk should reach the public prints.

Shortly after Platell's arrival in March 1999, Maude asked her out to dinner to establish a working relationship. She said something that stuck in his mind. 'When I took this job, all my friends in journalism told me that if you think Fleet Street is a snake pit, wait until you get into politics,' said Platell.

'It's not true for my part,' Maude told her. 'It is a misconception to think we are always at each other's throats. I regard politics as a calling. If I wanted to make money I would have stayed in the City. For the most part, we all get on together very well and work as team.'

Platell's experience at Central Office convinced her that her journalist friends were right, as she said in her first interview after stepping down from her post after the 2001 general election: 'People said I would find politics more vicious than newspapers and I don't think I would disagree with them.'[10]

She had been hired as head of news and media by Hague in March 1999 to replace Gregor Mackay. Australian-born Platell more than made up for Mackay's lack of glamour. In her twenties she had backpacked to Britain, and quickly rose through the ranks of Fleet Street. She joined the Tories after she was sacked from her job as editor of the *Sunday Express* when she fell out with *Express* editor-in-chief Rosie Boycott. Deteriorating relations between the two came to a head when the *Sunday Express* revealed the identity of Peter Mandelson's lover, Brazilian linguist Reinaldo Avila da Silva, and published a photograph of him. Boycott, a strong Labour supporter and friend of Mandelson, was angry, but bided her time before sacking Platell. Her dismissal, seen by many as 'Mandelson's revenge', gave her an added motive to work for the Tories. Hague asked her to revamp his media operation and use her intimate knowledge of Fleet Street, to help him achieve the impact that he had signally failed to do in the previous two and half years. She was employed to devise ways of projecting Hague's image and fighting Labour, but in the event found herself spending much of her time fighting those she saw as the enemy within.

Platell was not the kind to avoid confrontation, as Mandelson discovered when she clashed with him when they had dinner at the Labour conference in 1998. After Mandelson had made sarcastic remarks about her, she threw a half eaten *petit four* at the Minister, who picked it up and silently put it back on the table.

Platell demanded a £100,000 salary from Conservative chairman Michael Ancram – £30,000 more than her predecessor had earned – and got it, and after a shaky start secured Hague far better coverage in the popular press, particularly the *Sun*, whose cruel lampooning of Hague reached its climax – or nadir – at the 1998 party conference when it portrayed him as a dead parrot, borrowing from the famous *Monty Python* sketch: 'RIP Conservative Party . . . Born 1832, died 1998'.[11] It was only the last-minute intervention of a senior executive that dissuaded *Sun* editor David Yelland from allowing a reporter dressed as a parrot to run onto the platform during Hague's conference speech and pretend to drop dead beside him.

Platell introduced Hague to Yelland and the two found they had more in common than a bald head and a Yorkshire accent. Under the headline 'Hope For Hague', the *Sun* declared: 'On October 6, 1998, we likened it [the Tory party] to *Monty Python*'s dead parrot. Maybe we started something. Nobody is yet saying Hague will win. But there is no doubt the nation is warming to him.'[12]

One of Platell's few rows with Hague came when she managed to fix up a meeting for him with Rupert Murdoch, whose News International company owned the *Sun*, *News Of The World*, *Times* and *Sunday Times*. Murdoch phoned out of the blue from America and suggested meeting Hague, who was in Montana with his wife Ffion. Hague refused to interrupt his holiday to fly to New York and Murdoch did not repeat the offer.

Platell forged similar links with other newspaper editors, opinion formers and political correspondents, many of whom she had worked with and knew well. This only fuelled the suspicion in the minds of Portillo and Maude that any damaging story about them in the media must be her fault. 'There were endless reports saying William was the only one who was any good and the rest were crap,' said one Central Office source: 'It never occurred to them that the press had made up their own minds.'[13]

Platell's boast that she could use her media contacts to track down the source of any leak from inside the party was sufficiently intimidating to end a series of damaging leaks before her arrival. She was convinced that Portillo's tribe were responsible, and did not have to wait long to find concrete evidence of disloyalty.

One month after she arrived in March 1999, Michael Simmonds, Tory party director of marketing and membership, was caught leaking to the *Times* a draft copy of a speech by Hague's deputy Peter Lilley, in which the former Cabinet Minister tried to distance the party from Thatcherism and move to a more 'inclusive' approach.

Simmonds, who secretly helped Portillo with speechwriting and received a message of support from him during the leak investigation, was forced to sign a gagging clause before he was given a pay-off. Next to go in the purge of Portillistas was director of operations Andrew Cooper. Platell suspected him of leaking the damaging findings of focus group surveys of which he was in charge, which showed that people regarded Hague as weak. Once she discovered his computer 'screen saver' consisted of a picture of Portillo, he had little chance of persuading her of his innocence. Cooper left soon afterwards.

He was followed by another member of the tribe, Ceri Evans. Evans went on to lead the London mayoral campaign of Steve Norris (another Portillo supporter). Evans defected to Labour in March 2001 saying he felt let down by Hague.

After leaving Central Office, Cooper set up his own political consultancy which became a refuge for Portillista exiles from Smith Square: Simmonds, Evans and another ex-Central Office staffer, Kevin Culwick, who acted as Portillo's minder in the Kensington by-election and during the general election, went to work with Cooper.

To Hague loyalists, all this merely confirmed what they had believed all along: that the Portillo mafia inside Central Office had been in cahoots and were waiting for the day when they would get their jobs back under a Portillo-led party. They longed to do to Platell, Coe and Wood what they had done to them.

One of the most confusing aspects about the Portillo tribe is that they have two distinct political origins. Some, like right-wingers Gibb and Simmonds, are Thatcher's children. Others have their roots in David Owen's SDP. Cooper was a former SDP member who campaigned against Hague in the Richmond by-election in 1989 when Hague entered the Commons.

But two other SDP converts remained in key posts in Central Office right up to the 2001 general election.

Tory director of policy Danny Finkelstein was a former aide to SDP leader David Owen, and Hague's head of research Rick Nye, half brother of Gordon Brown's chief of staff Sue Nye, used to run an SDP think tank.

Cooper, Nye and Finkelstein defected to the Tories *en masse*, working for John Major, then Hague. But when a softer chastened version of Michael Portillo emerged after his shattering defeat in the 1997 election, combining Euroscepticism and social liberalism, the Gibb faction and the SDP faction in Smith Square found common cause.

Platell and Coe were suspicious of Nye and Finkelstein. Finkelstein was blamed by some over a leak in 1998 suggesting Redwood, Gillian Shephard and Michael Howard were to be sacked from the Shadow Cabinet, while Nye was accused of leaking information to the *Sunday Telegraph* about divisions over the party's approach to the euro and asylum. Neither allegation was proved.

'We didn't have a great deal of talent to draw on, and since Rick and Danny were two of our best thinkers and both did their jobs well, it was better to keep them on board,' said one Conservative source. 'Most of the awkward squad had gone.'[14]

The connections of the Portillistas spread further. *Times* political commentator Tim Hames, who received the leaked copy of the Lilley speech, was a Portillo supporter and is married to Simmonds's sister. Simmonds is a close friend of Nick Gibb, Tory MP and brother of Robbie Gibb. Nick Gibb is as devoted a Portillista as brother Robbie and a close confidant of Maude.

Another member of the *Times* Portillista circle is Michael Gove, Portillo's biographer and friend, who authored a scathing two-page attack on Platell two months before the 2001 general election, calling her a 'liability'. Gove is friends with Ivan Massow, the millionaire businessman who fought Jeffrey Archer and Steve Norris in the contest to choose a Tory candidate for the London mayoral election. Massow, another who is sympathetic to Portillo, defected to Labour in August 2000, describing the Tory party as 'bigoted'.

When Finkelstein left Central Office after the general election, having failed in his attempt to become Tory MP for Harrow West, he joined the *Times* leader-writing staff, alongside Hames and Gove.

The air of mistrust pervaded every corner of 32 Smith Square. 'The Portillistas operate like sharks,' Tim Collins told a friend: 'When one fin moves all the others move in the same direction.¹⁵

Nor did the purge mean an end to the leaks. They continued, though many were based on old research, prompting speculation that some of those forced out had simply taken their files with them and were drip-feeding information to the press, taking slow and calculated revenge.

As the row over Gibb raged in early February 2000, there were two leaks, leading some to think it was part of a tit-for-tat war over Gibb's treatment.

The first, leaked four days after Hague told Portillo he could not employ Gibb, revealed that some of Hague's team had nicknamed the Tory party the 'flatliners' – after the medical term for a dead patient. The word had been used in a confidential report for Hague compiled by senior aides a few months earlier as a means of describing the Tories' plight at being stuck at a lowly 30 per cent in the polls for month after month – a flat line on the graph.¹⁶

Interestingly, the only Tory politician to use the term publicly was Michael Portillo, in off-the-cuff remarks made to the Spanish newspaper *El Pais* in December 2000: 'For about eight years we never passed 30 per cent. It's what the Americans call flatlining, like a dead patient.' It was almost an echo of the *Sun*'s 'dead parrot' taunt. Hague was furious and saw it as evidence that the term 'flatlining' – which he had banned – was common parlance among Portillo and his supporters.

A week after Gibb's enforced departure, another internal report was leaked, revealing that Tory private polls showed voters regarded its policy on Europe as 'backward looking' and regarded Hague as 'weak'; Redwood was 'extreme and arrogant' and Widdecombe 'alienated men'. The public 'scarcely recognised' Francis Maude and Shadow Defence Secretary Iain Duncan Smith, both of whom should 'smarten up'.¹⁷

The mistrust was mutual. Maude constantly complained he was the victim of briefings by Platell. At one of the daily 9 a.m. 'Leader's Meetings' at Central Office, after another bout of press criticism of Maude's performance, Platell and Wood insisted they had strongly defended him in briefings to the media and had told journalists that Hague had ordered all Shadow Ministers to do the same.

Maude interpreted their actions as a slight and commented: 'It is not helpful to suggest that the Shadow Cabinet is disloyal.'

Hague sighed wearily: 'You just can't help some people, can you?'[18]

Just as Platell and Coe believed Maude and Portillo – or their supporters – were constantly sniping at them, so Maude and Portillo themselves were rarely out of Hague's office making the same complaint. On one occasion when Maude had been accused of 'underperfoming', he and Portillo marched into Hague's office – and left it livid when Hague refused to take their word over Platell's.

'We have incontrovertible proof that this was done by Amanda,' said Maude.

Hague: 'If you can prove to me that it was Amanda then I will act on it, but you must produce evidence.'

Portillo: 'William, we are telling you that we know it to be true. We have the highest placed sources and they have confirmed it to us.'

Hague: 'And I am equally confident that you are mistaken. I cannot act on hearsay. If you present me with the evidence then I will act. But not unless you can do that. It would be wrong.'

Maude: 'But we are your two most senior spokesmen. You must accept our word.'

Hague: 'I have explained to you that I will only act when I have clear evidence that what you are saying is accurate.'[19]

But they never did produce the evidence.

When the general election campaign began and Central Office needed all the troops it could get to man the 'war room', Portillo and Maude insisted that Robbie Gibb be allowed back in to help, and Hague could hardly refuse since he had put them in charge of the 'war room'. Gibb and Platell met at Westminster's Atrium restaurant to bury the hatchet. Platell drank Chablis and Gibb sipped tea as they agreed a truce. Gibb later joked that it was how he imagined it might be meeting an ex-wife.

Although both were stationed in the 'war room' for the four-week campaign, they managed to avoid each other most of the time. The moment Platell came in via one door, Gibb went out of the other, and *vice versa*.

Tory treasurer Michael Ashcroft once confronted Portillo over reports that the Portilistas had undermined Hague. 'If any of my people were doing things I didn't want them to do, they wouldn't be in the positions for very long. These people are paid by the party, they shouldn't be undermining it,' Ashcroft told him.[20]

Ashcroft later gave his verdict of who was to blame. 'Anyone could see that, taken as a whole, Portillo's actions would have difficulty in passing the test of being loyal.'[21]

A measure of Portillo's near obsession with Platell is provided in two incidents involving former Tory MP Michael Brown, formerly one of Portillo's closest friends.

Brown, a political columnist for the *Independent* newspaper, was taken aback to receive a phone call at his Pimlico flat late in the evening on 26 June , 2000.

'I haven't spoken to you for a long time, Michael,' said Brown.

'Have you seen the *Times*?' asked Portillo.

Brown hadn't.

Portillo told him it contained a report claiming 'Tory knives are out for low impact Portillo.'[22]

'How did it happen?' demanded a clearly flustered Portillo. 'Where did the story come from? It's all nonsense.'

It dawned on Brown that Portillo assumed that since he was now a political journalist, he must know the source of the story. Brown, who has an impulsive but warm and open nature, said without thinking: 'I should speak to Amanda.' He recalled: 'It was said in all innocence. I simply meant that she was Hague's press secretary so he should ask her, not me. The conversation petered out after that. With hindsight, I probably reinforced his paranoia about her.'[23]

On another occasion, Brown had lunch with Platell at the Reform Club and was spotted by Stephen Sherbourne, a former aide to Margaret Thatcher and one of Portillo's (and formerly Brown's) closest friends. 'I wondered whether Stephen told Michael he had seen me dining with Amanda and because I had written sympathetically about William once or twice, from then on I think Michael assumed I was in league with her.

It is how the Portillo mindset works, but there was nothing in it: they see conspiracies everywhere,' said Brown.24

The wounds left by the row over Gibb never healed, and created a mutual suspicion between the two factions that intensified as polling day approached. Tory hopes faded and minds turned to what would happen after the election.

Maude said: 'The reason Amanda wanted to get rid of Robbie was not because he had been disloyal – he hadn't – it was because they thought he wanted to make Michael leader of the party and that that was Michael's only ambition. It was not.'25 Platell would agree with most of that statement – apart from its declaration of Gibb's innocence and the last three words.

Malcolm Gooderham, the man recruited by Portillo as his spin doctor when Hague vetoed Gibb's appointment, was no more successful in proving the loyalty of Portillo's tribe than Gibb had been. Hague wanted Gooderham fired on the spot when he was caught briefing against the party leader in the middle of the election campaign, but Portillo refused, saying: 'If William was not prepared to take action against his staff who briefed against me, I will not take action against my staff.'

Like Hague, Portillo was determined to defend his tribe.

5   Back from the Brink

'The more we see of Hague, the more impressed we are. If he stands outside Number 10 in his mid 40s, remember this: you read it here first.'
The *Sun*, 20 July 2000

In the first weeks of the new millennium, one of William Hague's closest friends arranged to meet a Tory grandee at the Carlton Club in Pall Mall.

He had phoned him the previous day and asked to see him to discuss 'a problem with William'. The grandee had served both Margaret Thatcher and John Major in a career spanning three decades. 'I think William may resign,' said his colleague.

'Are you serious? Why?'

'He feels he is not making any headway, and what with Archer and everything else, he's low. Very low.'[1]

'Archer and everything else' was a reference to a spate of scandals and controversies in the last few weeks of 1999 that had more than dented Hague's natural resilience and good humour and made him give serious consideration to resigning as party leader.

As Hague saw in the New Year 2000 at the Millennium Dome with Ffion, he, like millions of others, assessed his life and prospects. He had been leader for more than two years, was well over the halfway point between the last general election and the next, and yet he felt he had achieved virtually nothing. He was still seen as the weird little boy in short trousers who knew every MP's name when he was at primary school and looked like – in the tasteless but authentic words of Labour MP Tony Banks – a foetus.

Early attempts at changing his fuddy-duddy image with a personalised baseball cap and trip to Notting Hill carnival had backfired disastrously. The Dome, a winter beds crisis in the National Health Service, a series of Labour 'cronyism' scandals, the first sustained complaints that New Labour had not delivered its grand promises – all had failed to cut Blair's lead in the polls. Every Saturday afternoon became a nightmare for Tory media staff as they waited for a fresh bombshell to be dropped in the next day's Sunday papers.

On the afternoon of Saturday 20 November, Hague took a phone call he had been dreading for months. The *News Of The World* was about to publish allegations that Jeffrey Archer, who was standing as Tory candidate in the London mayoral election, had lied in his 1987 libel case against the *Daily Star* over his affair with call-girl Monica Coghlan.

Archer phoned Hague at his home in Yorkshire and told him: 'I'm pretty confident I can get through this.'

'Oh no you can't, you're out, that's final,' replied Hague.

On 2 December, Hague fired Tory MP Shaun Woodward from his position as Shadow Spokesman for London for defying him over his hardline stance on Section 28 of the Local Government Act, which banned the promotion of homosexuality in schools. On 18 December, another Saturday, Hague and Ffion were leaving for Wales to celebrate their second wedding anniversary when he was phoned on the way and told by an aide: 'Woodward is defecting.'

Bernard Jenkin, Woodward's boss in the Tory environment team, knew of his sensitivities on gay issues, and warned Hague of pushing him too far, and Shadow Cabinet Office Minister Andrew Lansley had discussed a compromise deal with the leading gay rights group, Stonewall.

But Hague refused to water down the policy.

'I am not changing our position now. We support Section 28,' he told the Shadow Cabinet in a rare display of impatience.

At the same time, voters were reminded of old Tory sleaze and 'cash for questions' with daily coverage of former MP Neil Hamilton's unsuccessful libel case in the High Court against Mohammed Fayed. Hague's relations with the *Times* newspaper had broken down over the paper's year-long campaign against Conservative Party treasurer Michael Ashcroft and his mysterious financial dealings. And a Gallup poll in mid-January showed that only fourteen per cent of voters thought Hague would make 'the best Prime Minister'.

Alongside all this loomed the shadow of Portillo.

With the local elections looming in May, there was growing speculation that unless the Tories did well, Hague would not last until the general election, let alone beyond. Right-wing commentator Bruce Anderson, one of his most ardent admirers, wrote that the Conservative leader was at 'rock bottom.'[2]

Hague had to do something – fast. And it would have to be eye-catching, imaginative and popular, words not usually associated with him.

'Shut your eyes,' Amanda Platell said to Nick Wood as they sat in Central Office.

He did. She shoved a piece of paper towards him and said: 'Open them.'

Wood opened his eyes and saw a crude sketch of a lorry with a Union flag and the pound sterling symbol on it.

'What is it?' asked Wood.

'It's William's flat bed truck that is going to stop Tony Blair scrapping the pound,' she replied triumphantly.

And so Hague's single most memorable campaigning gimmick was born.

Platell started doodling when she received a panic phone call from the leader from his car on his way back to Central Office from Heathrow on 14 October 2000. An enraged Hague had heard on the radio how Kenneth Clarke and Michael Heseltine had sat either side of Blair that day at a news conference organised by Britain In Europe, a cross-party coalition to promote closer ties with the European Union.

Hague saw this as an act of outrageous personal treachery by two political foes from his own party who were determined to damage him: he felt humiliated and was desperate to find a way of hitting back. As his mobile phone line crackled, he told Platell: 'We must have something special so we can respond to what Heseltine and Clarke have done. It must be good, really good.'

She and Wood spent an hour or so tossing about ideas before she came up with the truck, and when Hague arrived at Smith Square, Platell performed the same trick on him. He was silent for a few seconds and then exclaimed: 'I like it, I like it. Yes, we'll do it' – then called in his full team of advisers, devised a message to go with the truck and launched the policy there and then in briefings to newspapers.

It had the required effect.

The front page headline of next morning's *Times* newspaper was not 'Blair and Clarke Humiliate Hague over EU' but 'Hague to Fly Flag against Blair's "Traitors"':

> William Hague last night put himself at the head of a national campaign to save the pound as he responded to the formation of Tony Blair's 'new patriotic alliance' on Europe. As Mr Blair, Michael Heseltine and Kenneth Clarke redrew the political map on Europe, Mr Hague proclaimed a fresh battle for Britain and promised to take his fight to keep sterling into the country's cities, towns and villages. In a move reminiscent of John Major's soapbox campaign in the 1992 general election, Mr Hague plans to address open-air meetings across the country. Armed with a loud hailer, he will speak from a platform on the back of a truck decorated with Union flags and balloons.[3]

Hague issued his rally cry: 'I will be leading a full blooded campaign – the Battle for the pound, the Battle for Britain.'

There was only one problem.

No one had told Francis Maude that war had been declared. Maude was then Shadow Chancellor and, in theory at least, the man in charge of the Tory policy on the single currency. The first he knew about the truck idea was when he was called by his deputy David Heathcoat-Amory, who had been challenged about the *Times* report in a late-night TV interview as the first edition of the paper arrived in the studio.

The interviewer held up the paper and asked Heathcoat-Amory to comment. He couldn't because he knew nothing about it. He waffled for a minute or two and, the moment the interview was over, phoned Maude – who immediately phoned Platell in a rage.

'This is a crappy way to behave!' he shouted. 'There is a group of us who have been working on this policy for a long time and yet something like this is announced out of nowhere which is quite liable to leave us open to ridicule. I am not prepared to put up with this kind of conduct.'

Platell: 'If you are saying you intend to resign, that is a matter you should discuss with William.'

The two continued yelling at each other, with Maude doing most of the shouting, for almost fifteen minutes.

The seeds of Maude's mistrust of Platell – and Hague – were sown. According to some reports it was during this conversation that Maude made his first threat to resign over her. He went on to make three more.

Maude said he was sick and tired of being kept in the dark about important decisions. Platell told him she was acting under Hague's orders.

One of Platell's colleagues said: 'She had only done what William had asked her to do. He was determined to produce something to show that he could top anything Heseltine and Clarke could throw at him. He wouldn't have thought of asking Francis because it took him ages to produce a proposal. William needed something dramatic and practical and Amanda produced it.'[4]

Maude took his complaint to Hague the next day and asked how long Hague had been planning the truck and was told: 'Since yesterday.' The Shadow Chancellor objected: 'We can't just go and do these things without thinking it through and discussing it with colleagues. We have to make sure that our actions are properly joined up.' He also expressed doubts about whether the truck would work, fearing it could make Hague a figure of fun.

Platell's first venture into politics and the euro had been a disaster. She arranged for Hague to give his wife an 18-carat yellow gold pendant in the shape of a pound sign to show the couple's shared patriotism – but nobody remembered to pay the £1,425 price tag and the disgruntled jeweller complained, leaving an embarrassed Platell to cough up. The entire incident was exposed as a crass publicity stunt.

But Hague was determined the truck would be a success. He was also beginning to doubt whether Maude shared his determination to make Europe the party's biggest single campaigning issue. 'More than once we had the impression that Francis was reluctant to talk up Europe in the way that William wanted him to,' said one senior party member. 'We couldn't risk telling him about the truck because he might have said no. Once William had announced it, he couldn't stop it.'[5]

Coe was given the task of finding a truck and driver. The idea had been dreamed up in five minutes, but it was four months before it was ready to hit the road.

The truck – or box van as it turned to be – was unveiled on 15 February 2000 in St Albans, where the leader was accompanied by his Shadow Chancellor of two weeks, Michael Portillo, who, judging by his awkward demeanour as he briefly stood alongside Hague on the podium in front of the van, appeared to be no more impressed than Maude.

The van kept on trucking right through to the general election campaign. One strategist said: 'For the first time in ages people were actually crossing the street to talk to Conservatives instead of crossing to the other side. The downside was that it reinforced the impression that we were a single issue party. But William loved it – and the activists loved it too.'[6]

Pleased by his successful foray into populist politics, Hague decided to repeat the trick. He launched a series of aggressive right-wing initiatives and stunts on asylum seekers, law and order and other issues which transformed his reputation with sections of the press, won him plaudits from the party faithful and, for a while, had Labour on the ropes.

But behind the scenes, Portillo, Maude, Norman and the 'liberal' wing of the Shadow Cabinet were alarmed by Hague's abrupt change of tactics.

They recalled his debut performance as Tory leader at the 1997 party conference when he talked of his passionate concern for the NHS, sent a message of support to the Tory gay rights group TORCHE, and met Portillo before the conference to make sure their speeches were in harmony. Then they seemed to be marching arm in arm down the same 'inclusive' road, as the *Times* reported:

> The Tory party is undergoing a transformation as much generational as ideological. The evolution of a more sceptical position on Europe and the adoption of a

more inclusive tone on social policy could be construed as simultaneous feints to the right and left. The policy changes are, however, better seen as the coming into their inheritance of Thatcher's children. William Hague has planted his standard on libertarian ground since coming to office and Michael Portillo's speech to the Centre for Policy Studies last night was also clearly in that territory.[7]

But two and half years later on 18 April 2000 there was little sign of a 'more inclusive tone on social policy' or of Hague occupying 'libertarian ground' when he launched one of most provocative initiatives of all.

A Conservative government led by Hague would round up all asylum seekers, detain them in converted army barracks and send them home 'within days' if their application proved bogus, he announced in a speech to the Social Market Foundation. The theme of the speech had less to do with including people than with excluding them from the country altogether.

Publicly, Labour accused Hague of playing the race card, but privately they knew Hague had struck a chord with many voters, and Home Secretary Jack Straw promptly announced plans to build three new holding centres for asylum seekers.

But there was no stopping the Conservative leader. Ten days later he seized on the life prison sentence for Norfolk farmer Tony Martin, who had shot dead a burglar, to attack Blair's law and order record: if the Tories won power, people who defended their homes would get more protection from the law, promised a rampant Hague. He found himself under siege from what he called the 'liberal establishment' – Labour, Liberal Democrats, civil liberties campaigners, trendy bishops and the chattering classes in general.

He was positively thrilled. At last, he had made an impact. People were talking about him. And this time they weren't laughing. He was beginning to look as hard as his Bruce Willis haircut.

'Great! We've got the whole liberal establishment railing against me. It's just what I wanted,' Hague told colleagues.[8]

He sounded more like his 'hang 'em and flog 'em' father Nigel than the modern, liberal inclusive William paraded at the 1997 Tory conference.

His message was aimed at provincial saloon bars, not the metropolitan salons favoured by the Portillos of this world.

Liberal was a word he spat out. 'It's time they were taken on. I shall never be browbeaten by them. Someone has to rebel against those attitudes, and I'm happy to lead that rebellion. I will not be put off by the abuse that is heaped on anyone who challenges the liberal orthodoxy of the day.'[9]

The transformation came as something of a shock to Portillo, Maude and Archie Norman. 'In 1997 William seemed genuinely progressive, but he suddenly changed,' said Norman. 'He wasn't the William I had known and worked with at McKinseys. He went back to his roots and became a Yorkshire poujadiste, a tub-thumping little Englishman.'[10]

When Norman, Maude and others challenged Hague's harsh new tone during one of their regular 'Strategy Group' meetings on Monday mornings, he replied: 'We need to take this approach to shore up the core vote. We will broaden our message afterwards.' But they claim he never did.

Even the loyal and normally monosyllabic James Arbuthnot questioned the wisdom of Hague's approach. 'We have to be careful with the voice and tone we adopt on issues like asylum,' he told the leader: 'It is not that what we're saying is wrong, but it is what it says about us. A party that adopts a strident tone in talking about things like asylum and Tony Martin and the like may stereotype us and prevent us from appealing to young people and single parents.'[11]

But he was slapped down by Hague: 'No, I know that my speeches on asylum are reaching out to people far beyond our natural supporters.'

Hague did also make speeches stressing his faith in the NHS and state education, but they were not always successful. The day after he addressed the faithful with a rabble-rousing speech focusing on crime, asylum seekers and tax cuts at Harrogate, he addressed the annual conference of the Royal College of Nursing and promised to match Labour spending on hospitals. But minutes after he left the stage, a snap poll of delegates revealed 85 per cent did not believe him, and it was that vote which dominated the following day's headlines – and frightened him off making similar overtures. 'Whenever it was suggested William should make a speech on health or education, people around him would say "look what good it did when we tried it last time,'" said a Tory strategist.[12]

But Hague had firm support from other Shadow Ministers including Widdecombe, Lansley and Duncan Smith, all of whom were sceptical about the 'inclusive' agenda being pursued by Portillo, Maude and Norman, who had now emerged as an anti-Hague alliance.

Portillo had no intention of echoing Hague's new strident tone. Indeed, he was about to add to the friction by doing the exact opposite.

'How dare anyone give instructions for one of my speeches not to be briefed?', an angry Portillo told a colleague on the evening of Friday 31 May 2000.

It was the eve of his first major address to a Tory gathering since returning to frontline politics, and he was determined to use the party's spring conference in Harrogate to show that he had turned his back for ever on the aggressive, arrogant right-wing style that had led to his downfall. His new buzz words were 'public services', 'the NHS', 'state schools'. He wanted to steal Labour's clothes by claiming that these were traditional Tory issues. This was the caring, sharing, touchy-feely new Portillo.

He also wanted it to be front page news.

But when Hague's office was sent a copy of the speech, his staff were deeply alarmed by its tone. It was totally at odds with the new hard-edged approach that Hague planned to demonstrate in his own conference speech twenty-four hours after Portillo.

The Portillo speech read like a rehashed version of the one delivered by Peter Lilley in 1999 in which he tried to show the Tories cherished the welfare state as much as Labour, was accused of renouncing Thatcherism and provoked a violent response from the very activists gathered in Harrogate. If Portillo's speech was 'spun' in the same way, there could be a disastrous clash with Hague, with reports of a split.

Hague told a colleague, 'I am uneasy. This is taking us back into the Lilley territory and we aren't ready for it', while some of his team saw even more sinister motives. They considered it a deliberate attempt by Portillo to sabotage the leader's plan to move to the right: behind the scenes, he was already pushing Hague to ditch the tax guarantee, and they could not risk any more humiliations or Portillo victories.

The job of briefing the press on the weekend speeches was the responsibility of Nick Wood. After seeking advice from other members of Hague's team, Wood told Portillo's press spokesman Michael Gooderham: 'I'm not going to brief on that speech. Surely you can understand that the last thing we need now is another U-turn. We can't risk it.'

Gooderham relayed this to Portillo, who was furious. He rang Hague to protest and told him: 'It is totally unacceptable that I am not allowed to make a speech without first clearing with officials at Central Office.'[13]

Eventually Hague told Wood to do as Portillo had asked, but by then it was late afternoon – too late to secure prominent coverage for the speech. It looked like just another speech on health and education and came and went virtually unnoticed, leaving Portillo seething with anger.

'It was his first big party rally since becoming Shadow Chancellor and he wanted it to be a big event for him, personally,' said one source. 'He never forgave the press office for thwarting him and spoke to them as little as possible afterwards. It was another stage in the general slide towards disunity.'[14]

Portillo met Hague privately afterwards to discuss the dispute, but from that moment the Shadow Chancellor had less and less contact with Central Office. 'He stayed away, particularly when he was angry,' said one Tory MP.[15]

It was to be another six months before Portillo achieved the impact he had sought in Harrogate. The 'inclusive' speech he delivered to the party conference in Bournemouth – and which secured banner headlines – was more or less the same as the one he had written for Harrogate. In Bournemouth, Portillo's own spin doctors were in charge of promoting the speech – and did so successfully, only to be plunged into a far bigger confrontation with another rival.

But back in the spring, the growing differences between Portillo and Hague remained largely below the surface. The Tories gained 600 seats in the town hall elections on 4 May 2000, and although they lost the Conservative stronghold Romsey to the Liberal Democrats in a by-election,

Labour lost its deposit. With Ken Livingstone elected as London mayor on the same day, there was no cheer for Blair.

Writing about this period, political commentator Andrew Rawnsley observed:

> William Hague, making an aggressively right-wing pitch about asylum seekers and crime, found a voice which resonated with some voters. Previously disaffected Tories began to return to the Conservatives while the Labour heartland remained sullen. Fear rippled the spine of the Government.[16]

One of Hague's main supporters in Fleet Street, the *Daily Telegraph*, went even further:

> The political equivalent of Clark Kent seems to have walked into a telephone box and been transformed. He may not have emerged with quite the powers of superman (or even Supermac) but William Hague has never looked so combative and robust. He is getting more attention in all the media and is regularly putting the Government on the defensive.[17]

'You know you really ought to do this for a living, William.'

Danny Finkelstein teased Hague after he had cleverly refined and improved yet another of Finkelstein's one liners that regularly made a monkey of Tony Blair in their confrontations in Prime Minister's Question Time at 3 p.m. every Wednesday in the Commons.

Buoyed by his successes outside Parliament, Hague was going through a purple patch at the despatch box. His performances may have looked effortless, but were the product of the same discipline, training and attention to detail that helped his friend Seb Coe win his Olympic medals. He and Hague would take a break from their Question Time rehearsals at 11 a.m. on Wednesday morning to go for a jog round Battersea Park to keep Hague's mind clear.

The preparations for the weekly Question Time started two days before the event.

On Mondays at 5 p.m., John Whittingdale would attend the 'Forward Look' meeting of Conservative MPs, chaired by Arbuthnot, to collect suggestions for possible questions for Hague to put to Blair.

At 3 p.m. on Tuesdays, Whittingdale would meet Hague, Finkelstein, George Osborne and Wood in Smith Square, where Wood would tell them what issues were likely to surface in Wednesday morning's papers. Hague would join the process at 10 a.m. in his office on Wednesday morning and apart from the break for a run, carry on practising over a working lunch until 2.40 p.m., when he left for the chamber. Finkelstein would play the part of Hague, firing questions at Old Etonian Osborne, acting as Blair. Finkelstein would try every conceivable question and Osborne would have to produce every answer, until they decided the best way for Hague to trap, tease or torment the real Blair.

Most of Hague's brilliant one liners came from Finkelstein, often conceived in his bath. They included the memorable putdown of Liberal Democrat leader Charles Kennedy: 'He has gone from "Have I Got News For You?" to "I'm Sorry I Haven't A Clue".' And during the London mayor shambles: 'Dobson is the day mare and Ken is the nightmare.'

Finkelstein would produce an idea for a gag and Hague would adapt it. 'It was like being a member of a successful TV sit com writing team,' said one official who took part in the sessions, though several jokes were dropped at the last minute for fear they were too risqué. One such was a planned putdown by Hague in his speech at the 1999 State Opening of Parliament about Peter Mandelson's role in charge of the Dome. Hague planned to round off an attack on the Government's handling of the project with the words: 'and at the centre of it all is a huge androgynous figure' – a *double entendre* linking Mandelson with the asexual Body Zone in the Dome.

Hague thought better of it.

On another occasion, a piece of quick thinking by his deputy private secretary Tina Stowell made a fool of Blair. Halfway through Prime Minister's Question Time on 10 February 2000, Stowell, sitting in Central Office, heard a news report that Labour's First Minister in Wales, Alun Michael, had resigned shortly before being defeated in a vote of no confidence.

She paged Whittingdale in the Commons, Whittingdale showed the message to Hague, who urged: 'Check it, quick.' Whittingdale grabbed Welsh Tory MP Nigel Evans, who dashed out of the chamber, phoned Welsh Tory leader Nick Bourne and received confirmation of the news. Evans dashed back in and told Whittingdale, who told Hague. The Tory leader tore up his prepared question, leapt to his feet and Blair, who did not know of Michael's announcement, was humiliated. In response to the Prime Minister's insistence that 'The Welsh First Secretary is doing an excellent job', the Opposition chorused with their Leader: 'He's resigned!'

Blair was so rattled by Hague's performances that he ordered his civil servants to provide better ammunition so that he could strike back. A leaked Number 10 memo written by Clare Sumner, Blair's private secretary responsible for briefing him before Question Time, blamed officials for making the PM fall into 'elephant traps' set by Hague. And it demanded more 'killer facts' with which to attack the Tory leader.[18]

Further confirmation that Blair was in trouble was provided by devastating leaked memos from the PM's polling guru Philip Gould, who described New Labour as a 'contaminated brand'.

By the time Hague was on his summer holidays, he was a different man from the one who had been on the brink of resigning in the New Year. He had clawed his way back by hard policies and hard graft.

The *Sun*, the paper that mocked him as a dead parrot, declared:

> It has been Hague's year. The more we see of Hague, the more impressed we are. If he stands outside Number 10 as Prime Minister in his mid-40s, remember this: you read it here first.[19]

6 Fuel on the Flames

'Watch me do Portillo.'
Liam Fox, 18 September 2000

William Hague bounded up the stairs of the £160-a-night four-star Hartwell House Hotel near Aylesbury and strode into his suite on the first floor.

A few moments later there was a knock at the door and Michael Portillo, wearing a blue open-necked shirt, walked in. Hague invited him to sit opposite him on the sofa.

The Conservative leader had asked Portillo to come to his room during a Shadow Cabinet gathering in the Buckinghamshire countryside to discuss a sensitive issue. They had some serious talking to do, and neither of them wanted the rest of the Tory front bench team present.

The subject of their discussion was an event that had caused the most severe civil disorder in Britain since the poll tax riots, visibly shaken Blair's nerve, and thrown the Tory party a lifeline: the fuel blockade, when mounting anger over rising petrol prices saw pickets preventing tankers leaving oil refineries.

Downstairs in the dining room, Shadow Cabinet Ministers had queued up to plead with Portillo to support a big cut in petrol tax in order to capitalise on the uprising. But the Shadow Chancellor refused. Now Hague wanted to make one last attempt – in private.

As was their custom when they had important negotiations, they would do it alone, with no aides, note-takers or officials present. Only they knew what went on and who said what to whom. Only one other relationship in Westminster is conducted along similar lines and for the same reason:

that between Tony Blair and Gordon Brown. Blair was party leader, but he could not rule without Brown's consent. The same was true of Hague and Portillo.

There was another reason for conducting such affairs in private: if only the two of them were present, details could not be leaked. If they were, each would know who was responsible.

Hague's spring revival had proved short-lived. Superman had turned back into Clark Kent. His hopes that he had made a breakthrough collapsed when a MORI survey on 24 August showed Conservative support down by 4 per cent since its peak of 33 per cent in July. Labour had gone through the 50 per cent barrier, while the Tories were back below 30 per cent for the first time in four months – 'flatlining' again. It was a severe blow, all the worse because it showed that the Philip Gould memos, some of the most damaging Government leaks of all time, had had no impact on Blair's standing. All the populist headlines on asylum, Section 28, Tony Martin and Europe had gained Hague nothing.

But the biggest blow of all that summer was inflicted by Hague himself in an interview with the style magazine *GQ* published on 8 August, when he tried too hard to win the laddish vote.

'Anyone who thinks I used to spend my holidays reading political tracts should have come with me for a week,' he boasted, recalling his teenage days when he worked as a driver's mate for the family firm, Hague's Soft Drinks in Rotherham: 'We used to have a pint at every stop . . . and we used to have about ten stops a day. You'd work so hard you didn't feel you'd drunk ten pints by four o'clock.' And after tea, he would go the pub, bringing his daily up to a manly fourteen pints.

It was a clumsy attempt to turn the Milky Bar Kid into Dirty Harry. Terry Glossop, manager of the Angel pub in Rotherham, called Hague a 'lying little toad'.

In addition, the Tories had failed dismally to live up to their promise of keeping up the 'summer heat on Labour'. The previous summer, Ann Widdecombe had blow-torched Labour, but now she was on holiday. Hague's gaffe made it hard for him – or anyone – to fill the gap.

'Once the kerfuffle over William's fourteen pints interview had started, it was hard for him to do anything,' said one strategist. 'The moment we put him up for an interview, the only question he would get would be about fourteen pints, so we had to wait until it died down. Unfortunately, it also meant it looked as though we weren't doing anything.'[1]

The Times summed up the renewed gloom:

> If there is not an atmosphere of despondence inside Conservative Central office this morning, then what the psychologists call denial has triumphed over the opinion poll evidence. The very modest Conservative recovery over the past six months has not only stalled but might be in the process of reversing.[2]

Hague needed a break – or there was every likelihood that he would face a crisis of confidence at the party conference. With no hope of victory in the election, it would only take one speaker to rise to the platform and attack him for his entire leadership to unravel there and then. His aides had already discussed how to meet such a contingency.

But by the time the Shadow Cabinet met at Hartwell House three weeks later, Hague got the break he had prayed for.

Eight long hard years of 'flatlining' ended dramatically on 17 September 2000 when the Tory ratings went off the Richter Scale. A MORI poll put them two points ahead of Labour, the first time they had been in the lead for eight years – since just before Black Wednesday in September 1992.[3]

The cause of the turnaround was the fuel blockade.

As the Shadow Cabinet gathered at Hartwell House to prepare for the coming party conference in Bournemouth, much of the nation was paralysed. Hague had shrewdly identified increasing anger among drivers as a potential problem for Tony Blair earlier in the year and supported a petition to complain about rises in fuel duty, and Tory transport spokesman Bernard Jenkin had repeatedly told Hague that the party must capitalise on public opinion on the issue by promising lower fuel taxes if the party won power. Hague was won round to the argument, but Portillo vetoed it, arguing it was 'too expensive' and 'gimmicky'.

Tony Blair brushed aside a nationwide demonstration calling for a 2p cut in fuel duty in July: 'It's easy for campaigners to put up signs outside garages saying so much goes to the Treasury. But you don't hear them talking about putting up signs outside hospitals saying the number of nurses and doctors should be cut because the Government doesn't have enough money.'

But no one, including Hague, foresaw the crisis that exploded as suddenly and violently as a lighted match thrown into a petrol can when the fuel blockade that started in France in early September spread to Britain.

By 11 September the nation was virtually at a standstill. A week later the Conservatives were ahead in the polls.

It was amid this heady atmosphere that on Monday 18 September, the Shadow Cabinet gathered. The main item on the agenda was a document drawn up by Hague and Portillo aimed at identifying public spending savings to finance tax cuts, but when Hague arrived, he had only one tax cut on his mind. From the moment the UK fuel blockade had started, Hague stepped up pressure on Portillo to act on the advice he had been pressing on him for months: make a pledge to cut fuel taxes by 6p a litre.

Portillo refused, arguing it was tantamount to giving in to civil disorder. When the dispute started in France, there was anger in Britain when French police stood aside as farmers and hauliers' union leaders blockaded the Channel ports, preventing British holidaymakers from getting home. But when the dispute spread to the UK, the public rallied round. British hauliers and farmers were protesting for the same reason, but their action was seen as a spontaneous uprising provoked by a genuine grievance, not engineered by union militants who used any excuse to block the Channel ports and disrupt the Brits.

'Michael thought the petrol tax cut was a typical product of the "let's get a quick headline" faction in Hague's office,' said one Shadow Minister. 'It was the sort of initiative he regarded as a substitute for serious politics.'[4]

But for once Hague's Shadow Cabinet allies were not prepared to take no for an answer. Led by health spokesman Liam Fox, they plotted a carefully rehearsed 'sting' over dinner at Hartwell House.

Hague was adamant. Since the Tories had been campaigning all year against high petrol prices, they could argue they had been consistent. The

Conservative leader had signalled his support for the fuel protesters the previous day, 17 September, in an interview on GMTV, describing them as 'fine upstanding citizens'. Interviewed later the same day, he struck a very different tone and conspicuously avoided committing himself to cutting petrol tax.

As shadow ministers arrived at Hartwell House, Fox handed lists of names to the conspirators so that they could co-ordinate their attack: 'Watch me do Portillo,' he said to one.[5]

The following night, as soon as the main course was over, with the £15 a bottle Chardonnay flowing, 'sting' leader Fox swung into action. Renowned for his fiery temperament, he had frequently crossed swords with Portillo and now tore into the Shadow Chancellor. 'This is an absolutely huge opportunity for us and we have to go for it. The Government is having a terrible time and we can win the argument on fuel. We are staring at an open goal.' Fox winked at his allies as Portillo came under siege.

Ann Widdecombe said: 'We will never have such a heaven-sent opportunity again. The Government may announce a cut in fuel duty itself very soon. We must get in first.'[6]

But Portillo disagreed: 'I cannot promise that. It would cost billions to take 1p off the price of petrol. We cannot find that sort of money. I don't know where it is going to come from. And we cannot condone the behaviour of some of the protesters.'

Another Shadow Minister remonstrated with Portillo: 'We have got to act, the blockade has been going on for two weeks and we aren't even in the story.'

Portillo said that announcing a price cut now would 'tie his hands' and the party could be out-manoeuvred if Brown cut fuel duties in one of the two budgets he would announce between then and the election. The Tories should delay making their own commitment on fuel taxes until much closer to polling day.

Fox returned to the debate: 'We need to do something now. This would really capture people's imagination.'

Widdecombe said: 'This is simply stupid. We obviously don't want to win the election if we can't agree on something as straightforward as this.'

It was stalemate.

Eventually, Portillo and Hague adjourned upstairs suite to thrash it out alone. In the privacy of his suite, Hague again set out his arguments for a 6p petrol tax cut – now. It was the best chance they had had for months to put Labour on the back foot – and keep them there. The protesters had won overwhelming support from the public. Blair and Brown, the honeymoon couple, were public enemies numbers one and two. The Tories had to show they were the friends of everyone who suffered from the crippling cost of fuel.

But Portillo still refused. He shared Labour's disdain for Hague's description of the protesters as 'fine upstanding citizens' and the rallying cry for a 'taxpayer's revolt' – and tackled his leader head on: 'If we cut petrol taxes, it is tantamount to giving in to civil disobedience and I cannot condone that.'[7]

They had discussed the issue over and again. Neither would bend to the other's will. At one point, two Shadow Ministers interrupted the meeting. One mentioned he had just watched a BBC TV news bulletin in the hotel sitting room which included a report suggesting the Government could easily afford a large cut in petrol taxes. All that was needed was the political will. Hague shrugged his shoulders and looked at them as if to say: 'That is what I have been trying to tell him.'

With mounting pressure from other Shadow Ministers who backed Hague, Portillo finally agreed to meet him halfway with a cut of 3p per litre, worth 13p per gallon. 'Michael came down and told us he agreed to the 3p, but it was pretty grudging,' said one source who was present.

Hague dared not push the issue any further. Only two months earlier, Portillo had threatened to resign, forcing Hague to abandon his 'tax guarantee' commitment, and the Shadow Chancellor would probably do the same if he tried to overrule him on petrol duty.

The day after Hague and Portillo had sat arguing on the sofa, the *Sun*, the paper whose support Hague was desperate to woo away from Labour, gave its damning verdict in an article headlined: 'How Hague Shot Himself In The Foot Over Fuel Tax':

Petrol tax has been an increasingly explosive issue for the last 18 months. It was part of the Tory campaign against stealth taxes which was causing the Government so much pain. Yet, just as it turned into a crunch issue, the Tories abandoned their tax guarantee. As Labour faced its biggest crisis, the paralysed Tories were unable to promise they would slash fuel duty. It was a disastrous own goal by a party, which above all, should be battling for small government and low taxes.[8]

Two days later, a *Sun* editorial rubbed salt into Hague's wounds, declaring of the 3p cut: 'Where was this policy last week when the country was on its knees?'[9]

'We were constantly being accused of jumping on bandwagons,' said one Shadow Minister. 'It was a fair point, but one of the reasons was that every time we tried to do something, Michael would delay it, with the result that by the time we did it, it did look like a response to popular opinion. If William had been given a free hand he would have acted in advance of public opinion. We took so long to do anything that by the time we did it, we got precious little credit.'

Portillo's enemies claimed there was another reason for his reluctance to cut fuel duty: his association with American oil giant Kerr–McGee. He had worked for the company in the early 1980s before entering Parliament, and since 1997 had been employed by them to advise on international affairs.

When he returned to the Commons in 1999, he declared his earnings with Kerr–McGee in the Commons Register as 'between £5,001 and £10,000' for 'Parliamentary services'. It later emerged that this sum was only a fraction of much larger earnings from the company. A leaked letter written twelve months earlier by Kerr–McGee chairman Frank Sharratt stated that the payment was a 'small proportion of a much wider agreement'. In April 2000 Portillo had to apologise to the Commons for speaking about petrol taxes in the budget debate without declaring his interest in Kerr–McGee. He told the House: 'On Monday, March 27th, at the conclusion of the budget debate, I made some remarks regarding the taxation of petrol without reminding the House that I have a registered interest as an adviser to an oil producing company. It was an oversight for which I apologise to the House.'[10]

The issue of Portillo's oil firm connections was raised less than two weeks before the fuel blockade, when he came under fire after launching a Tory campaign at the end of August to scrap the Government's new energy tax. Labour said Portillo had a conflict of interest because Kerr–McGee, who have substantial interests in North Sea oil, were one of the firms who would be hit by the tax.

No sooner had Portillo announced the 3p petrol tax cut, than Labour launched another attack. On 21 September, Labour MP Denis MacShane wrote to Hague demanding that Portillo be barred from 'making statements on the level of fuel duty which will have a direct bearing on the sales and profitability of the industry that employs him.'

In April 2001, it was reported that Portillo had enjoyed a series of 'jaunts' around the world financed by Kerr–McGee. On one of these trips, Portillo reportedly flew to Philadelphia with three leading members of his fan club, former Central Office aides Robbie Gibb, Andrew Cooper and Michael Simmonds, with the bill picked up by Kerr–McGee. They were chauffeur driven round the city in limousines. All three had left Smith Square following doubts about their loyalty to Hague. Portillo could not have provided a clearer demonstration of his loyalty to them.

Mr Sharratt said the free trip was one of several Portillo had enjoyed, describing the Shadow Chancellor as 'an oil man in so far as he is anything' before adding: 'Mr Portillo is an employee of ours. He often travels with us and did on the Philadelphia occasion. In the course of a year he travels with us quite frequently. Like me, he works on oil and gas matters in the oil and gas division.'[11]

'Michael was very sensitive about any criticism of his connections with the oil industry and suggestions that it might affect his judgement over petrol tax,' said a source.

Portillo's detractors pointed to another reason for the difference in attitude between him and Hague towards the fuel protesters. 'The blockade started far away from London, places like North Wales and rural areas where petrol costs hit people hard,' said one Conservative MP. 'It was of far less concern in metropolitan areas like Kensington. I don't suppose

Michael had many suicidal farmers or hauliers at his weekly surgery.'

In the end, the Tories did promise to cut fuel tax by 6p per litre. The decision was announced during the 2001 general election campaign.

By then, no one was listening.

7   Gone to Pot

'There you are, Ann – you have got a camp.'
'One person? One person does not make a camp.'
Michael Portillo and Ann Widdecombe, October 2000

The warning signs of the drugs fiasco that wrecked the Tory conference in Bournemouth in October 2000 were visible when Ann Widdecombe and Michael Portillo met in secret shortly before the annual gathering by the seaside.

Two weeks before the start of the conference, a group of Shadow Ministers who needed Portillo's approval for spending commitments in their speeches met the Shadow Chancellor in Birmingham. Widdecombe asked Portillo to approve a £250 million package to pay for more policing for a new drugs crackdown.

Portillo said: 'There is no way I can allow you to spend that much money.'

Widdecombe taunted him: 'You are always talking about inclusiveness. This will help people on council estates whose lives are ruined by drugs. What about including them, Michael?'

Portillo retorted: 'I disagree with you, Ann.'

Widdecombe: 'Are you trying to stop me from doing my job?'

Portillo: 'No. I am trying to save on our public expenditure commitments.'

Widdecombe: 'If you don't agree to this, I may have to take it up with the leader.'

Portillo: 'It's up to you.'[1]

According to the Widdecombe camp, she did get permission from Hague. According to the Portillo camp, she didn't.

There were further sharp exchanges when Archie Norman asked

Portillo for extra money for his inner city regeneration plan. As Norman pressed his case to a sceptical Portillo, Widdecombe muttered an aside: 'Quite right too, Archie.'

Portillo said: 'Not only do you want more money for your own scheme, but you are supporting other spending by Archie, too. I heard you say "Quite right too" when he was talking.'

Widdecombe was so cross that she wrote a letter of complaint to Hague stating: 'Michael has refused to give me more money and I believe it is partly because he is angry because I supported Archie Norman's request for more money.' She asked Hague to arbitrate between herself and Portillo.

Others give a different account. 'Michael turned down her request for more money and she stomped off in a huff and announced it anyway. That is why it all went wrong,' said Norman.[2]

The weeks leading up to the party conference saw a fiercely contested behind-the-scenes struggle between the two wings of the party, who were now becoming the Portillo faction and the Hague faction. The fuel blockade had shaken Tony Blair and suggested that his seemingly impregnable position was more vulnerable than anyone – including the Conservative Party – had imagined, and for the first time since Hague became leader people were beginning to contemplate whether he might, just might, become Prime Minister.

All eyes were on the Conservatives. If they could use their Bournemouth gathering to show they were a united party, fit to run the country, they might be able to give Blair a run for his money after all.

But a week later, by the time the delegates were packing their bags to return home to the shires, their hopes had gone up in a cloud of cannabis smoke as the feud between Portillo and Widdecombe boiled over, culminating in eight Shadow Ministers admitting they had taken drugs in their past. The fragile alliance between the traditionalist wing of the party, represented by Widdecombe, Duncan Smith and Lansley, and the reformist wing, led by Portillo, Maude and Norman, with Hague perched uncomfortably in the middle, leaning ever further to the right, was smashed to smithereens.

In the weeks leading up to the conference, before the fuel blockade gave the Tories a momentary though illusory glimpse of victory, Portillo, Norman and Maude had used the party's renewed slump in the opinion polls to challenge Hague over his pursuit of a right-wing agenda based on asylum, law and order, Section 28 and other so called 'core' issues. He must change the tone and broaden the party's appeal, they told him, and after a series of keenly fought debates Hague agreed once again to modify his approach to satisfy them.

The theme of the 2000 conference would be 'One Nation' – an old-fashioned term for the trendy new version of moderate Toryism they favoured. Francis Maude had special reason to be pleased with the decision: his father Angus Maude was one of the co-authors of the book *One Nation*, published in 1950, that established it as the creed of Conservatives who supported not *laissez faire* private enterprise but what Rab Butler described as 'private enterprise in the public interest'.

Portillo and Maude were confident that they had slammed the brakes on Hague's populist bandwagon, and Hague duly kept to the agreed script. The 'I'm in it for you' soundbite in his Bournemouth speech was meant to be an appeal to all voters, not just Tories. A large section was devoted to explaining how he would tackle hospital waiting lists and inner city decay and help the poor, the very kind of 'inclusive' messages which Portillo, Maude and co. had been urging him to adopt for the previous nine months.

They were confident they had secured a major victory, but they reckoned without Widdecombe.

Before Portillo's return to the Shadow Cabinet, Widdecombe was seen as the favourite to succeed Hague if he stood down. She had emerged as the somewhat unlikely successor to Michael Heseltine as the darling of the conference, and was proud of her virtuoso performance at the previous year's event in Blackpool where she delivered a word-perfect speech without notes, striding up and down the stage like a bantam.

Widdecombe used mnemonics, a system of using initials to remember a sequence of subjects, and in 1999 her mnemonic had been APPYVS – asylum, prisons, punishment, youth crime, victims and sentencing.

While her colleagues talked of how best to tackle Labour, Widdecombe was out there handbagging them, performing a passable imitation of another well-known female Tory who believed in deeds not words.

The prospect of Widdecombe emulating Thatcher alarmed some. A. N Wilson wrote:

> Something must be done to get rid of this ghastly woman. It would take a small swing to the Tories in some marginal seats and we could have Doris for PM. Anyone who is as embarrassed by her as I am would see what a calamity this would be. Why should we suppose that it is a virtue in some insufferable bossyboots if she has given 138 interviews in the space of three summer weeks. Should we not think it is a sure sign that she is deranged, a deformed personality?[3]

Widdecombe may not have been leader, but she had effectively ousted Hague's nominal number two, Maude: Her biographer Nicholas Kochan said: 'The swashbuckling confidence she displayed over the summer, and again at the conference, allowed Widdecombe to be regarded as the "unacknowledged deputy leader of the Conservative Party".'[4]

Inevitably, stories that she was out to oust Hague soon appeared in the press, and Widdecombe had no doubt where they were coming from. 'Portillo's supporters would do it to anyone they regarded as a threat,' said Widdecombe.[5]

Embarrassed by the reports, she approached Hague and told him: 'I enjoyed the summer, William, but I can assure you I am certainly not after your job.'

Hague replied: 'If people are saying that kind of thing about you, they are certainly not friends of mine. I don't mind if you do want this job when I give it up, but I know that you are not after it now.'[6]

There is no evidence that Widdecombe was trying to undermine Hague, though equally there is no dispute that her ambition was to lead the party should the chance arise. And the moment Portillo returned to the front line, each saw the other as their chief rival to Hague's crown.

Widdecombe would tend to side with Hague in disputes – though not always – she had argued against the tax guarantee long before Portillo became Shadow Chancellor.[7]

The Portillo camp always had difficulty in coming to terms both with her personality and her politics. 'She would rant and rave in meetings but she was often very inconsistent and incoherent,' said one Shadow Minister, while Francis Maude observed: 'Ann has a pathological dislike of Michael which was not returned. I don't know why she feels like that.'[8]

As the Bournemouth conference approached, Widdecombe and Portillo knew it was likely to be their last chance to display their talents to the party faithful. Both had a very clear idea as to how they would achieve their aim, though neither knew the other's plans. They were on collision course.

Portillo was first to address the conference, on the opening Tuesday. Just as he had been at the spring conference in Harrogate, he was cross at the way his own speech had been briefed to the press in advance by Tory officials. He had hoped the media would focus on his new caring approach to health and education, including his own brief spell as a hospital porter. Instead, his plan for increased involvement by the private sector in the NHS made front page news on Tuesday morning, the day of the speech. Privatisation was way down the agenda with the new Portillo.

But his anger at the briefing was as nothing compared with his fury when his speech was knocked off the front of the following day's papers by another briefing which revealed Widdecombe's controversial plan for £100 on-the-spot fines for drug takers twenty-four hours ahead of her own speech on Wednesday. Portillo and his supporters were convinced she did it to put his own speech in the shade.

Portillo's speech was hailed as a daring break with the Tory past and an attempt not merely to upstage Hague and Widdecombe, but Blair too, and the Shadow Chancellor showed that, like Widdecombe, he too could deliver a bravura address without notes. But while he mimicked her style, the content could not have been more different.

'We are for people whatever their sexual orientation. The Conservative Party isn't merely a party of tolerance; it's a party willing to accord every one of our citizens respect. Why should people respect us if we withhold respect from them?' he declared in an intimate and at times emotional performance. It was nothing like any speech she had ever delivered – with or without notes. He used the words 'I', 'me' or 'my' fifty times; he spoke in his father's native Spanish; he talked of his 'devastation' in defeat. The speech used language drawn from a different lexicon from Widdecombe's – and Hague's. Two of the Portillista officials forced to leave Central Office by Hague, Andrew Cooper and Michael Simmonds, had been consulted on the speech by Portillo, and Hague's former press secretary Gregor Mackay was reported to have helped as well.

Portillo did not mention drug takers. But had he done so, it would have been to suggest not new criminal penalties to deter them but that it was time to consider decriminalising cannabis, a view he expressed nine months later during the leadership contest. Incredibly, he barely mentioned his own portfolio, economics, which led *Times* columnist Peter Riddell to describe the economic content of the speech as 'evasive waffle'.9

Kenneth Clarke was even more outspoken, calling it 'blithering nonsense'.

Others saw the dangers ahead. Peter Oborne wrote in the *Daily Express*:

> Portillo's speech was the exact opposite to the style and content that Hague has brought to his job as Leader of the Opposition. Conference has never heard this kind of advanced talk before. Portillo thinks that the Tories have no choice but to learn from the open and emotional style of Tony Blair. Hague by contrast, feels voters are ready for a return to traditional values. Above all, he feels that New Labour has allowed itself to become too close to the enlightened but brittle values of a London based elite. In the long term, conflict between Hague and Portillo is inevitable.10

Widdecombe wasted little time in displaying her disapproval in her own words. Interviewed on the BBC the following morning, she was asked about Portillo's call for 'social tolerance' towards gays and other minorities. 'I have never been quite sure what is meant by that phrase "social tolerance",' she replied: 'The state should have a preferred model and promote family life.'11 She was still bristling with indignation about being described in Tuesday's *Times* as 'the Blue Nun, a strain of Conservatism with all the qualities of cheap hock' – in an article by Michael Gove,

Portillo's biographer and confidant, and had berated one of Gove's colleagues in the corridor of the Highcliffe Hotel and said: 'We all know what silly game he is playing.'

But it was not Portillo who dominated Wednesday morning's headlines. It was Widdecombe's own drugs plan – even though she was not due to reveal it until her speech later that day. Conservative officials had given an advance briefing to several newspapers that she was to announce the toughest ever crackdown on drug users and dealers. A new zero tolerance approach would lead to anyone caught possessing drugs, no matter how small the amount, being punished with a £100 fine and a criminal record – the kind of initiative born of the constant battle between Labour and Tory for the honour of being tougher on crime.

Officials insist that the advance briefing was routine practice for all speeches by senior party spokesmen, but Portillo's allies insist that the drugs fines were added on at the last minute – without getting clearance from him – for no other reason than to knock him off the front page, and Portillo himself was furious. 'This is a ludicrous policy dreamed up in two minutes to get some cheap headlines,' complained to one Tory aide.[12]

Widdecombe's speech went ahead as planned.

There would be no mercy for those who traded in the misery, despair and death caused by drugs or for those caught in possession of even a single cannabis cigarette. 'It means zero tolerance for possession,' she said. 'No more getting away with just a caution, no more hoping that a blind eye will be turned. From the possession of the most minimal amount of soft drugs, right up the chain to the large importer, there will be no hiding place.'

She won a standing ovation, capped with a bottle of champagne uncorked on stage to celebrate her fifty-third birthday. Hague hugged her. Portillo kept his distance.

But even before Widdecombe delivered it, the plan was condemned as unworkable. The Police Federation, which represents rank and file officers, challenged the 'practical implications', while the Police Superintendents Association stated: 'We would not support this proposal.'

Even some Tory supporters in Bournemouth criticised it. Tory student delegate Cara Cuthbertson, aged eighteen, said she had smoked cannabis – and her parents didn't mind. 'They'd rather I had a few joints than got drunk.'

Widdecombe – and Hague – were in trouble, and anger in the Portillo camp turned to glee as the Shadow Home Secretary came unstuck.

Other Tories turned on her. Lord Cranborne, former Conservative leader in the House of Lords, called for cannabis to be decriminalised, telling the BBC: 'I don't like the idea of people using drugs which are illegal any more than Ann Widdecombe does. But what I do think you do is you play into the hands of criminals if you make the law into an ass when nobody wants to obey the law and, indeed, regard breaking the law as a bit of a challenge.'

As pandemonium broke out at the conference, chairman Michael Ancram, a close ally of Widdecombe's, ordered her to retreat. Party officials, horrified by the realisation that the entire conference was disintegrating, urged her not to give media interviews. Nick Wood was seen on the Bournemouth promenade remonstrating with her. She marched straight into the press centre, where chaos ensued as she was assailed on all sides by a crowd of some fifty journalists. One with known right-wing political affiliations shouted abuse at her.

Hague had to repair the damage and gave a hastily arranged interview that evening to Channel 4 News in which he defended the Shadow Home Secretary but stressed the Tories were not declaring war on young people. And he made it clear that the party would now, belatedly, seek the advice of the people who would have to implement the policy before going ahead with the mandatory fines. 'We want to talk to the police about how you do it. They have to fight harder against drugs, not surrender.'

By Friday Widdecombe had made one concession, expressing regret that Tory officials had said her policy would mean that everyone caught with cannabis 'will receive a criminal record'. But she insisted that there would be no U-turn, and claimed that Hague, Portillo, Norman and Lansley had all cleared the policy before the conference. There was, however, a slight softening in her tone: 'A fixed penalty is a very sharp warning that you are doing something wrong. It doesn't mean we are going to send the police into every student's digs looking for drugs, or that every seventeen-year-old who smokes dope is going to be shanghaied into court or have a record which is going to blight their employment.'[13]

The row completely overshadowed Hague's own speech to the conference on Thursday, in which he tiptoed between the Portillo and Widdecombe wings of the party. There was the usual tough talk on asylum, law and order and Europe. But he also talked of the poor, inner city ghettos, run-down schools and how he would listen to black teenagers on sink estates. It could have been Tony Blair speaking.

Hague knew the Portillo–Widdecombe row had exposed the schism in his party. Working on his speech overnight in his suite at the Highcliffe, he added just one paragraph in a desperate attempt to paper over the cracks. 'There are some who say there is a contradiction between traditional Conservative issues and winning new Tory audiences; between tolerance and mutual respect for all people and championing the mainstream values of the country. There is no contradiction.'

Widdecombe and Portillo appeared to be determined to prove the opposite.

Hague's aides conceded the speech was a move away from his usual right-wing message to a more inclusive approach, and the change in tone brought press comment. Michael White in the *Guardian* wrote that Hague had 'sacrificed a ritual Conservative conference triumph with a speech that reached out beyond the Tory heartlands in an attempt to woo disaffected blue collar Labour voters',[14] while under the headline 'How El Caudillo Drew Blood' the equally left-leaning *Observer* said: 'Last week's party conference saw the final triumph of a gentler brand of ideology – welcoming to gays and worried about the inner cities – over Ann Widdecombe's moral authoritarianism.'[15]

But there was nothing gentle about what Widdecombe's enemies were about to do to her. Even before the Tory delegates left the seaside resort, the undercurrent stirred up by the tensions between Widdecombe and Portillo during the week was building up into a tidal wave of anger powerful enough to sweep Bournemouth pier into the English Channel.

No sooner had the conference ended than the *Mail On Sunday* disclosed that seven of Hague's front bench team had used cannabis when they were young.

Widdecombe was convinced that the story was leaked by someone in the Portillo camp in a deliberate attempt to kill her off as a potential leadership rival to their man, and friends say she was so devastated by the affair that she was on the brink of resigning. Reporter Jonathan Oliver said a 'senior party aide' had told him over a drink in the small hours of Thursday morning in the bar of the Highcliffe Hotel, where most senior Tories were staying, that half the Shadow Cabinet was furious with Widdecombe's plan to target cannabis smokers. He described in Raymond Chandler-style prose how the aide had planted the idea: '"Ask some of them whether they smoked dope when they were younger. I promise you will receive some fascinating responses," he murmured before disappearing into the crowd.'[16]

Over the next thirty-six hours the paper set about contacting every member of the Shadow Cabinet and was astonished when seven freely volunteered the fact that they had taken drugs. Francis Maude was first to come clean, followed by Bernard Jenkin and Archie Norman.

James Arbuthnot inadvertently played his part in the disclosures. The moment he learned of the newspaper's inquiries, he issued instructions to all Shadow Ministers to tell the truth if asked if they had taken drugs in the past. If he had told them to do what politicians normally do when asked awkward questions about their private life – say nothing – the story could have been closed down. But it was too late: the seven who admitted having experimented with drugs were Maude, Jenkin, Norman, Peter Ainsworth, Oliver Letwin, David Willetts and Lord Strathclyde.

Maude said: 'Like many of my generation, it was quite hard to go through Cambridge in the 1970s without doing it a few times.'

Norman said: 'I don't regret having done it. You expect human beings to explore and experiment. If you don't you haven't been young.'[17]

The seven insisted they had not colluded with one another, but few believed there was not some element of collaboration, and five of them later joined Portillo's leadership campaign. The seven became eight on

Monday when agriculture spokesman Tim Yeo, later to become a senior lieutenant in Portillo's leadership campaign team, joined them, confidently declaring he had found the experience 'agreeable'. In what could only be seen as a cheeky reference to non-pot smoking Hague's fourteen pints, Yeo declared: 'I enjoyed it. I think it can be a much pleasanter experience than having too much to drink.' Portillo himself remained aloof from the debate, having flown to Morocco for a holiday the moment the conference was over, a convenient escape route he was to use again the day after the 2001 general election.

But there was no doubt in Widdecombe's mind: Portillo, or at least the Portillistas, had ganged up on her. Her opponents were not motivated solely by a desire to avenge her for trying to steal the limelight from Portillo's speech. Most of them, and certainly those who instigated the drugs revelations, genuinely believed that all their hard work in winning over Hague to their updated version of One Nation Toryism had been single-handedly sabotaged by Widdecombe.

The mass drugs confession by the Tory frontbenchers ruined her political career. 'It was a spiteful attempt to damage me,' said Widdecombe. 'They saw me as a rival and set out to damage me. They had done the same to others like Liam Fox and John Redwood when they looked like potential rivals to Portillo. I have no doubt about it.'[18]

Widdecombe was not the only potential future leader who was angry with Portillo at the conference. Liam Fox raged in private, accusing Portillo of 'stealing' his announcement on hospitals. And Duncan Smith was furious when he discovered Portillo had blocked his plan to announce new spending for the armed forces.

Asked about her response to the drugs disclosures, Widdecombe stood her ground: 'It's all very well talking about what educated, articulate people did at university, but I'm talking about housing estates where drugs ruin people's lives.' But behind the bluster, she acknowledged she would have to think again. 'I have no doubt that in view of the uproar we will wish to have a full Shadow Cabinet discussion. If anybody can come up with a better way to tackle the demand side of drugs, I will be happy to look at it.'[19]

It was a far cry from the days when she told Portillo she would vote for him to be party leader. She had admired his ability when she was appointed junior Employment Minister to his Secretary of State in John Major's government, although there were times when she was dismayed by his haughty manner, such as the occasion when he was angry with a junior civil servant who refused to disclose a set of unemployment statistics to him, claiming it was against civil service rules. Widdecombe was horrified when Portillo summoned the official's Permanent Secretary boss and had the official disciplined.

'When I served with him in John Major's government, I decided that if for any reason Major stepped down, I would vote for Michael to replace him. When he came back I was expecting to find the same man. But he had changed. I had read all this stuff about a personal journey but I didn't believe it. He lives in a world where he is at the middle of the circle.'[20]

Some commentators believe that Catholic convert Widdecombe's distaste for Portillo is more to do with his private life than his public life. 'She cannot reconcile herself to his inclusive Conservatism that stretches out to homosexuals and other minority groups in society', observed Nicholas Kochan.[21] Widdecombe herself disputes claims that she turned against Portillo after he admitted to gay experiences in his past.

However, when Portillo stood in Kensington and Chelsea, she put aside her reservations and volunteered to campaign for him in the by-election. Weeks after his victory, he asked her if she would address a fund-raising dinner in his constituency. She readily agreed. Not long afterwards, she wrote to him asking if he would be kind enough to return the favour and visit her Maidstone constituency. A week later she received a letter from Portillo's office informing her that, no, Portillo would not address her constituency. She assumed there had been an innocent slip-up by his office and sought out Portillo after a Shadow Cabinet meeting.

'Your office said you could not do the dinner. I assume it was a mistake,' she said.

'No, it was not a mistake. Doing dinners is not a productive use of time.'

Widdecombe was furious and retorted: 'But I did one for you, Michael!'

'Yes, but Kensington is in London and it is not so much effort to get there. You are in Maidstone,' Portillo replied.[22]

Months later he asked her to address a breakfast in his constituency. She did so, and the next time he saw her at a Shadow Cabinet meeting, he thanked her. One source said Widdecombe replied: 'That is the third time I have visited your constituency and you haven't been to mine once yet.' Portillo ignored her and walked away, leaving the Shadow Home Secretary complaining out loud: 'It's just Portillo, Portillo, Portillo with him, that is all he thinks about.'

Portillo and Widdecombe were all Hague could think about in Central Office when he surveyed the wreckage of the previous week's conference in Bournemouth. His despondency at the beginning of the year, when he was close to throwing in the towel, returned. He knew how essential it had been for the Tories to have a successful pre-election conference if they were to be taken seriously in the campaign itself. Now they were a laughing stock. He had no choice but to try and clear up the mess at a post-conference meeting of the 'Strategy Group.'

This turned out to be one of the most acrimonious meetings ever staged at Central Office.

By now, Portillo had discovered that Widdecombe had written a formal letter of complaint about him to Hague over the way she claimed he had snubbed her before the conference when they clashed over funding for her drugs package. He turned on her and said: 'I hear you wrote a note to William saying that I refused to give you money because I was angry with you. I was not angry.' He continued to deny he had given his approval for the drugs scheme: Widdecombe continued to insist that he had.

Portillo claimed that he, and not Widdecombe, had been the main victim of the hostile press coverage in recent days. (Several later reports blamed the Portillistas for the leak about Shadow Ministers and their drug taking past.)

'I have never read such shitty rubbish about myself as I have in the last few days,' he said.[23]

Widdecombe exploded: 'Ha! I thought it was me who had been getting it in the press!'

Portillo hit back by reading out one press report which quoted an anonymous source, referred to as 'a friend of Ann Widdecombe'.

'There you are, Ann,' he harrumphed, '*you* have got a camp.'

'One person?' Widdecombe exclaimed in disbelief. 'One person does not make a camp' – at which point Hague looked away in embarrassment and changed the subject to stop the dispute getting further out of hand.

Certainly, if Widdecombe did have a camp, it was fairly well camouflaged. Her lack of one was one of the main reasons she was unable to mount a serious leadership challenge when Hague resigned in June 2001. Unlike Portillo, she failed to cultivate or attract the band of supporters needed to convert leadership ambitions into leadership. The party faithful love her, but there are no Widdecombistas prepared to die for the cause.

By comparison with the Portillistas – battle-hardened spin doctors, masters in the black arts, heavyweight political strategists, financiers and groupies – Widdecombe was on her own.

8   The Last Supper

'There are millions of people in this country who are white,
Anglo-Saxon and bigoted, and they need to be represented.'
Tory MP Eric Forth, 24 October 2000

'Well, Eric, what did you think of Michael's speech?'
The question by a smiling Robbie Gibb to right-wing Tory MP Eric
Forth when they bumped into each other in the foyer of Bournemouth's
Royal Bath Hotel seemed straightforward enough. It was tea time on 3
October 2000, the day of Portillo's dramatic 'reaching out' speech to the
party conference.

For years, Bromley and Chislehurst MP Forth had been the most ardent
and outspoken of all Portillo's backbench supporters, and his reply to
Gibb was the prelude to a bloody backlash that resulted in a spectacular
break between Portillo and his former diehard right-wing allies.

'He's gone completely bloody mad,' ranted Forth in typically forthright
terms. 'What is all this nonsense about gays and minorities? I have never
heard such rubbish in all my life!' An embarrassed Gibb tried to persuade
Forth that he should study the speech again. But Forth would have none
of it.

Over the next few weeks Forth discussed the matter with like-minded
colleagues, and they too were horrified by the New Portillo.

Ann Widdecombe received her come-uppance for her misjudgement on
drugs the moment the conference ended, with the Portillistas celebrating
her annihilation. The backlash to Portillo's own speech took longer, but was
no less fatal: just as Widdecombe's error killed off any realistic hope she may
have had of becoming Tory leader, so the violent response to Portillo's
speech did exactly the same, for it cost him the handful of votes that, in all
probability, would have guaranteed that he inherited Hague's crown.

Unlike Widdecombe's enemies, who struck like lightning in Bournemouth, Portillo's bided their time. It was not until three weeks later on 24 October, at a dinner held by the No Turning Back Group, a dining group of Thatcherite MPs, that he reaped the whirlwind.

The impact of what happened at the NTB dinner at the Institute for Economic Affairs, the free market think tank, was so shattering that it led Portillo seriously to consider quitting politics altogether, and some of his allies believe that it brought him to the brink of a nervous breakdown. It was no less traumatic for Francis Maude, one of the founders of the NTB group in 1983, who was also present at the dinner: what happened there led him to make another resignation threat, followed a few weeks later by yet another, during which he stormed into Hague's office, hurling allegations, before turning on his heels and slamming the door.

The event that started it all was the £28-a-head dinner at the IEA hosted by No Turning Back group chairman Eric Forth.

Forth, an Elvis Presley fanatic whose colourful opinions are surpassed only by his colourful ties, is renowned for his robust approach to politics. Once billed as a spiritual successor to Norman Tebbit, he had been a junior minister in John Major's government and since the 1997 general election had earned a formidable reputation as an exponent of Parliamentary wrecking tactics – or, as Forth would put it, performing his democratic duty in holding the executive to account at all times. And if that meant keeping the debate going until 4 a.m. and depriving the Blair Babes of their beauty sleep, then so much the better.

Forth customarily kicked off the NTB dinners with a provocative statement and then threw it open for general discussion. But he had never made an opening statement as provocative as the one he made that Tuesday after the guests had assembled at 7.30 p.m.

Sitting between Maude and Portillo, Forth's introductory comments were inflammatory, even by his standards, and led to one of the most spectacular, bad-tempered, abusive and at times, comical bust-ups in the history of Parliamentary dining clubs.

'Well, gentlemen, I see we have a good gathering tonight,' said side-burned Forth, like a Teddy Boy relishing a dust-up with some mods at the local disco. 'I think we ought to have a discussion about what this group believes in. I must say I always thought we believed in lower taxes, locking up more criminals, and standing up for Britain. But now I am told we stand for something called *REACHING OUT*.' He shrieked the words with melodramatic disgust.

He turned to Portillo: 'What was your conference speech all about? You should be attacking the Labour government and cutting taxes, not talking about yourself. This touchy-feely stuff is just rubbish, total rubbish.'

Portillo spoke with exaggerated composure, as though addressing an unruly pupil: 'Of course we believe in lower taxes, individual initiative and less government. But if we are going to win an election we must recognise that society has changed. Ethnic minorities are a much bigger part of the population – presumably you want them to support Conservative principles, Eric? Presumably you want homosexuals and lesbians to vote for us? We don't want to say to them, "We don't like you, we don't want your vote".'

Shropshire North MP Owen Paterson barged in: 'But it's a tiny market out there and it is already staked out by other parties. We go on and on about these minority social issues when they are of no real interest to the vast majority of the population.'

Alan Duncan, one of the most passionate advocates of Portillo's new brand of progressive Toryism, leapt to Portillo's defence. 'Michael is right. We have got to appeal to other groups such as ethnic minorities.'

Paterson interrupted him: 'You're wrong, we have to go back to family values. You are obsessed by a few issues which are of great interest to the metropolitan elite, but they are of no concern to most of our members who don't live in London. My voters are worried about more basic things, issues like fuel prices, how much tax they pay, government red tape. Why can't you address those issues instead of going on about minorities?'

Duncan flashed back: 'For f***'s sake, Owen, I know we are supposed to be the stupid party, but you don't have to prove your virility by being nasty to people.'

(Duncan was no fan of Paterson, whom he referred to as 'wooden top'. Dislike between them had surfaced during a similar discussion at an earlier NTB dinner when Paterson interrupted Duncan's speech in defence of gay rights with the memorable put-down, 'But biddies don't like botties, Alan' – a reference to the homophobic tendencies of the blue rinse brigade. Duncan snarled: 'That is a low grade barb, wooden top.')

Now Maude intervened, saying that if the Tories did not adopt inclusive policies, they had no hope of a revival.

Paterson: 'I don't give a damn what anybody gets up to as long as it's legal and it's in the privacy of their own home.'

Duncan: 'The trouble with you lot is that you are bigots.'

It was all too much for Forth. 'All this sucking up to minorities is ridiculous. There are millions of people in this country who are white, Anglo-Saxon and bigoted, and they need to be represented.' He was sending himself up – or was he?

Portillo refused to rise to the bait. 'We are a One Nation party, Eric, and that One Nation means not just white Anglo-Saxon Protestants. We have to represent people of all races and sexualities.'

New Forest MP Julian Lewis said: 'But why this obsession with appealing to the gay vote?'

He was answered by Buckingham MP John Bercow, young Turk of the Thatcherite right, one of the newest converts to Portillo's inclusiveness. Bercow had been applauded by Portillo earlier in the year when he candidly told the Commons that he had been wrong to oppose gay rights in the past and voted to lower the age of consent for homosexuals to sixteen. Portillo made the U-turn on the same day.

'Of course we want gay people who are Conservatives to vote for us,' said Bercow. 'But it's also about attracting floating voters. If we give them the impression that we are bigoted about gays or people of other races, then we will lose floating voters too.'

Redwood, relishing the sight of his right-wing adversary being roasted on the spit, gave it another turn. 'We are not bigots. We simply don't want to make these issues a big part of Conservative policies. I am certainly not intolerant towards gays or ethnic minorities but we are wrong to go on and on about it.'

Bernard Jenkin: 'Yes, we shouldn't bang on about homosexuals all the time.'

The meeting descended into bickering as Maude tried to make light of it all, saying: 'Look, the thing about this game . . .'

But he was cut short by the terrier-like Bercow: 'It's not a game, Francis.'

Duncan to Bercow: 'Down boy, down boy.'

Bercow: 'You two might think it's trivial . . .'

Maude: 'I do.'

Bercow: 'Politics is not a game. It is a very serious business.'

The discussion turned ugly again when Forth, Redwood and Paterson claimed that Portillo and Maude's obsession with 'reaching out' and 'inclusiveness' had damaged the party. Perhaps it was why they 'hadn't laid a glove' on Gordon Brown, said Forth, referring to press comments that neither Maude nor Portillo had been able to match the mighty Chancellor.

'You should be finding ways to cut taxes,' said Forth: 'Are we a tax cutting party or not?'

Maude replied: 'We have to be realistic. We could go into the general election offering big cuts in public spending and tax cuts, but we haven't got time. It would frighten people.'

Redwood took up the gauntlet: 'There are lots of ways of cutting public expenditure.'

'Perhaps you'd like to put in a document on the subject. Feel free to do so,' said Maude facetiously.

'I'd be delighted,' said Redwood. He meant it.

Maude was targeted again when some claimed he had tried to water down the Tories' commitment to revoke the EU's Nice Treaty which gave more power to Brussels.

Eventually the conversation petered out, with the room clearly divided into two camps. Right-wingers such as Gerald Howarth, Chris Chope and Julian Brazier said little, but were closer to Forth than Portillo. Others, like Oliver Letwin, were moving Portillo's way. Public Accounts Committee chairman David Davis, who arrived late, sat back and enjoyed the spectacle of his best friend Forth making a fool of Portillo, whom he had long held in contempt.

The split in the NTB was a long time coming, but the gap between

Portillo and Forth, the opposite ends of what was once a united right wing, had become a chasm, and Forth's forthrightness had become too much for some to stomach. Nick Gibb had stopped attending the NTB dinners a year earlier for precisely that reason.

But Portillo and Maude's fury at the ambush was nothing compared with their fury when a sketchy version of the exchanges was leaked to *The Times* four days later. An account headlined 'Night The Right Had Portillo For Dinner' described how Portillo was 'battered from all sides by critics who accused him of deliberately setting himself up as the leader of what Tory MPs are now calling the new "social radicals".'[1]

Westminster's golden rule – all MPs' dining clubs are supposed to be strictly confidential – had been broken.

At a drinks party on 31 October, John Whittingdale, who had also attended the dinner, told a senior Tory official: 'Francis and Michael have resigned from the NTB. If it gets out we are in big trouble.' Less than twelve hours later their resignations were all over the morning papers, and Portillo told friends that he was resigning on principle because he had the right to 'take part in discussions and thrash out matters of contention without them ending up in the press.'

The day after his resignation Maude publicly attacked the NTB group, claiming they failed to understand what was needed to protect Thatcher's legacy. He likened the Tories' need to support gays and ethnic minorities to the way Thatcher had tried to win over trade unionists and others who had been hostile to the party.

Meanwhile, behind the scenes, Maude and Portillo launched a witch hunt to track down the mole who had leaked the dinner debacle. Their first suspect was Redwood. Portillo knew Redwood disliked him, and Maude believed Redwood had undermined him when he was Shadow Chancellor by meddling in interest rates and other economic issues.

However, unlike certain other members of the NTB group, Redwood did not have a reputation for sharing his insights with the 'Fourth Estate.'

Portillo contacted Whittingdale, his former close ally who now worked as Hague's Private Parliamentary Secretary, his Commons 'eyes and ears.'

Whittingdale, who had arrived late at the dinner and did not hear the first half of the exchanges, was asked by Portillo if he had told anyone about what had happened. Whittingdale told him 'No' before correcting himself. Yes, he told Portillo, he had mentioned it briefly to Coe. It was enough to convince Portillo that he had tracked down the source of the leak. He reported back to Maude and the pair formed their own elaborate theory as to how the meeting was leaked.

They decided that after Whittingdale told Coe, Coe then told Platell and Platell told *The Times*. There was only one problem with this theory: Whittingdale missed the start of the dinner and Platell was not at the dinner. But Portillo and Maude devised an answer to this: Platell had a mole on the group who filled in the relevant details.

Maude and Portillo had not a shred of evidence that she was guilty but they were simmering with rage. The author of the *Times* article, Andrew Pierce, had worked briefly for Platell at the *Sunday Express*, but he was also known to have extensive contacts in the Tory party and had written stories equally embarrassing to Hague.

After attending the annual service of remembrance at the Cenotaph on Remembrance Day, Hague told a colleague: 'Michael and Francis are on the warpath over the NTB leak. They think it was Amanda.'[2]

Portillo and Maude demanded, and were granted a meeting with the leader, at which both threatened to resign unless Platell was fired. She was enraged to be told that she was being accused of leaking the No Turning Back dinner and denied responsibility. Once again, Hague refused to sack her.

Now it was Platell's turn to be outraged. She explained she had not been at work at the time of the leak: she had told colleagues she was taking a holiday, but in fact had been on sick leave. She even offered to produce her mobile phone records to show she had been completely out of contact at the time.

After accepting her explanation, Arbuthnot told her that Portillo and Maude had made a 'terrible mistake'. They withdrew their resignation threat, but were still angry about the affair.

Forth was convinced that the whole thing was a set-up, and that Portillo and Maude not only engineered the row but also leaked it to provide them with an excuse to leave the No Turning Back group – and that blaming Platell was part of an elaborate ruse.

Hague was confused. Maude and Portillo were constantly accusing Central Office of briefing against them, and yet it was Portillo's own supporters who were generally regarded as the most persistent plotters.

The leader was so fed up with Maude's constant resignation threats, that he seriously considered firing him, only to be talked out of it by his advisers. 'We did everything to try and make Francis happy,' said a source: 'James Arbuthnot was constantly taking him and Michael [Portillo] out to dinner to try and placate them, but it never had any lasting effect.'

By now the entire party establishment was gripped by a collective paranoia, with each side convinced the other was plotting against them. But within a fortnight, Portillo was on the warpath again.

On 29 November, a report suggesting he was on the brink of giving up politics altogether caused a sensation.

A story which took up almost the entire front page of the *Daily Telegraph*, and was headlined: 'Portillo: I Don't Want To be Leader,' declared that he had told friends he had 'no ambition' to be Tory leader, attributing this feeling partly to his lack of success as Shadow Chancellor. An editorial headlined 'Portillo Agonistes' said:

> His friends, and indeed his opponents, have noticed an unhappiness that partially disables his efforts to take on the Labour government. For someone who is so intelligent, Mr Portillo seems surprisingly uneasy in his role as Shadow Chancellor.[3]

Portillo saw this story as a dirty tricks operation masterminded by his Central Office enemies. It came twenty-four hours after another report claiming that Portillo and his allies were already plotting to stop Widdecombe beating him in the battle to succeed Hague. A frenzied new round of backbiting was under way.

The *Telegraph* insisted the 'Portillo to quit' story had come from reliable sources. Sources close to the paper said the account was similar to remarks allegedly made to editor Charles Moore by Conservative MP Nicholas

Soames, who was reported to have told Moore that Portillo was fed up with all the backbiting and wondered whether he had made a mistake in returning to Parliament.[4]

Soames wished Portillo no harm – he wanted him to be the next leader of the party. He had formed a close friendship with Portillo when he served under him at the Ministry of Defence: ex-Guardsman Soames had advised Portillo on how to carry out formal duties such as inspecting troops, and was to introduce Portillo at the launch of his leadership campaign in June 2001.

The controversy over whether or not Portillo was about to resign is all the more surprising since his friends freely admit he was on the verge of packing up politics for good at that time, and indeed had been at several times since his comeback in 1999. He was worn down by the media's constant references to his gay past, his inability to shrug off his reputation as someone who was 'untrustworthy', and his being worsted by Gordon Brown. To cap it all, he had now been disowned by some of those who had been his strongest devotees. On the day that the NTB row was leaked, *The Times* ran a separate report stating that Lady Thatcher, his former mentor, had lost faith in him. '"He has become very confused," the former Prime Minister has told friends. She "no longer understands" his beliefs.'[5]

Five days before the *Telegraph* story, Norman Tebbit, another former ally of Portillo who now constantly goaded him, poured scorn on the 'coming out of the new touchy-feely pink pound Portillo'.

With the Tories almost certain to lose the next election, what future did he have even if did succeed Hague? It was not as though he did not have another life outside waiting for him. He had switched effortlessly into the role of an ex-MP when he lost his Commons seat in 1997, making highly acclaimed television programmes and writing. There would be no shortage of offers.

His mood was frequently melancholy. Earlier in 2000 he had confided in one colleague: 'We are like John the Baptist. We are leading the way for somebody else to come after us.'[6] It was not the voice of someone who was convinced that William Hague was going to be Prime Minister. Perhaps not Portillo either. Or did he see Hague as John the Baptist, and himself as Christ, who would lead the Tories back to the promised land?

He told one confidant in the autumn of 2000. 'Until now I have enjoyed every year of my life more than the last. But this year has just been a torment.'[7]

Portillo's supporters were so fearful that he intended to give up that Nick Gibb started canvassing support to switch the leader-in-waiting mantle to Francis Maude. Gibb received a lukewarm response. It was Portillo or no one. Several MPs went to see him, urging him to carry on. In the end he agreed.

When the *Telegraph* challenged him over the reports that he was about to step down. Portillo hesitated before acting, which merely served to convince the paper's editor Charles Moore that their information was correct. Portillo remained convinced it was black propaganda, based partially on the truth but deliberately twisted to damage him.

Or was he seeing demons everywhere?

He had been criticised by people who had not the remotest connection with Hague's Central Office team, such as political commentator Anthony Howard:

> It's odd how quickly the air can go out of a political reputation. Michael Portillo's strikes me at the moment as very much a case in point. I hold no view on whether he was right to flounce out of the No Turning Back dining group. What has recently gone wrong with the Tories' 'king over the water' is, however, far more fundamental than any peevishness displayed by that episode. There is no more dangerous change to attempt in politics than a wholesale image makeover. Very few have brought it off. The same charge of lack of consistency now applies to Michael Portillo. My guess is that he will need to let his skin stretch a bit – and the 'tucks' become a little less visible – before he can confront his colleagues with a countenance that guarantees their support for him as a successor to (let alone a replacement for) William Hague.[8]

Later the same month, the *Sun* accused Portillo of 'failing to repair the Tory reputation for economic management' but went on to attack Hague's 'isolated leadership' and Ancram's 'dithering' – hardly the sort of propaganda Central Office would spread.[9]

It was twenty-four hours before 'Portillo Agonistes' pulled himself together. He gave a round of media interviews the following day, cheerfully proclaiming he was as keen as ever to stay in politics; talk that he wanted to give it all up was 'absurd tittle tattle'. He confirmed part of the *Telegraph* story by saying he had 'no ambition' to lead the Tories, although this was little more than a standard politician's denial.'

The episode had only served to reinforce Portillo's wariness of his enemies, and, according to some friends, his unhappiness. Francis Maude was certain that the whole affair had been orchestrated by Central Office, driven by their ever growing fear of defeat in the election and their determination to destroy anyone who might be in a position to challenge Hague afterwards.

Two weeks after Portillo's crisis, on 13 December, Maude exploded yet again. This time he stormed into Hague's office visibly furious over a press report suggesting that he was 'going soft' on Hague's demands for a referendum on the EU's Nice Treaty. As with the Portillo report, it was not a novel observation. For months there had been speculation among senior Tories that Maude was uneasy with Hague's hard line position on Europe.

This was the last straw for Maude. First the No Turning Back group, then the Portillo story in the *Telegraph*, and now he believed he too was the victim of a piece of malicious gossip put about by Platell. 'Every minute of my life I'm trying to target Labour and yet I am being picked on by my own side,' he told a friend.[10]

Maude freely admits to being an emotional man: 'If I have something to say to somebody then I prefer to be upfront about it.'[11]

One witness of the latest confrontation described how 'the door flew open and Francis barged in, shouting at William and holding up the offending press report. He believed everything critical about him that appeared in print was part of a giant conspiracy against him. We got used to hosing him down.'[12]

Maude told Hague: 'I am not going to put up with this any more, William. I've had enough. I have had it from the highest sources that Amanda was responsible for this. I will not put up with any longer. I'm off.'[13]

With that, he marched out, leaving Hague to wonder whether 'I'm off' meant he was leaving Hague's office or whether it meant he was resigning.

Hague tried to soothe Maude's ruffled feathers by praising him in his address to the 1922 Committee that evening, lauding the way Maude had handled Europe.

Platell was having lunch at The Savoy the following day when she was contacted by Central Office and told not to return. For a moment she thought she had been fired, but was later given the all-clear to go back after Maude had backed down. Hague had refused to sack her, though he promised Maude that if he ever caught any member of staff briefing against Shadow Cabinet Ministers, he would dismiss them.

But Maude was determined to vent his feelings in public and launched a devastating attack on the 'poison' in the party, while carefully omitting to identify the poisoners. 'I find it breathtaking that some people apparently think it is appropriate or helpful to spread poison in this way,' he said in a radio interview: 'Whoever is doing it is inflicting grave damage on the party. William has assured me that anyone proved to have done this kind of thing would be dismissed immediately and quite right too. It would be outrageous conduct and it is not just wrong – it is stupid.'[14]

'I lost count of the times that Francis and Michael would walk into William's office and say, "We have incontrovertible proof that your aides are briefing against us and you must do something about it or we will resign",' said a source close to Hague. 'They would say that they had it from impeccable sources but that they could never reveal them. William had a stock reply. Unless they were prepared to name their sources and provide the evidence that it was happening and was not just a figment of their imagination, then he was not prepared to act.'[15]

Unlike Portillo and Maude, Hague, who had suffered more personal abuse than both put together, rarely worried about what appeared about him in the press, something that impressed Tina Stowell, who had worked for the hypersensitive John Major when his leadership was under constant attack from elements of his own party:

'I'd have been suicidal by now. I think most people would. I mean, Christ, he's had everything about him completely pulled apart. But this is what is so remarkable about him – he has the skin of a rhino.'[16]

Inside Central Office, the volcanic relationship between Platell and Portillo was a source of fascination. 'I sometimes think you have been sent to us to get rid of Portillo,' George Osborne told her.[17]

Portillo used every ounce of his considerable powers of persuasion to force Hague to get rid of Platell, but the leader repelled him every time.

Francis Maude's last resignation threat was to have a major effect in shaping the Tory election strategy.

Portillo and Norman used the incident to demand promises from Hague as to how the election was to be run – and more significantly, who was to run it. They told him that Maude had been treated abominably and that Hague must do something to make him feel both a valued and trusted member of the team.

But the trio were seeking much more than a gesture from the Tory leader. They were still anxious that during the election campaign, he might do what – in their view – he had been doing for much of the last twelve months: make all the right noises when they talked about the need for a One Nation, or, in modern jargon, 'inclusive' approach, then go off at a tangent and make a hard hitting speech about the 'flood of bogus asylum seekers' or attack the liberal elite as the scourge of mankind.

Norman and Maude went jointly to see Hague and suggested a way to address the two issues: Maude's wounded pride and their desire to have a 'lock' on policy projection in the run up to polling day. They said Portillo and Maude should be in charge of policy on a day-to-day basis in the 'war room', the large second-floor office from where the campaign would be controlled. As a 'balancing measure' Widdecombe and Duncan Smith, their two main right-wing Shadow Cabinet opponents, would be sent out and about, touring constituencies as 'barnstormers'. It was a significant tactical victory for Portillo and Maude (and Norman). They had got Widdecombe and Duncan Smith where they wanted them – out of Central Office.

Andrew Lansley and Tim Collins, the right-wing junior equivalents of Widdecombe and Duncan Smith, would be in the 'war room' but in charge of tactics – how to make the most of the policy decisions made by Portillo and Maude and how to respond to crises.

Platell and Wood, who acted to protect each other as well as Hague, would also be in the 'war room' to keep an eye on Portillo and Maude.

But there was a sting in the tail for Platell. Robbie Gibb was to be allowed back in Smith Square for the election.

Portillo and Maude wanted control of the 'war room' to make sure Hague kept to the strategy they believed he had agreed in the last major discussion on the issue following the drugs row at Bournemouth. After much to-ing and fro-ing, the leader had made a presentation to the Shadow Cabinet using a slide and projector to declare his 'final' decision on the election strategy. According to one Shadow Cabinet Minister it was 'a shade more Portillo-ite than Hague-ite' in content. There would be less emphasis on his 'save the pound' and asylum hobby horses. They agreed that their theme should be 'compassion that people respect', a reworking of Labour's 'tough on crime and tough on the causes of crime' slogan.

The party should avoid talking about tax cuts in crude '2p off tax' headlines which prompted Labour scare stories of how the Tories would cut schools and hospitals to pay for them. Instead they should stress the benefits of any tax cuts. For example, the Conservative plan to cut tax on pensioners' savings must be billed as how pensioners would be, say, £5 a week better off, instead of dry statistics about tax cuts.

But by Christmas 2000, at the same time that Maude was threatening to resign again, Portillo, Maude and Norman were still not convinced that Hague was fully committed to what they had agreed, and used the Maude resignation crisis to put pressure on him.

'William was told that he must act on the election team and that it was important to make Francis and Michael feel they were a central part of it,' said a Conservative strategist. 'We were still drifting along. It was then that William was persuaded to put Francis and Michael in charge of policy projection and send Iain and Ann into the country.'[18]

Norman told Hague: 'Even though we have agreed a strategy, we don't seem to be ready to implement it. Here we are coming up to the election, but how are we going to fight it? One of the things you have to do is to make Francis feel comfortable, and you can do that by giving him a serious role in the election.'[19]

9   The Liberal Elite

'I am a liberal. And I am a member of the elite.'
Michael Portillo, December 2000

The meeting of the Tory high command was in full swing. William Hague was accepting congratulations from colleagues for his ferocious assault on Britain's 'liberal elite', linking that elite to a fall in police morale in the wake of the Macpherson Report on the death of black teenager Stephen Lawrence.

At first, hardly anyone noticed that Michael Portillo was making curious stabbing gestures. And he was mouthing something indecipherable.

The Tory official who was addressing the group continued his analysis of the morning press coverage. He read out an article by the *Guardian*'s Polly Toynbee, doyenne of the chattering classes. She had been referred to in person in Hague's speech and responded by posing the question: 'Who Is The Liberal Elite?'[1]

Still Portillo carried on his strange pantomime. Gradually, all eyes settled on him. The official fell silent. 'What are you doing Michael?', asked one shadow minister.

'I am,' said Portillo, defiantly puffing out his chest.

'You are what?'

'I am a liberal. And I am a member of the elite.'

Jaws dropped. One or two burst into nervous laughter. Ann Widdecombe slapped her arms on the table and hooted: 'God preserve us!'

William Hague stared. Portillo returned his gaze, head tilted upwards, grinning.

It was six months earlier that a Labour Party attack on William Hague's *alma mater*, Magdalen College, Oxford, had provoked the Conservative leader into making his first attack on the 'liberal elite'. Chancellor Gordon Brown had claimed that the college's decision to refuse a place to Laura Spence, a comprehensive school pupil from Tyneside, was an example of the 'elitist' attitude of parts of the education system. Oxford's treatment of Laura, who won a medical scholarship to study at Harvard in the USA, was 'an absolute scandal', he said.

Brown's comments, at a TUC reception in London on 25 May 2000, caused an outcry among leading Oxford academics, including Roy Jenkins. Nor were his views received with great enthusiasm in Number 10, where the Oxford-educated Prime Minister, a regular dining companion of Jenkins, feared that they might undermine all his efforts to promote Labour as the friend, not the enemy, of excellence in education.

Brown's speech was a glimpse of the fangs of Old Labour, the party which tried to destroy grammar schools. Middle England thought Tony Blair had got rid of all that: but here was Gordon Brown talking as though he would tear down Oxford and Cambridge brick by brick, given half a chance.

Labour was in further trouble when Leader of the Lords Baroness Jay was accused of lying over her education, saying she went to a 'pretty standard grammar school' – when in fact she had attended a fee-paying independent school, Blackheath High School, even though she had been a direct grant pupil who had not paid fees.

Conservative private polls said their core voters strongly disapproved of Brown's comments, and this was a heaven-sent opportunity for Hague to claim Labour was riddled with envy and hypocrisy. Two weeks after Brown's outburst, the Tory leader counter-attacked with his own assault on Labour's 'liberal elite', claiming it had destroyed Britain's education system.

For once, he was in a good position to attack Labour on its own ground. Unlike Baroness Jay, Hague had had a genuine state education, attending Wath-on-Dearne Comprehensive, Rotherham. Choosing his venue carefully, Hague went to Archbishop Tenison's School, a Church of England inner-city comprehensive in South London, to announce proposals to give head teachers new powers to exclude rowdy pupils.

But the real purpose was to attack Brown and his 'elitist Oxford' jibe. 'The next Conservative government will not just turn the tide. We will defeat the liberal elite that has brought our education system to its knees,' he said. 'Ignorant Chancellors of the Exchequer who lecture our best universities about elitism should come to inner-city comprehensives like this one to find out what a liberal elite did to destroy standards in our schools.' Members of the liberal elite were leading 'Labour Party activists in a war against our excellent grammar schools. For decades we have had to put up with the classroom obsessions of the Labour Party and the liberal elite. And we have paid the price in our schools with falling standards, poor discipline and children who can't spell the word Oxford, let alone aspire to go there.'

The tactic was another stolen from the Bushes. George W.'s father, former President George Bush, attacked Bill Clinton's links with 'liberal elites' in the 1992 US presidential election. It failed to stop Clinton ousting Bush from the White House, but Republican Newt Gingrich won the Congressional elections in 1994 after repeated attacks on Clinton and 'lifestyle liberal elites' – an attempt to link the phrase's damaging political connotation with Clinton's personal conduct.

The Tories were convinced that the 'liberal elite' could be New Labour's Achilles Heel. Baroness Jay, Blair's former flatmate Lord Falconer and the Lord Chancellor Lord Irvine could all be portrayed as high handed, unelected, arrogant and wealthy – and as elitists and liberals. Blair and wife Cherie were the archetypal Islington couple. Their ability to reconcile left-wing roots with highly paid jobs, getting their children into elite schools without the nuisance of paying school fees and enjoying expensive holidays with flights on the Queen's aircraft paid for by taxpayers, irked some.

The millions wasted on the Dome, Bernie Ecclestone's £1 million contribution to Labour coffers and the Formula One row, blind trusts to fund Blair's activities in Opposition, £300 rolls of wallpaper for Irvine's official residence, Peter Mandelson's secret £373,000 home loan from fellow minister Geoffrey Robinson, Robinson's own murky links with Robert

Maxwell, cocky young spin doctors, some of whom were caught trying to 'sell' access to ministers: it was not so long ago that Blair was condemning such activity as Tory sleaze, the product of an arrogant and out of touch Government that had one set or rules for itself and another for the rest of the country.

Now New Labour was acting just like the last lot.

Hague had been called a lot of things: out of touch, odd looking, weak. But not an elitist. He had tried hard to convince people he was down to earth. But for all his faults, opinion polls showed most people saw him as genuine, compared to 'smarmy' and 'insincere' Blair. Hague had few means of attacking the Prime Minister; he had to make the best of what slim opportunities were presented to him.

If New Labour was the new establishment, then Hague would speak up for the little man against the governing class. The role of little man suited him.

But to achieve his aim, Hague was to embark on yet another right turn, the very direction Portillo, Maude and Norman thought they had steered him away from. Days after his first 'liberal elite' speech in June, the Tory leader was asked if he, like Portillo, described himself as a 'social liberal'.

His reply was unequivocal: 'No, I'm a Conservative. I believe in people being able to have the lifestyle that they wish but I do believe the Government is responsible for making sure there are some standards of order and responsibility in society. People are sick and tired of being taken for a ride and that's different from being intolerant or illiberal. Peter Mandelson, Lady Jay, Tony Blair are part of the liberal elite, the intelligentsia that is out of touch with the country and has failed to deal with the problems.'[2]

Satisfied with acclaim in the popular press for his first 'liberal elite' speech, Hague widened his assault when he addressed the Scottish Tory party conference in Dundee later that month. He attacked the 'politically-correct liberal elite beloved of this Government', contrasting it with the Tories' support for the 'common sense instincts of the British people.' His comments were applauded by Tory supporters – and caused little controversy.

When, six months later, he returned to the subject of the 'liberal elite', it caused a political sensation.

But the political and personal emotions raised by the murder of black teenager Stephen Lawrence were always extreme. Lawrence's death in 1993 at the hands of racist white youths, and the failure by police to bring them to justice, became a *cause célèbre*. Labour used it to attack the Tory government's record on law and order. Four months after winning power, Home Secretary Jack Straw set up an inquiry into the police handling of the affair, and the report by Sir William Macpherson, published in 1999, accused the police of 'institutionalised racism'. It caused deep resentment among some policemen and was blamed for a drop in stop-and-search powers and an increase in muggings.

In November 2000, there was another horrific killing with racial implications. A ten-year-old Nigerian boy named Damilola Taylor was murdered in Peckham, south London, on his way home from school. This time the murder was blamed not on whites but on black youths.

It was into this political minefield that Hague stepped when he addressed the Centre for Policy Studies, on 14 December.

Having tried out his 'liberal elite' attack earlier in the year, he now made his most controversial attack on Labour since becoming Conservative leader, and in doing so he knew full well that it would outrage Portillo every bit as much as Blair. Portillo, Maude and Norman had persuaded him to tone down his right-wing rhetoric in the run-up to the party conference, and again, after the drugs debacle in Bournemouth, they told Hague he must stick to a more inclusive approach.

Hague agreed because he had no choice: he was outnumbered. He later defied them – out of desperation as much as anything else – convinced that it was the only way he could make an impact. Hague shared many of the sentiments of Portillo, Maude and Norman, but did not believe it prevented him from speaking out on issues like race.

As he had told the party conference two months earlier, he believed it was possible to be both a mainstream traditionalist Tory and show tolerance and reach out to new voters, and he decided to make a speech arguing that the Macpherson Report had contributed directly to a collapse of police morale and recruitment. It had led to a crisis on the streets and was another example of how the 'liberal elite' were out of touch with ordinary people.

The decision was taken shortly after yet another discussion with Portillo and Maude, during which they had criticised his repeated outspoken attacks on asylum seekers. He did not tell them that he planned to make a speech about Macpherson, but he did tell one member of the Shadow Cabinet.

Early in December, Hague called in Widdecombe for a confidential discussion. 'I want to go big on Macpherson and say that it is having a deleterious effect on police morale and hindering the operation of stop-and-search laws,' he told her: 'I know that some people will say that I have reverted to type, but it is what I believe and it is what I want to do.'[3] Widdecombe offered her wholehearted support, and Portillo, Maude and Norman were kept out of the loop because Hague knew that they would try and stop him.

He knew what Blair's reaction would be, but before delivering it he would learn of Portillo's response. Portillo and Hague always sent each other advance copies of their speeches; it was one of the things they agreed when Portillo returned to the Shadow Cabinet to help avoid misunderstandings. Occasionally Hague would ask for some clarification or minor change to a speech being delivered by Portillo, and Portillo would occasionally make observations on Hague's speeches. But his response on receiving a copy of Hague's speech on Macpherson was more than an observation.

Hague had sent Portillo an advance copy and his speech-writer George Osborne discussed it with the Shadow Chancellor, who made it clear that he strongly disagreed with the tone and content of the speech and told Osborne that Hague must change certain parts. Osborne was so taken aback by the comments that he jotted them down on the back of his own copy of the speech, then went to see Hague, who was in his office with Seb Coe and Danny Finkelstein.

'What did he say?' Hague asked Osborne, though it was clear from Osborne's expression that it was not: 'Congratulate William on a marvellous speech.'

Hague had half expected Portillo to disapprove – but he was not prepared for what Osborne had to say. Before reading out the remarks, Osborne held up the piece of paper on which he had jotted them down, as though to emphasise they were Portillo's words, not his own. Hague sat in silence as Osborne told him that Portillo objected to the section of the speech in which Hague attacked the 'liberal elite'.

'He said: "But I am a liberal, I am the elite", and said that "William should refer to the left-wing elite, but not the liberal elite".'

Hague replied instantly: 'Well I'm not a liberal, nor am I a member of any elite – liberal elite stays in' – and a smile spread across his face as he added: 'It's the bit I like best.'

Hague was furious that Portillo had the nerve to try and force him to delete the most important part of the speech. But he was also pleased to know he had struck home. 'Liberal elite' stayed in.

It was not the only threat to disrupt the speech. Keen to produce visible evidence that its tone was not racist, Hague wanted his speech to coincide with a visit to Brixton police on the same day. If he was photographed with black policemen, it would be that much harder for opponents to denounce him as racist. After being warned that the police might not allow Hague's visit, Widdecombe contacted Metropolitan Police Commissioner Sir John Stevens, who gave his support to Hague and told him to carry on speaking out on Macpherson.4

'The next Conservative government will tackle the whole attitude of the liberal elite to the behaviour of criminals, which for the last forty years has oscillated between denial and despair,' Hague told the Centre for Policy Studies. Macpherson was right to acknowledge that the police do make mistakes on occasions. 'But the liberal elite have seized on the report as a stick with which to beat the police . . . We will take on and defeat a liberal elite that has always given more consideration to the rights of criminals than the rights of victims.'

Hague's repeated use of the term was seen as a deliberate attempt to provoke Tony Blair and Jack Straw. But, given his demand that it be removed, Portillo could only have seen Hague's refusal to do so as a deliberate act of provocation against him.

In public, the Conservative leader and his Shadow Chancellor were fighting the Labour Party. But in private, increasingly, they were fighting each other.

Portillo had laid out his new credentials as a liberal at the party conference only six weeks earlier in Bournemouth. Now Hague was laying out his as an anti-liberal. He made a conscious decision to make it clear that he despised liberalism and those London-based elitists and their brittle values: people like Blair the liberal elitist from Islington, and, by implication, Portillo, the liberal elitist from Kensington.

Labour critics were quick to denounce the Conservative leader.

'That William Hague sought to jump on this particular bandwagon is further evidence of his weakness as a leader,' said Jack Straw. Stephen Lawrence's father Neville accused the Tory leader of 'playing the race card'. And Damilola's parents Richard and Gloria Taylor criticised Hague. 'Mr and Mrs Taylor are very unhappy that Mr Hague decided to use their son's death in his recent article and speeches,' said the couple's solicitor Neil O'May: 'They did not hear anything by way of condolences from Mr Hague after Damilola's death.'

But the Conservative leader was supported by Police Federation Chairman Fred Broughton who said: 'Some [police officers] feel a sense of vulnerability when dealing with minority ethnic suspects.'[5]

Hague did not help his argument by getting his facts wrong. In his speech he claimed that in February 1999, when the Macpherson Report was published, the Metropolitan Police 'made 18,752 arrests following stop and searches'. In fact the number of stop and searches was 18,518 and only 2,609 resulted in arrests. Hague made a similar error in describing the fall in stop and searches and arrests by September 2000. But he was not so wide of the mark about the trend in Peckham, where Damilola was murdered. Between April 1999 and April 2000 in Southwark, which includes Peckham, there were 13,838 stop and searches resulting in 1,989 arrests. This represented a substantial fall from the previous year in which there were 22,890 stop and searches in the area with 3,362 arrests.

Hague stood his ground. 'There will be more crime if police numbers and police morale continue to fall and that will mean, yes, there are more tragedies which we all end up discussing.' The Macpherson Report, he said, was part of the culture of 'political correctness' that had undermined institutions like the police. In private, one of his favourite expressions was: 'What we need is less PC and more PCs.'

While Portillo kept quiet, Steve Norris, Tory vice chairman responsible for ethnic minorities and a man rapidly emerging as one of the Shadow Chancellor's most powerful allies, pointedly refused to defend his party leader.

'I don't think you can say that the Macpherson Report led to a rise in street crime. Of course there has been a rise in crime, but that does not undermine the thrust of the report.' It was a replay of Norris' performance at the conference when he had attacked the 'homophobic nonsense' of Hague's stance on Section 28.

When senior ministers met in the Central Office boardroom after the speech, Portillo repeated his 'liberal elite' boast in front of them all, starting with his silent chest jabbing gesture, before saying it out loud: 'I am liberal, and I am a member of the elite.'

The speech had been one of the most important of Hague's career as party leader, yet Portillo was prepared to mock it to his face. Some of his colleagues claimed it was meant as a joke, but Hague did not find it funny.

Nor did he have any intention of backing down, and three days later delivered another provocative attack on the 'liberal elite'. He wrote a newspaper article in which he linked the murder of Damilola Taylor to Labour cuts in police numbers. In an article for the *Sunday Telegraph* he described Jack Straw as part of a 'liberal elite' that had failed to recognise that the main victims of muggings, thefts and assaults were blacks and Asians.

He said of the Government: 'They like to brand everyone who takes a critical look at the impact of Macpherson as racists, rather than confront the truth that it is members of the ethnic minority communities them-selves who are suffering the most from the post-Macpherson collapse in police morale and rise in street crime.'[6]

Again he came under heavy fire from opponents, with Transport Union leader Bill Morris comparing Hague's remarks to Enoch Powell's 'rivers of blood' speech in 1968. Portillo kept quiet, though he was reported to have described Hague's speech as a disgrace.

'We liberals are closer to the majority,' wrote Polly Toynbee. 'Hague is marooned in yesteryear with his shrinking blue-rinse party while we are swimming in the sea of pluralism, multiculturalism, complex families, difficult choices, all the muddle born of freedom.'

Portillo would have agreed with her.

10 Jackets or No Jackets?

'I got this Parliament the wrong way round. I should have spent the first year or so shoring up the base Conservative vote and then reached out later on.'

William Hague

'I'm sorry, but if Francis hasn't got a jacket, then we can't do the photo call,' said Hague.

The Conservative leader was standing on the sweeping staircase at an English country house at the start of one of the Shadow Cabinet 'away days', where members are supposed to 'bond' with each other and be inspired by the relaxed and comfortable setting (and fine wines and *à la carte* menus) to come up with fresh and original ideas that can never be thought of in the hidebound wood-panelled world of Westminster.

Dressed in a tweed jacket and open-necked shirt, Hague was waiting to appear in a photo call with Maude, his number two. They had agreed to be filmed walking down the grand staircase, in casual conversation about the state of the world.

Not for the first time, Maude was late. When Hague saw him striding briskly down the hallway, the Tory leader frowned. Along with Norman and Portillo, Maude was joint leader of the Tories 'no jackets' brigade. You looked younger, less stuffy and more modern without a jacket than with: it was like a facelift, only cheaper and less painful. Nor was it only about appearance. It made you more open minded, more creative, more radical.

Hague had rather more conservative ideas about dress code. He was no pin-striped stereotype, and often worked in shirtsleeves. But he had been brought up to believe that when you were 'on parade' you should be 'properly dressed' – even if it was at the weekend. He was happy to go tieless, but he drew the line at going jacketless.

When Maude breezed up the stairs towards him in a pink shirt and no jacket, Hague asked him if he had brought one with him. No, said Maude. Hague said it was impossible for the photo call to go ahead with him wearing a jacket and Maude without one. Nor was he prepared to take his off and pose jacketless with his Shadow Chancellor. Maude, much to his chagrin, was banned from taking part in the photo call, like a pupil barred by the headmaster from appearing in the annual school photograph because he had forgotten his cap. Hague posed alone, *avec* jacket.

'You think differently if you aren't wearing a suit and tie,' said Maude: 'It makes you less buttoned up and enables you to be more imaginative.'[1]

There is nothing new in the 'no jackets' theory. Bill Clinton, followed as ever by Tony Blair, set the trend, appearing jacketless at informal public occasions, schools, hospitals, walkabouts. Blair took it further, strolling out of Downing Street in jeans, holding a mug of tea with his children's photographs on it, or ostentatiously loading his Fender Stratocaster guitar into his people carrier car for a weekend at Chequers.

Tory chairman Michael Ancram's brave attempt to match him with camp fire style singsongs at party gatherings were risible by comparison.

Politicians looked more casual and approachable without jackets than with them, went the argument, and Maude was enthusiastically supported by Archie Norman, who as Tory vice chairman pioneered 'dress down Fridays' at Central Office, when staff were encouraged to come to work in casual gear. He also introduced 'black bag' Mondays when they were urged to bring in a bin liner and clear all the waste and clutter from their desks. The old guard like Cecil Parkinson – Tory chairman when Norman waltzed into Smith Square in his Chinos – bristled.

Portillo believed that changing the way the Tories looked was essential to changing their fortunes. 'Michael thinks that you have to make voters realise that we are like them. We have to make them feel we belong in their living rooms and are not a bunch of stuffed shirts who sit in gentlemen's clubs drinking port. We have to show them we are nice, normal people – like them,' said one of his allies. 'Appearing in public without a jacket is synonymous with being modern and open. Most people do not wear jackets.'[2]

Portillo showed his own faith in jacketless politics when he visited Brick Lane in London's East End, the heart of the capital's Asian immigrant population, at the height of the row over Tory MP John Townend, who had been accused of making racist remarks.

It was a classic piece of visual politics by Portillo. He went there without informing Hague and promanaded down the street, jacketless, his white shirt gleaming in the sunshine, mobbed by cheering waiters who poured out of the Indian restaurants to greet him. Accompanied by the Tory candidate for Bethnal Green and Bow, Shahagir Faruk, he inspected the halal meats in the Taj Stores, where he embraced the owner before moving on to meet worshippers arriving for Friday prayers at the local mosque.

Hague acknowledged the Tories had to look different, but not too different. One of Amanda Platell's first instructions on taking up her post was to issue an edict that no Tory MP was to wear a pin-striped suit.

They were encouraged to wear jumpers and open necked shirts at 'away days', though not if they were being interviewed for television. Some found it hard to adjust to such liberated ideas. Hague's first away day in Eastbourne was boycotted by three MPs, including Nicholas Soames (who probably wears pin-striped pyjamas). Shadow Attorney General Edward Garnier protested at one of the gatherings: 'I'm not a Tony Blair type denim shirt wearing character and I won't pretend to be what I'm not.'

Some were rather too keen to embrace the new style. Elegant Education spokeswoman Theresa May and her husband Philip were advised that their habit of appearing in colour co-ordinated outfits was a little over the top.

Eventually, Norman despaired of changing dyed-in-the-wool attitudes. 'I have sat around more often than I care to remember discussing whether we should wear jackets and jeans and we are no further forward than when we discussed it the first time,' he said. 'The truth is we are who we are in our jackets and suits and let's stop wasting time on this.'[3]

The biggest image problem the Tories had was the leader's image.

How Hague looked and how he spoke, was a talking point in pubs and at dinner parties. The focus groups told the brutal truth. *Nerd, weird, geek* and *anorak* were four of the more unflattering words commonly used to describe him. A fifth was *gay*. He was not helped by smears put about by his Tory enemies during the 1997 leadership contest implying he may be a homosexual. His marriage to Ffion should have buried that myth.

He might have got away with the baseball cap he wore on a water chute at a Cornish theme park had not some bright spark among his aides made sure it was a customised version with HAGUE printed on it in capital letters. He should have stuck to the suggestion made by his friend and adviser Alan Duncan that a Panama Hat would look better.

'But I always wear baseball caps,' Hague told him. He really was being himself.

There was more ridicule when he and Ffion turned up at the Notting Hill carnival where they posed drinking rum punch from coconuts.

Cecil Parkinson, brought back by Hague as party chairman for his experience, was horrified at the amateurish attempts to remodel the leader. 'Someone has got to tell William that he can't let his people present him in this ridiculous way,' he said when he saw the baseball cap photos. 'They haven't got a clue what they are doing. Can't they see it isn't working?' Parkinson marched off down the corridor to tell Hague in person and found Hague and his circle of male advisers, some of whom were not born when Parkinson's political career began, huddled around Hague. On his return Parkinson sighed: 'I can't believe the people who are advising him.'[4]

Tim Collins said: 'If a leader is not well known, the first few months of their leadership defines their image. People thought William was this nerdy bookworm whereas in fact he is a modern man with modern views and a lovely wife, so we thought: Let's show him as he is. It was very unfair but Notting Hill and the baseball cap seemed flippant and shallow. The TV was forever showing those pictures, William could never escape them.'[5]

Catching up with the post-Mandelson age of politics by focus group, the Tories spent a fortune trying to find out how people saw their leader: the results were so depressing that they eventually stopped doing it.

Voters would be asked which drinks, cars, music they associated with the parties and party leaders. Hague invariably came out badly. He was perceived as a gin and tonic drinker who drove a Jaguar and listened to 'Land of Hope and Glory' for fun. Hence Notting Hill, baseball caps, photos of Hague in a frogman's suit diving in Red Sea, the Bruce Willis haircut, judo sessions with Seb Coe, and fourteen pints. None of them worked. By the time he resigned after the June 2001 general election, he was still stuck on the rostrum in front of Mrs Thatcher, aged sixteen going on sixty.

Michael Ashcroft said: 'William had a Herculean task. He had a remarkable brain, great ability, was deeply patriotic and could outdebate Blair easily. But he was very inexperienced when he got the job and doesn't have the looks or the voice for the TV age. One of the focus groups said he didn't pass the 'snoggability' test, which matters for women voters. John Major had his faults, but women felt they could cuddle him. Others said they didn't like the way he pronounced his vowels. He never had long enough to convince people that he was a deeply principled, talented man who had all the attributes needed to become a great Prime Minister.'[6]

In his four years as Conservative leader, Hague experimented with more brand images for himself and his party than are found on the shelves at one of Norman's supermarkets. He started with 'kitchen table conservatism' – an attempt to 'reconnect' with voters by concentrating on bread-and-butter issues that people talked about around the kitchen table: health, education and transport. The clever concept, devised by Cooper and Finkelstein, led to a Tory party political broadcast featuring Chris and Debbie, a fictional young married couple meant to be everyday modern Tories chatting over their kitchen table about everyday issues.

Kitchen Table Conservatism became Compassionate Conservatism, an idea Hague picked up after visiting George W. Bush in 1999. Next stop was the Common Sense Revolution. Later came 'pebble dash' Conservatism, a patronising attempt to identify with Mr and Mrs Average in suburbia.

Along with the down-to-earth policies came Platell's attempt to rebrand Hague. First came 'regular guy' Hague or 'Bill the Bloke', intended to get away from William the Nerd. Then came 'Project Hague' – a comprehensive plan drawn up by Platell and Ffion aimed at showing him in a wide range of roles, from action man to loving husband. It contained some good ideas, but had to be cancelled when it was leaked in a deliberate act of sabotage.

This was all designed to show the Tories and Hague were more in touch with modern Britain, and one of his first acts as leader was to send a message of support to the Gay Pride rally of homosexuals in London in July 1997. Hague was trying to 'reach out', to be 'inclusive' – long before Portillo had even bought a ticket for his own exotic voyage of discovery, let alone arrived at the destination.

But it didn't work.

Archie Norman believes that Hague's early public relations mistakes played a critical role in the problems that beset the second half of his leadership. 'It was a tragedy for William because he never really overcame his image problem. People laughed at him, he was portrayed as a little boy in shorts. Having failed to change his image by such means, he tried to do so by changing his politics.'

'Are you sure, Danny? This is devastating!'

The response of Nick Wood when told by Danny Finkelstein about Peter Lilley's Rab Butler Memorial Lecture should have alerted the Tories to the catastrophe that was about to engulf them. The speech by the Tory deputy leader to the Coningsby Society at the Carlton Club had been cleared by Hague. It was meant to be a philosophical exposition of 'Kitchen Table Conservatism', showing how the party of Margaret Thatcher was able to embrace the welfare state.

But that is not the version that appeared in the press the day before the speech was delivered. Instead, it was seen as a U-turn on Thatcherism.

Hague knew that if he was to be taken seriously as a political leader, his party had to move on from Margaret Thatcher. He would always be the first child of Thatcherism, but she represented the past and he had to represent the future. However, to perform such a manoeuvre would require most delicate skills, careful planning and the right timing – none of which qualities were displayed by Lilley when he blundered into a political minefield on 20 April 1999.

The Tories decided to brief the speech along the lines of 'this is our

Clause 4' – referring to the Marxist doctrine in Labour's rule book which was abandoned by Tony Blair. Except Margaret Thatcher was not Karl Marx, something that Wood, a Thatcherite Tory to his nicotine-stained fingertips, appreciated.

Ann Widdecombe was aghast when told of the Lilley speech two days in advance. 'It says what?!' she exclaimed. Lilley watered it down, but it was too late.

He could not have chosen a worse moment to deliver the speech. On the same night that more than 1,000 Tories attended a party at London's Hilton Hotel to celebrate the twentieth anniversary of Margaret Thatcher's election as Prime Minister. It came slap bang in the middle of the town hall elections, not the ideal time to perform the party's biggest somersault in a quarter of a century.

When the balloon went up Hague tried to calm things, insisting that reports of the death of Thatcherism were exaggerated. But he was proud to have 'slain the myth we wanted to abolish the NHS and the state education system.'

The Shadow Cabinet was in revolt. Michael Howard, Widdecombe and Duncan Smith led the attack on Lilley. Howard complained it impugned his reputation as a minister who had served under Thatcher. Widdecombe said it made a mockery of her attempts, at Lilley's behest, to call for the 'Berlin Wall' between public and private health finance to be knocked down.

'It is not so long ago, Peter, that you were telling us to get more private money into the health service, now you are telling us we must make it clear we would never privatise it,' she said. Told the Lilley anti-Thatcher speech was 'the new line,' she replied: 'It might be, but it's not mine.'[7]

Thatcher stepped up the pressure on Hague, her aides telling his office that she had gone 'ballistic' over the Lilley speech.

'It had all got terribly out of hand,' said a Shadow Minister. 'William is a Thatcherite; he never meant to repudiate her. We hadn't thought it through properly. He blamed himself for the screw-up, but he felt badly let down by a lot of the people around him.'[8]

Hague tried to row back on the earlier claim that the speech was a U-turn on Thatcherism, but the ploy was blown out of the water when a copy of an earlier draft of Lilley's speech was leaked, showing he had planned to go even further.

The party was in turmoil. Activists were pounding the streets trying to drum up support for the local elections on 6 May only to receive a hostile welcome from Tory supporters outraged that Thatcher's name was being trashed, and derision from potential supporters turned off by the latest bout of Conservative blood-letting.

Archie Norman ordered a check on e-mails sent from Central Office and found the culprit. Michael Simmonds, the party's director of marketing, had e-mailed the speech to his brother-in-law, *Times* writer Tim Hames.

Hague was seared by the experience. Having tried, tentatively, to take one step out of the towering shadow of Margaret Thatcher, he had been forced to go running back to mummy. He was too scared to step out of line again.

Simmonds was fired. Hague sacked Lilley in a Shadow Cabinet reshuffle on 15 June. Cooper left the next day.

'We didn't spin the speech as a U-turn on Thatcherism: it was meant to slay one of the myths of Thatcherism, i.e. that we did not want to dismantle the public services,' said a Shadow Minister. 'Liam Fox and Ann Widdecombe went ballistic because they had been arguing that the only way to save the NHS was to get private money into it. The reason it went wrong was because of the timing, the leak and because William was in a weak position. The right wing was fed up with what it saw as his drift to the left. One of the few things that held us together was the belief in Thatcherism, yet he appeared to be throwing that out too.'

Hague used the reshuffle to sweep out the Tory old guard, Michael Howard and Norman Fowler, and make two appointments which changed not just the style but the entire direction of his leadership.

Andrew Lansley, a former adviser to Norman Tebbit who shared most of his former boss's more-Thatcherite-than-Thatcher views, was made Shadow Cabinet Office Minister, effectively replacing Finkelstein as Hague's main policy adviser. From that day forth, there would be no more renunciations of Thatcher, only reaffirmations.

Lansley brought with him his 'grid' – a detailed timetable outlining every major speech, event – even royal and sporting occasions – on the calendar. Never again would the Tories be caught out by spur-of-the-moment briefings, sloppy planning and rogue speeches. In future no one could open their mouths, unless they were booked into Lansley's 'Stalingrid', as it became known.

No less significant was the appointment of Tory MP Tim Collins, a former spin doctor, as senior party vice chairman. Like Lansley, Collins was a dyed-in-the-wool right-winger and seasoned campaigner.

The Portillista kids were out, replaced by Thatcherite grown-ups.

Hague knew he had to try something different, something more in keeping with his own Thatcherite past. And he was now surrounded by people around him who shared his belief in it.

'At the beginning, William did buy the touchy-feely argument in a way,' said Collins. 'What was Notting Hill and sending a message of support to Gay Pride if not reaching out? And what happened? William was ridiculed and Labour went forty points ahead in the polls.'[9]

Over the next year, others around Hague who would have preferred to see Thatcherism interred gradually noticed the change.

'At the outset, William genuinely wanted to change the party,' said Norman. 'But he discovered it was difficult to lead it in a direction that its underlying culture and tradition found hard to accept. Increasingly, he would decide to make speeches on issues like asylum without involving other members of the Shadow Cabinet. We would sit there and he would agree with us that we had to be more inclusive and tone down our language and then he would go off at a tangent and make a speech about asylum or Macpherson without telling us. The speech would be made available in the Whips' Office and we would be expected to be loyal to him and support him.'[10]

Maude and Norman would frequently complain that Hague's only strategy with Platell was to make headlines, regardless of whether or not they took the party in the right direction, but Platell had a ready answer to such criticism: 'When Nick and I arrived the complaint was that no matter what the Tory party did, it never made headlines. By the end the complaint was that we got too many headlines.'

Hague's new populist streak would in all probability not have been challenged by the Shadow Cabinet, since for all his failings no one member was powerful enough to be a serious threat to him. At least, not before the election.

That all changed when Michael Portillo returned to politics following the death of Kensington and Chelsea MP Alan Clark in September 1999, three months after Hague had been crucified over the Lilley speech. The new Portillo cruised into Central Office, determined to take the Tory party on his magical mystery tour to the promised land of gays, ethnic minorities and single mums. The tax guarantee, one of Hague's key populist policies, was thrown out of the window the moment Portillo took his seat at the Shadow Cabinet table.

It was precisely at this moment that Hague, frustrated that his half-hearted attempts to be inclusive had stalled, decided to get off the touchy-feely bus and switch to a different mode of transport.

It was less comfortable. At times it seemed to be careering downhill out of control, but at least it was going somewhere, fast. And boy, it was exciting! It was a bandwagon.

Some of the passengers were thrown out. Others leapt off. Asylum seekers, the liberal elite and Brussels bureaucrats were knocked over in its path. Crowds stood at the roadside, some cheering, some booing as 'Wee Willie' Hague, egged on by Annie 'Get Your Gun' Widdecombe,' Marshall Duncan Smith and deputies, Lansley and Collins, cracked the whip.

The suave, sophisticated and jacketless three, Portillo, Maude and Norman, retired to their stretch limos.

Francis Maude was fed up with Hague's dithering.

'William, please can we have a strategy? I don't even mind if it's the wrong one, because at least we would know what we are supposed to be doing. And that is better than no strategy at all.'[11]

The Tory 'Strategy Group' met every Monday morning at 10.00 a.m. Week after week they would thrash out what the party stood for, what its policies should be, what words it should use, what its image should be, its slogans, how they should dress. The meetings would often go on for up to two hours.

Left: Francis Maude's spin doctor Robbie Gibb leaving a wake at Michael Portillo's Belgravia home after his defeat in the leadership contest. Hague's refusal to let Gibb work for Portillo led to resignation threats from Portillo and Maude.

Below, clockwise from top left: Mark Field – helped Portillo win the Kensington selection battle and later became MP for Westminster amid controversy (Universal Press); Nick Gibb – a Tory MP and brother of Robbie Gibb who also promoted Portillo's cause (Universal Press); Danny Finkelstein – the Conservative Policy Director; Malcolm Gooderham – Portillo's spin doctor accused of encouraging the *Mirror* to ridicule Hague.

Clockwise from top left: Former Social Security Minister Andrew Mitchell, who complained to Party Chairman Michael Ancram about 'dirty tricks' used to stop him becoming a Tory Parliamentary candidate (Universal Press); Jill Andrew, who was the victim of anonymous hate mail sent to Tory chiefs (Universal Press); right-wing MEP Daniel Hannan, who told a senior local official in Sutton Coldfield Conservatives how to get information on Mitchell (Universal Press); former Minister Derek Conway, who believed that Portillo supporters tried to wreck his bid to become MP for Kensington.

Archie Norman leaving Michael Portillo's house after the collapse of Portillo's leadership bid.

Francis Maude, suitably relaxed without jacket and tie.

Hague's Shadow Cabinet are all smiles as they meet at Hartwell House Hotel in Buckinghamshire in September 2000. They fell out during dinner over Portillo's stance on the fuel blockade.

Novice MP Iain Duncan Smith joins Cabinet Ministers Michael Portillo and Peter Lilley at a weekend gathering at Lilley's French farmhouse in October 1993 after the Maastricht Treaty revolt. *Back row from left*: Michael Forsyth, Portillo, Lilley, Neil Hamilton, Edward Leigh and Mary Leigh; *front row from left*: Bernard Jenkin, Anne Jenkin, Sue Forsyth, Gail Lilley, Carolyn Portillo, Christine Hamilton, Michael Brown and Iain Duncan Smith.

Hague shares an election platform with Margaret Thatcher in Plymouth, rejecting Portillo's call to disown her. (*Daily Mail*)

Portillo, alongside the Majors and the Hagues, salutes Tory activists at a rally in Brighton moments before losing his cool with a party aide. (Reuters)

Widdecombe and Hague toast her controversial anti-drugs speech at the 2000 Party Conference before the bubble burst. (*Evening Standard*)

Hague launches his Save the Pound truck in St Albans on 15 February 2000. (PA)

Hague with his election 'A' team: Portillo, Maude, Widdecombe, Ancram, Lansley and Duncan Smith. (PA)

Hague and Portillo's loyalty pledge in an Essex farm yard. (PA)

Portillo dines with *Times* editor Peter Stothard at Le Caprice restaurant after the newspaper had attacked Amanda Platell.

The Blairs on 8 June 2001. (PA)

The Hagues (and Seb Coe) on 8 June 2001. (PA)

Amanda Platell leaving Smith Square the day after the 2001 landslide. (PA)

Iain Duncan Smith in Rhodesia/Zimbabwe in his army days with Andrew Parker Bowles (then married to Camilla).

Oliver Letwin – the Shadow Chief Secretary to the Treasury who went missing during the election after telling the *Financial Times* that the Tories wanted to cut £20 billion from public spending. (PA)

Ann Widdecombe gives her support to Kenneth Clarke in the battle to become party leader.

Iain Duncan Smith eyes up Kenneth Clarke during the leadership election. (PA)

With 21 votes each, Michael Ancram and David Davis drew for last place in the first round of the leadership contest, forcing another vote. (PA)

Kenneth Clarke congratulates Iain Duncan Smith on his victory

By the winter of 2000, with the election approaching fast, they were no closer to deciding on a strategy than when they had first sat down in the Conservative boardroom on the first floor of Smith Square.

Maude wasn't the only one who was frustrated. Widdecombe, who had spent most of the previous two years arguing against him, told one meeting: 'I have sat on this body for two years and I am sick and tired of these discussions which get nowhere. Can we please reach a decision and go away and start making some policies? The election is only six months away and we have done nothing!'[12]

When the group met a few weeks after the Bournemouth drugs debacle, the shaky edifice that was the Conservative Party's election strategy came crashing down in an avalanche of insults. Widdecombe was still raw over the cannabis debacle. She was face to face with her colleagues for the first time since it happened.

There was yet another argument over how to fight the election. Hague was filled with despair. Polling day was only months away and his senior spokesmen were too busy slugging it out with each other to aim any blows at Labour. To rescue the situation, he told Archie Norman to speak individually with each member of the 'Strategy Group' to try and reach a peace deal.

Norman visited all the key players. The 'Strategy Group' met again and Norman gave a presentation, setting out his conclusions. Instead of bringing peace, it sparked another war. 'There are other things we could be doing on law and order, such as talking about rehabilitation,' he said.

Widdecombe bristled. 'You haven't been listening to my speeches, Archie. I have covered that issue.'

Norman: 'We don't do enough to mention genuine asylum seekers.'

Widdecombe: 'I do.'

Norman: 'Well, I've never heard you.'

Norman changed tack. 'On education, we should do more to stress how our proposals will help deprived pupils.'

Theresa May was not a member of the 'Strategy Group', but Widdecombe leapt to her defence: 'Theresa did that the other night.'

One witness said: 'We were all punch drunk. We had spent so long arguing about what we should say and what we should stand for and we had not made a single decision.'13

The meetings frequently saw angry exchanges, usually with Portillo, Maude and Norman pitched against Widdecombe and Lansley, who were backed occasionally by Ancram and later by Duncan Smith. Hague himself rarely got involved, and would usually point out that the issues where the Tories had a lead over Labour were asylum and law and order, his favourite topics. The Portillo wing would argue it was not enough. The party had to broaden its appeal. The Strategy Group went round the same course again and again.

The group had been set up in 1999, when after two years as leader Hague faced complaints from Shadow Ministers that the party was nowhere near developing a coherent image, either for himself or his party. It started out discussing policy, but as the months went by, and more specifically after Portillo joined it in February 2000, it turned into something different, becoming a battle for the heart and soul of the Tory party. On one side were the libertarians – or Portillistas: Portillo, Maude and Norman. On the other were the authoritarians – or Thatcherites: Widdecombe, Lansley, and in most cases Ancram. Modernisers – or 'Mods' – versus reactionaries – or 'Rockers'.

Hague started out trying to straddle the two, but ended up siding with the rockers, though he never told the mods.

Portillo, Maude and Norman would make speeches about reaching out, changing the party's image, looking different, sounding different and dreaming up new slogans and soundbites. Widdecombe saw all that as pointless navel-gazing, but to Portillo it was the only way to prevent the party 'flatlining' to oblivion. The public despised the Tories, he would argue. They had to do something drastic to win back their affection; the party had to be 'for people, not against people'.

Norman would tell the group: 'People have a very negative impression of the Conservatives. They think we only care about a small number of issues that they don't care about themselves. We must make them think we are more accessible and user friendly.'

The discussions ran into the buffers as Portillo, Maude and Norman stuck to their inclusive agenda, with Widdecombe and Lansley demanding more hard-hitting traditional policies – and Hague pretending to agree with them all. Unlike the Leader's Meeting, where there were as many advisers as politicians, advisers were excluded from the Strategy Group, with the exception of director of research Rick Nye.

As a result of the deadlock, Hague set up an 'inner Strategy Group' consisting of Portillo, Maude and Widdecombe and given the task of producing a new language for the Tories, and it was this group that produced the slogan 'Safe haven, not a soft touch' – intended to demonstrate that they were not against all asylum seekers, merely against those who were not genuine.

Maude and Norman said Hague and Widdecombe must stop talking about a 'flood' of asylum seekers and 'bogus' asylum seekers. Hague was also told to tone down his virulent anti-EU rhetoric. It was suggested he talk about a 'Common Market, not Common Government' – providing a positive pro-European message as well as a patriotic anti-Brussels one.

The Portillo faction stepped up their campaign for more 'inclusive' policies after the local elections in May 2000, when Hague took a sharp right turn and concentrated on asylum, Section 28 and Tony Martin. They were determined to steer him back towards the centre ground – the mainstream, as they called it – and they were convinced they had succeeded by the time they gathered in Bournemouth for the all important pre-election conference.

'The real tragedy of the drugs debacle was that until Bournemouth, we had been getting somewhere,' said Norman. 'William had made subtle changes to his style. The main theme of his conference speech, "I'm in it for you", echoed what Michael and others had been suggesting for some time – that we had to be for people, not against them. We had progressive policies on pensions, inner cities and of course, there was Michael's speech. But the drugs row ruined everything.'14

Tim Collins disagreed. He claimed the switch to a more inclusive Conservatism failed. 'From the May elections right up to the start of the general election campaign the following year we campaigned on what I call "fluffy bunny Conservatism". To my mind it is no coincidence that having done well in the May elections, we never came within twenty points of Labour again.'[15]

But others say it was Hague who undermined the Strategy Group's plans.

'We would have long debates about broadening our appeal and developing a more user friendly image – and we were winning the argument,' said Norman: 'Then William would go off on his own and do the opposite.'[16]

One of the main bones of contention was how the Tories should tackle their Achilles Heel – health and education. During the election campaign, there were frequent reports that Portillo and Maude wanted Hague to focus more closely on schools and hospitals, the bread-and-butter issues at the centre of the long since abandoned 'Kitchen Table Conservatism.' But some members of the Strategy Group claim that as the election approached, both men were less than committed to such tactics. It led to angry exchanges at one of the post-Bournemouth meetings.

Maude said: 'I don't think there is any chance that we can persuade people we are more trusted than Labour on health and education.'

Portillo said: 'We cannot take the high ground from Labour because their lead is too commanding, but nor can we campaign on our core issues because it makes us too narrow. We have to decide what we are for, what sort of people we want to be, who we want to appeal to.'[17]

Widdecombe replied: 'Oh no, not again! We are never going to win this argument now so we might as well get back to core issues.'

Portillo fired back: 'Well, you say not again, Ann, but we have to resolve this.'

Widdecombe: 'It's too damned late.'

Ancram intervened to stop the bickering. 'Look, this is getting nowhere.'

Arbuthnot sighed wearily: 'We really do have to come to a conclusion.'

And so another meeting broke up with no agreement having been reached.

Hague said afterwards: 'I never ever want to be part of another meeting like that. We have got to know where we are going.'[18]

'When we got to Bournemouth, the Strategy Group had set the

agenda,' said Archie Norman. William's "I'm in it for you" theme was the kind of inclusive message we had been urging him to adopt for a long time. We had policies to go with it on pensions, inner cities – and then Ann wrecked it with her drugs speech. After that it became very acrimonious.'[19]

Tim Collins said: 'William made a grave miscalculation when he changed the make-up of the Shadow Cabinet. He thought that promoting Maude and bringing Portillo back would make it more right wing. It didn't, it made it more left wing.'

Widdecombe believed Portillo was using the Strategy Group deliberately to undermine and outmanoeuvre Hague. 'We were not making any headway with the PC approach. Portillo and co. were not allowing us to make any progress. We kept going round in circles.'[20]

Widdecombe and her fellow Hague loyalists tried to take on Portillo and co., but they were less well organised. She had strong opinions and an even stronger personality, but was not a political 'player'; Lansley was relatively junior in status; and Ancram had right-wing instincts and was deeply sceptical about Portillo but lacked intellectual fire power. By contrast, Portillo, Maude and Norman were sophisticated operators, working to a plan.

Around the New Year, Iain Duncan Smith was drafted into the Strategy Group, on the grounds that he was a key member of the election team, though many Shadow Ministers believe the real reason was because Hague felt outnumbered. Another Portillo ally, David Willetts, who wrote the election manifesto, joined them for discussions.

Many senior Tories believe that for as long as a year before the election, Hague's approach was dictated not by strategy, but by survival. 'Hague and his team were no longer concentrating on how to win the general election but on how to secure the leadership of the party for William,' said a source close to Maude. 'William had got locked into a negative public image. Doing all the populist stuff – asylum and the rest – was a way of getting him some kind of prominence in the media. There was a greater desire to appeal to the activist base than to the wider electorate. It was more about William's position than benefiting the party. The activists loved all the stuff about asylum, Europe and the liberal elite but it was never going to win us any new voters.'[21]

The analysis is not restricted to Hague's enemies. One of his allies on the Strategy Group said: 'By mid-2000 William decided that his own position with the Conservative Party was so weak and the media attacks on him so strong that he had to show results – and fast, both to the media and the membership.'[22]

Hague is at one and the same time a social liberal and a social authoritarian. He is young and modern, yet old-fashioned. The advantage of this was that it enabled him to form a bridge between the Widdecombe, Duncan Smith and Lansley authoritarian wing and the Maude and Portillo liberal wing. The disadvantage, in the words of one party director, is that such an approach was 'incompatible with consistency'.

Archie Norman said: 'William didn't like disagreement. He would close down a subject whenever it came to the sharp end. He never realised that agreeing with one thing meant disagreeing with another. He felt that having a strategy was a limiting factor, not a releasing one. His advisers would tell him how he could get a headline and he would make the necessary speech. We had great affection for him and that is why we let him do it. '[23]

Several Tories argue that the real divide in the Tory Strategy Group was not between Hague and Portillo but between Lansley, chief advocate of the 'bandwagon' approach, and Norman, who wanted a 'core narrative'.

One of Hague's most loyal allies, Bernard Jenkin, who became Duncan Smith's campaign manager for the 2001 leadership bid, said: 'William started out trying to develop a core narrative, and when it failed, he switched to the bandwagon approach. Our approach was inconsistent. One minute we stood for freedom, the next we wanted to lock more people up. One minute we attacked the liberal elite, the next we all smoked pot.'[24]

Tom Strathclyde said of the Strategy Group: 'In the beginning we went looking for the holy grail, but in the end there was this awful feeling that what we had found was silver plate and not solid gold.' Cynics said that the obsession with strategy inflicted a form of paralysis on the party machine, so that when a real crisis erupted, such as the fuel protest, it failed miserably to react fast enough.

Hague's experience of reaching out in the early years, only to have his hand bitten off, left a wound that never healed. When he changed tack and followed his gut instinct, concentrating on traditional Tory issues, he got the quick fix he was looking for, but as the general election showed, it was not a solution. He admitted he had made a fatal strategic error, telling a friend: 'I got this Parliament the wrong way round. I should have spent the first year or so shoring up the base Conservative vote and then reached out later on.'25

11   Dirty Tricks

'I have not come across the kind of dirty tricks that seemed to crop up this time'
Sir Norman Fowler

Michael Ancram was by no means certain that he wanted to enter the Tory leadership contest when, following the crushing defeat in the general election, William Hague resigned on the morning of 8 June 2001.

He was hugely respected by the party faithful for his loyalty, affability, ability to stay calm in a crisis – and for being a blue-blood. Ancram, heir of the twelfth Marquess of Lothian, was a Tory grandee, last of a dying breed. His role was to serve, not to lead. Leading was for others, with bigger ideas and bigger egos.

A few days after the general election, Ancram discussed with wife Jane, and later with close friends, whether he should throw his hat in the ring. He explained to a colleague why he decided to do so: 'I am standing because of the way he and his supporters have constantly undermined everything we have tried to do. Some of the things they have done have been very unpleasant.'[1]

The 'he' Ancram was referring to was Michael Portillo.

The 'unpleasant things' done were not just connected with the alleged briefings, leaks and conspiracies involving the Portillistas and their enemies that had made Ancram's job as chairman almost impossible at times. The phrase was also a reference to files kept in the bowels of Central Office. They have nothing to do with the policy divisions, Shadow Cabinet splits and other disagreements that contributed to Hague's downfall. The files contain a catalogue of complaints of dirty tricks used to ensure that Tory associations picked right-wing, Eurosceptic and pro-

Portillo Parliamentary candidates. Those considered moderate, Europhile or anti-Portillo were ruthlessly targeted. Ancram described the activities of the right as 'exitism' – they spent as much time plotting to keep out their 'enemies' as they did trying to get their 'allies' in. It was to be expected that the Portilistas and their Eurosceptic allies would operate to ensure that what was being done on Portillo's behalf as the Eurosceptics' champion would be done without his being aware and thereby tainted.

The files include correspondence relating to a number of seats where claims of foul play – including anonymous allegations about candidates sent to local parties in brown envelopes – were investigated. Ancram believed Portillo's supporters were at the heart of the trouble and ordered all Tory area agents throughout Britain to be on the alert for such activity: 'I was concerned about allegations that were being made in a number of selections and decided to initiate further inquiries, all of which at the end were inconclusive, but equally were disturbing,' he said.[2]

A senior Central Office aide said: 'The trail always led back to the same individuals, but we could never get the concrete evidence necessary to do anything about it.'

Two ex-Ministers, Derek Conway and Andrew Mitchell, considered suing right-wing opponents who they claimed tried to smear them. And leading Tory candidate Jill Andrew, a lawyer was the victim of vicious anonymous hate mail sent to party chiefs, making false and personal allegations against her.

Derek Conway warned Portillo to stop his supporters smearing him. Andrew Mitchell complained to Ancram after right-wing Tory MEP Daniel Hannan intervened in his attempt to become Conservative Parliamentary candidate for Sutton Coldfield. When Mitchell asked why he was being targeted in seat after seat, Lord Freeman, Tory vice chairman and head of the party's candidates' list, told him it was because he was 'the most high profile returnee after Portillo' – and was 'a moderate'.

Ancram ordered an investigation by Central Office into claims that the selection process was being rigged and considered ordering Westminster Conservative Association to re-run the contest won by Mark Field. Ancram was disturbed by some of the activities uncovered by his inquiry, but decided there was not enough proof to take action. Given the sensitivity of the allegations and the names of some of those involved, it would have caused the most grave damage to the party's reputation in the run-up to a general election.

The allegations include anonymous phone calls and letters to party officials, alleging that a candidate is corrupt or gay; claims that a candidate is involved in a scandal about to be exposed by the press; infiltrating selection panels to ensure certain candidates not on the 'pro-Portillo' or 'anti-euro' list are blackballed and undermined with hostile questions and lies about their past; and weeding out other serious contenders before the final stages.

Some candidates found their personal voting record in the town hall and European elections had been trawled through – a complex operation that involves access to voting files kept at local town halls and normally used only by party officials.

Former Conservative chairman Sir Norman Fowler believes the party should order a full investigation into the claims of seat rigging. Sir Norman saw at first hand the lengths some right-wing activists are prepared to go to destroy Tory rivals when he stood down as Sutton Coldfield MP to be succeeded by Mitchell, who had been rejected in five other seats, including four in which dirty tricks were allegedly used against him. 'It would be wise for the party to look at the selection process and take evidence from candidates around the country to find out exactly what happened,' said Sir Norman. 'The last thing the Tory party needs is this kind of dirty tricks campaign or factionalism. There is enough evidence to suggest that this sort of thing did go on in some places. The chairman should order an inquiry to see what took place so that safeguards can be introduced to prevent it ever happening again.'[3]

The Ancram inquiry studied allegations about the activities of some activists who attached themselves to Conservative Way Forward, a right-wing Tory pressure group which had been set up to promote Thatcherite policies but was later used by some members to promote Portillo's leadership ambitions. CWF activists played a large part in helping a number of right-wing and Eurosceptic candidates get picked in safe or marginal seats in the 2001 general election. Two of its main driving forces are Robbie Gibb and fellow Portillista Mark MacGregor, a CWF executive committee member who fought – and lost – Thanet South in the election.

Gibb and MacGregor have been friends and political allies since their days in the Federation of Conservative Students: MacGregor became chairman of the FCS just before it was closed in 1986 by party chairman Norman Tebbit, and Gibb was deputy chairman. The closure came after a riotous conference, when the FCS was forced to pay £1,400 damages to Loughborough University as a result of damage done to its halls of residence.

Causes embraced by members of the right-wing libertarian organisation included legalising hard drugs, incest, and privatising the Royal Family. Members wore 'Hang Nelson Mandela' T-shirts at gatherings. When the FCS closed, many of its members surfaced in other Tory fringe organisations. Many joined CWF and the National Association of Conservative Graduates.

Trying to stitch up a rival to win a plum seat is nothing new in politics. In some cases, spoiling tactics are merely part of the personal rivalry between competing candidates and their supporters. But Tory sources say the operation at the 2001 election by a hard core of right-wing activists to make sure Eurosceptics got selected and Europhiles were kept out was the most sophisticated – and successful – ever conducted inside the party.

Only eleven of the 170 candidates standing in seats the Conservatives needed to take to win power at the 2001 general election were in favour of the euro. Of the twenty top target seats, eighteen were fought by hardline Eurosceptics.

Some of the right-wing activists had another motive: they wanted Portillo to be next leader. Once they had achieved their first objective – getting him returned to the Commons via the Kensington and Chelsea by-election – their next aim was to get as many right-wing Eurosceptics (and where possible pro-Portillo) candidates selected as possible, to maximise the Shadow Chancellor's chances of succeeding Hague as leader – and to keep out opponents who would vote for someone else.

From the moment Portillo lost his Enfield Southgate seat in 1997, his supporters scoured the country for a safe seat for his re-entry. They had lined up the constituency of Cities of London and Westminster, where former minister Sir Peter Brooke had announced his retirement, making sure they had enough supporters in key positions on the local Tory Association to vote for Portillo. But their carefully laid plans were abandoned when Kensington MP Alan Clark died in September 1999. Portillo, still haunted by jibes that he had 'bottled out' in the 1995 leadership contest, could not afford to do the same again. His campaign to win the Kensington selection contest was led by Mark Field, a Kensington and Chelsea councillor and solicitor by profession who is also a leading member of CWF.

More than 150 people applied for the seat. Eventually Derek Conway, a former whip who had been Vice Chamberlain of Her Majesty's Household in the Major government, a post which involved keeping the Queen informed about Parliamentary business, emerged as the main heavyweight challenger to Portillo.

Conway was shocked when he was told by a member of Kensington Tories that an article about him that had appeared in the satirical magazine *Private Eye* was being circulated among party members. The magazine had alleged in 1982 that Conway had lied during his application to be nominated as Tory Parliamentary candidate for Hartlepool in 1974. But the allegation was untrue: *Private Eye* apologised and paid damages. Conway confronted Field and accused him of circulating the article.

Later in the contest, when Conway made it through to the final six, there was fresh controversy. Kensington Tories' executive council held a drinks party at their local office so that members could chat informally with the candidates and their spouses. A senior Conservative source alleged that one of Portillo's supporters was found sifting through incoming correspondence in the agent's office nearby and was holding in his hand a letter which referred to Conway. When challenged, the individual replied: 'I'm just checking to see if there's any mail.'

There was another surprise for Conway when he made it to the last four and had to appear in front of 1,000 Kensington and Chelsea Conservatives at a packed meeting. He was asked why he had not voted in the previous year's European elections in Westminster, his London home, where he was registered to vote. Finding out if an individual has voted in a parish, town hall, European or general election is a complex matter. Every citizen's vote is recorded (though not who they voted for) and political parties often check the list to find out how many of their expected supporters turned out. Someone had checked Conway's record and discovered he did not vote in the 1999 European elections. When asked why, as a loyal Tory, he had not done so, Conway said he had unexpectedly been called away on business.

Conway stated: 'There is no doubt where the nobbling was coming from, though I don't say that Portillo was personally involved,'[4] and was so angry that he made sure Portillo was told to curb the activities of his supporters: 'He was warned that he was being stupid and that if his people went round duffing up people like Conway and Mitchell then there could be serious consequences,' said a source.[5]

Mr Field said he made it clear form the start of the Kensington selection contest that he would support Portillo. 'Friends who knew Michael were in touch with me immediately that Alan Clark died and I said "Listen, my view is that they want a high-profile figure there" and I said if Michael goes for it he has a good chance.'[6]

He denied circulating the article. 'I had a word with Derek at that time,' he said: 'Someone had tipped him off to say that the *Private Eye* article was being circulated.' Mr Field said Conway contacted the party agent in Kensington, and the agent then contacted Field. 'The agent got in touch with me and said"what the hell is going on here?" I said "I have absolutely nothing to do with this." I have never had a copy of that article in my possession. I had in fact seen a copy that had been circulating – not by me – in the run-up to the Kensington and Chealsea selection. In my experience, if you try to undermine a candidate through any dirty tricks, it is normally counterproductive. The idea that it [the selection] can be fixed when you have three or four hundred people turning up at a final meeting is a bit fanciful. There are always shenanigans that go on, but once you start to play silly games . . . it just doesn't produce the goods.'

Claims of foul play often stemmed from people bitter at losing out, he said 'It is often disappointed people looking for excuses why they haven't been selected. Often they are the self same people who are happy to promote their own candidacy or put the knife in others, and when things go wrong they try to point the finger elsewhere.'

Derek Conway's crime was not his political stance – he is not a pro-European – but that he stood in Portillo's way. He was later selected for Sir Edward Heath's old seat of Old Bexley and Sidcup. Like Mitchell, Conway opposed Portillo in the Tory leadership contest in 2001: both men played a leading role in David Davis's bid before switching to Kenneth Clarke.

The campaign against Andrew Mitchell followed him all over the country. He went from one seat to another, only to find the smears followed him. A moderate on Europe, he had lost his Gedling seat in the 1997 general election and was determined to get back to the Commons, and as one of the younger and brighter 'retreads' the former whip and Social Security Minister was expected to get a safe seat. But nearly every time he put his name forward he was hit by dirty tricks.

One of the seats where wrecking tactics were deployed was Westminster, where the local party executive included a group of Portillo supporters who were determined to get Mark Field selected. To help him, they deliberately voted for a number of weak and inexperienced candidates to ensure that when Field reached the final stage, any strong potential opponents, including ex-ministers who had put their names forward, were already knocked out. Ancram was horrified by the 'block vote' ploy – similar to the tactics used in Labour conferences when that party was in the grip of the trade unions. He was told he had no power to stop it because the tactic was not illegal. Several local party members wanted a re-run, but the association rejected the demand.

Like Conway, Mitchell received a shock when he appeared before the local party selection panel. Westminster Tory chairman Nicholas Cooper told him: 'I have got an important question for you, but I am going to leave it until the end.' When the other panel members had finished, Cooper said: 'Your file has gone missing from Central Office, Mr Mitchell. This is a serious matter. What is in it and what caused it to go missing? What have you got to hide?' Mitchell had no idea what was in his file or whether it had gone missing. Knowing glances were exchanged between panel members.

Mitchell immediately contacted Lord Freeman. Central Office keeps a routine file on every candidate, which is shredded when the MP retires. Mitchell was a former vice chairman who had been in charge of the candidates' list. His file was mistakenly burned after the last election when, after losing his seat, it was mixed up with those relating to retiring MPs. There was nothing sinister: it was an error, for which Freeman apologised.

The final five candidates in Westminster were all right wing, and a member of the selection committee told Mitchell: 'You were stitched up, it's as simple as that'. *The Times* reported the infighting at Westminster:

> Tory activists have accused leading right wingers of rigging the selection of a candidate for the safe seat of the Cities of London and Westminster. Amid internal party feuding reminiscent of Labour in the early 1980s, some angry activists are considering taking legal action against senior officials for allegedly breaking mandatory party selection rules to block the path of moderates. They are also hoping to persuade local Conservative executive next week to ditch the current selection process and start all over again. To the amazement of ordinary members, the selection committee decided to reject out of hand three former ministers, seven other former MPs and two senior local officers – without even giving them an interview. Of the 15 people actually interviewed – ten fewer than usual – few could be described as high flyers.7

The *Independent* on 11 December described Field's selection in Westminster as 'giving Michael Portillo another reason to celebrate. Mr Field, 35, is a Kensington and Chelsea councillor who was doing the dirty work to knock out Mr Portillo's short-listed rivals. Similar methods were employed on Mr Field's behalf to knock out his own rivals in Westminster.'

Nicholas Cooper insisted the selection process had been carried out properly. 'People are making a lot of accusations, but there are a lot of bad losers around. If people who lost badly want to whinge about it, so be it.' Cooper is listed on the CWF website as a member of its ruling executive committee.

Andrew Mitchell's ordeal continued in Wealden in Sussex. This time he came under fire from a senior member of the local party who said at a selection meeting: 'Mr Mitchell, sleaze destroyed the last Conservative Government. Since you were found guilty by a Parliamentary inquiry of being involved in cash for questions, surely it would be bad for us to have you as our MP.' Mitchell denied the charge, a gross distortion of a technical inquiry into Labour claims that while a member of a Commons committee investigating Tory MP Neil Hamilton in 1994, Mitchell had used his position as a Government whip to try and influence other MPs on the committee. In 1997, an all-party inquiry unanimously dismissed the allegations of improper behaviour against Mitchell.

Mitchell came top in the first round at Wealden when the final twenty candidates were reduced to six. But the following morning, he was awoken at 7 a.m. by the local agent, who told him that the 'sleaze' allegations had not ceased.

'You had better get a copy of that [House of Commons] report,' the agent told Mitchell.

Mitchell complained to Ancram, who told Wealden Tory officials to stop the 'outrageous and untrue' allegations. While careful to express no view on the merits of the candidates, Chief Whip James Arbuthnot backed up Ancram's warning. When Mitchell asked a senior Tory politician with links to the individual making the allegations to cease doing so, he was told such a move 'could backfire'. However, the politician agreed to pass on a message to the person in question.

When Mitchell reached the last six in Wealden and addressed the executive meeting, he could see his accuser pointing at him and muttering, hand in front of face, to colleagues. He was defeated.

The 'sleaze' allegation came up again when Mitchell put his name down for Witney, the seat vacated by defector Shaun Woodward. When Mitchell addressed a selection meeting, a local party member challenged him with a question almost identical to the one asked in Wealden. 'Mr Mitchell: Sleaze destroyed the Conservative Party in the last Parliament. You were heavily involved in it. I want a one word answer: were you the subject of a Parliamentary inquiry? Yes or no?'

Mitchell's wife, Sharon, a doctor, was outraged. Mitchell protested: 'Of course I wasn't involved in anything like that.' The truthful answer to the question was: yes – even though that would have been totally misleading. Mitchell had been involved in an inquiry – which had found him innocent. He was defeated in Witney

By now Mitchell was regretting ever having tried to get back into Parliament. A director of a leading bank, he feared the repeated allegations against him would damage his reputation in the City on the 'no smoke without fire' principle. Mrs Mitchell was horrified at her husband's name being unjustly dragged through the mud and pleaded with him to give up politics. Mitchell, whose father David was a minister in the Thatcher government, said: 'If I had known what was going to happen I would never have sought another seat. But I decided that having started, rather like Magnus Magnusson I had better finish.'[8]

In Faversham, Kent, the 'anonymous' individual who tried to smear him made a crass error. A senior Tory in the local party contacted Mitchell and told him that a man had phoned him and said: 'Don't select Mitchell, he is not the sort of person we want back in Parliament – he's thoroughly sleazy', and put the phone down without leaving a name. The official dialled 1471 and the caller's number was read out. Once the selection process was finished the official gave the number to Mitchell. He dialled the number, and after the individual at the other end of the phone had given his name, Mitchell said: 'This is Andrew Mitchell. I gather you have been bad-mouthing me around town.' The man stammered, clearly shocked to hear from his 'victim', before mumbling: 'I may have said something . . .'

Mitchell said: 'I told him that if he or any of his friends did such a thing to me or anyone else, I would take the matter straight to Michael Ancram. He said it had taught him not to gossip.'[9] The individual is listed on the CWF website as a member of the organisation.

Further evidence of CWF's activities came when a right-wing Eurosceptic in the Faversham contest received a surprise phone call from a stranger who introduced himself as a CWF activist. The caller said: 'We have checked your record and decided that you will be the CWF candidate in Faversham. We have a man on the Faversham executive and I suggest you make contact with him to discuss tactics' – and the caller then provided the phone number of the CWF 'mole' on the executive of Faversham Tories. The individual did not take up the offer.

There was yet more mud-slinging when Mitchell applied for Sutton Coldfield, where Sir Norman Fowler was stepping down as MP. Just before the local party met to interview the candidates, Daniel Hannan rang a senior member of Sutton Coldfield Tories. Hannan had advised the individual to ring two people whom he said could provide her with more information about Mitchell: Douglas Smith and Sean Gabb. Smith had been one of Mark MacGregor's deputies in the FCS and is well known for his right-wing views.

Sutton Coldfield agent Martyn Punyer said the individual did not contact either Gabb or Smith, adding: 'At every stage of the selection process the association chairman stressed that there must be no lobbying for or against individual candidates. I received a phone call late one evening from one member who was very distressed. She said she had received a phone call from someone making certain allegations against Mr Mitchell. The allegation was that he had been involved in "cash for questions", that there had been an inquiry and he was unsound in every way.'[10]

The incident was reported to Norman Fowler who told the local party that the allegation against Mitchell was completely untrue. Fowler and Mitchell raised the issue with Ancram.

Fowler said: 'Sutton Coldfield Conservatives showed that if the local party decides it will not put up with this kind of tactic, then it can be stopped. It can be difficult if "fellow travellers" in a local party are used to help a particular candidate, but the only way to fight it is to do so openly.'[11]

Hardline Eurosceptic Hannan had been blamed by Tory Euro Commissioner Chris Patten for contributing to his downfall as an MP. Patten narrowly lost his Bath seat in the 1992 election when he sacrificed key votes to the anti-EU United Kingdom Independence Party candidate Alan Sked: Hannan worked on Sked's campaign.

Hannan was in the firing line in the run-up to the 2001 general election when he was credited with writing parts of the Conservative leader's controversial 'foreign land' speech, which was criticised by Labour as 'racist'. He had received CWF support when he was chosen as Tory candidate for South East England in the 1999 European elections, when he became one of the few CWF successes in its fight to send more Eurosceptic candidates to Brussels.

Hannan denies having made allegations about Mitchell, or having phoned a member of the Sutton Coldfield Conservatives to challenge Mitchell's credentials. 'It is an extraordinary claim.' He says he had been phoned by a member of the local party and asked about the final three candidates in the selection contest, one of whom was Mitchell. 'I said I didn't know anything about any of them, but if they wanted to speak to someone who does, I would refer them to them. I have no possible motive to have it in for Andrew Mitchell. I have never met the guy, I have no animus against him, I have not made any allegations of any kind against any of the candidates.' Hannan says he told the individual, whom he declined to name, to contact Dr Sean Gabb, an anti-EU Tory academic who keeps records of candidates' views on Europe. Asked if he had advised the individual to contact Douglas Smith, he said: 'I have nothing further to add.'[12]

Gabb runs a controversial Eurosceptic website named 'Candidlist', whose aim is to flush out pro-European Tories. Gabb, who believes Britain should leave the EU, recorded the views of more than 1,000 candidates on the Tory selection list, and makes no secret of his motivation: 'The [Tory] leadership is impotent to stop us from doing and saying as we like. Give us another five years of this, and we can probably capture the Conservative Party more surely than the left captured the Labour Party in the 1980s.'[13]

Nor was he deterred by claims that he was conducting a 'McCarthyite witch hunt'. Dr Gabb said of his list in December 1999: 'I have been likened to Joseph McCarthy and the Spanish Inquisition – which is a measure of its success.'[14]

When Mid-Worcestershire Conservative MP Peter Luff complained at being categorised as a 'Europhile', Gabb replied abruptly: 'Examination of your past as a personal and political assistant to Edward Heath and your record as an MP does not allow us to re-categorise you.' A founder member of the right-wing Libertarian Alliance, Gabb defended its submission to the Cullen inquiry into the massacre of sixteen children at Dunblane in 1996, when he called for any adult to be allowed to buy as many guns and as much ammunition as they could afford without showing any permit or identification, and be allowed to carry them freely in public. 'I dare say the parents might find our stand grossly offensive,' he said: 'But change in legislation needs to be considered with a cool mind.'[15]

The Eurosceptics' victories over Europhiles did not go unnoticed. The *Guardian* observed:

> The Conservatives are picking known Eurosceptics, Portillo-ites and candidates with strong local connections to fight their safe and winnable seats at the general election – at the expense of ex-MPs and pro-Europeans. Though some high profile supporters of William Hague look set to enter Parliament, the pro-Michael Portillo Conservative Way Forward group has been exercising a powerful, if discreet influence in some selection battles, it is claimed. 'They're the ones who delivered Kensington and Chelsea to Michael. They always have someone on the selection panel to sift potential rivals out of the short list. They can deliver 50 votes in the ballot and have "planted snipers" to ask tricky questions,' explained one MP.[16]

The BBC *Panorama* programme launched an investigation into allegations of a right-wing plot to stop moderate Tories being selected, but abandoned plans for a documentary, reportedly after failing to uncover sufficient evidence.

Jill Andrew, who describes herself as 'a Ken Clarke supporter', met opposition – not all of it discreet – when she tried to become a Tory candidate. Mrs Andrew, an employment solicitor, contested several Tory strongholds. But it was in Huntingdon, where she was bidding to succeed John Major, that she came across the most fierce – and in her view underhand – wrecking tactics. Huntingdon was another seat on the CWF hitlist. Mrs Andrew was the victim of smears contained in an anonymous letter sent to senior members of Huntingdon Conservatives. The letter read:

> Mrs Jill Andrew – potential PPC [Prospective Parliamentary Candidate] for Huntingdon Conservative Association.

Please forgive the anonymous nature of this communication, but as an active Conservative supporter, I thought you should know some pertinent facts about the individual in question given that she has made it through to the last six in the selection process. For an important, high profile seat like Huntingdon, with the winning candidate for the Conservative PPCship [sic] bound to receive lots of publicity, I felt it important that you should be aware of the following:

Mrs Andrew resigned the Conservative whip when a member of Bromley Council between 1994-8. Given John Major's removal of the whip from the Maastricht rebels, this could be embarrassing for the local association in Huntingdon (please feel free to check this out).

Mrs Andrew believes in the legalisation of cannabis, as she told members of the Kensington and Chelsea Conservative Association when interviewed there recently for the by-election (please feel free to check this out).

Mrs Andrew achieved the highest swing against any Conservative candidate in Greater London at the last General Election (documented fact).

Mrs Andrew received funding from Paul Sykes, the anti-EU campaigner, at the last General Election, which rather undermines the fact that she has signed a memo to the Huntingdon Association saying that she would have supported the Maastricht Treaty (please feel free to check this out).

Mrs Andrew is completely unable to keep any confidence or secret (speak to anyone who knows her).

Mrs Andrew was recently fired as a solicitor by [a client].

Mrs Andrew has been involved in minimal activity for her local Conservative Association, whilst devoting considerable energies to mixing with senior figures in the national party as well as being a frequent interlocutor with Cherie Blair on the employment law circuit.

Mrs Andrew is the next Shaun Woodward. Please believe me. Her selection would be a disaster for the local association as well as for the national party.

Mrs Andrew said that, save for the allegation about the voting swing, the allegations were malicious lies and distortions. Both she and another pro-European Tory who stood in Huntingdon, businessman David Platt, were targeted by the CWF. She said that on 13 June, four days after the selection contest, she was phoned by a Tory politician with very close links to Portillo who told her that 'they got David Platt on two grounds'. Mrs Andrew said the politician, who is a Tory MP, mentioned Section 28, adding 'Mr Platt is unmarried', and he also told her that they had 'got him for spinning with the press', claiming Platt had helped the BBC TV *Panorama* programme and that Platt 'got what he deserved'.

Platt was angry that rumours were spread about him suggesting he was gay and that he was a 'mad Europhile'. He is neither. 'David's opponents were strategically placed around the hall,' said one witness, 'and having put it about that he was gay, he was then asked about his view on Section 28 – code language in party circles for suggesting someone is homosexual. A prurient "oooh!" went round the room – it was their nudge-nudge way of suggesting he was gay.' Platt, an unmarried thirty-six-year-old London barrister, is described by colleagues as 'thoroughly heterosexual'. Platt, who went on to campaign for Kenneth Clarke in the leadership contest, told friends he had no doubt that he had been targeted by right-wing opponents. Some members of Huntingdon Tory association wrote telling him they felt 'ashamed' at the way he had been treated.

Another anonymous letter about Mrs Andrew was sent to Henley, where both she and Platt were bidding to succeed Michael Heseltine as Tory candidate. The letter claimed she was 'a close friend of Cherie Blair'. Mrs Andrew said that on 16 June she was phoned by the same Portillo supporter, who asked her about Henley and told her that 'the right had been working hard there' and 'had managed to get ten CWF members on the interview list.'

On 20 June 2000 Mrs Andrew was so concerned that she swore an affidavit, a contemporaneous record of what had occurred. In it she said: 'I was in no doubt in my mind that a pattern of conduct was emerging. Information of a potentially adverse nature was being actively gathered to stop candidates whom they saw as threats to people they wished to get selected.

'I was seen as someone who was seen as a possible contender who had to be eliminated for their favoured son. I am not naive enough to believe that the selection process has never been influenced by outsiders. However, the events referred to above display such a degree of cynical manipulation as to totally undermine the whole integrity of the selection process. The use of anonymous letters, carefully timed to prevent proper investigation, circulated by people who cannot be identified, containing clearly demonstrable falsehoods means that any candidate is vulnerable.

'The whole selection process now seems to be controlled to a significant degree by those who are prepared to engage in such conduct for their own political ends.' Sir Norman Fowler said: 'There have always been instances of candidates bussing in supporters or finding out what questions might come up, but I have not come across the kind of dirty tricks that seemed to crop up this time.'[17]

There is no suggestion that the main CWF organisation is involved in any of the activities linked to the selection process.

Conservative Way Forward, according to one member, 'was established as a network of like-minded people who believed that it was important for Margaret Thatcher's views, and in particular her views on Europe, to continue to be well represented on the Conservative benches in Parliament. Its objectives were honourable and its activities open and above board. But in recent years, some activists have tried to use it as a covert campaigning wing to make Portillo leader of a Eurosceptic party, and have used dubious methods.'

One senior right-wing MP with close links to CWF said: 'In the 2001 election CWF made a significant effort to get its candidates selected. There may have been some skulduggery going on last time round. They certainly made a very considerable effort to help Mark Field get chosen in Westminster.'

But the Eurosceptics can turn on their own. There was panic among some Portillistas when former Milton Keynes MP Barry Legg made it to the last five in Westminster. Few could match Legg's fervent anti-EU views, but to the Portillistas he was not 'one of us'. He was very close to John Redwood, and if Legg rather than Field got the seat he would vote for Redwood in any leadership contest.(At that stage Redwood had not given up his leadership ambitions.) According to the CWF source, Portillo supporters ensured that Legg faced some 'hostile bowling and the occasional bouncer' from Westminster Tories to embarrass him. He duly lost.

Mark MacGregor was another priority candidate, and moreover one who could rely on the support of close friend and Pimlico neighbour Robbie Gibb, who had been best man at his wedding. The two were at the heart of the so called 'Pimlico Portillistas'. Gibb is said by tories from all sectors of the party to have played a leading role in helping get Eurosceptics selected in key seats. Before the 1997 general election he put considerable effort into helping brother Nick, also active in the CWF and close to Francis Maude, picked as candidate in the Tory stronghold of Bognor Regis.

Disgraced right-wing former Cabinet member Jonathan Aitken was asked by a friend in CWF to use his influence in his old Thanet South constituency – a key Tory target seat – where the ex-MP is still well regarded, to help make sure MacGregor was interviewed. MacGregor, a former aide to Maude, won the selection contest but narrowly lost to Labour in the 2001 general election. He went on to play a leading part in Portillo's leadership campaign team.

A study of how the 33-strong new intake of Tory MPs in 2001 voted in the leadership election reveals the extent of the Eurosceptic bias of the new boys (and one girl). Only five are believed to have voted for Clarke in the final ballot of MPs, while twenty-five are believed to have voted for Portillo or Duncan Smith. The bias is even more marked when former MPs making a Commons comeback are excluded. Only one debutant Conservative backbencher, Henley MP and *Spectator* editor Boris Johnson, is known to have voted for Clarke.

Ancram's theory is that most of the dirty tricks were 'Portillo-centric' and stemmed from Westminster. 'They set up an elaborate framework to get him in in Westminster, then when thay didn't need it and got him in in Kensington, they thought they might well use the machinery they had set up in Westminster anyway,' he said.[18] They were so pleased with their results that they started using it elsewhere.

Some of Portillo's own supporters were appalled by the dirty tricks used in the selection process. One senior moderate Tory MP who supported his leadership bid said after the general election: 'The campaign to purge the party of anyone who is pro-Europe, often using the most unpleasant methods, has driven many highly talented people away. We need people of talent from both sides of the argument. Instead we have more and more right-wingers, chosen not because they are good, but simply because they are anti-Europe. It is tragic.'

The well orchestrated right-wing campaign to use the 2001 general election to maximise the number of Eurosceptics on the Tory back-benches – and minimise the number of Europhiles – was a success. The proportion of Eurosceptics rose sharply, the number of Europhiles fell. The Portillistas who were mainly responsible for the campaign took it for granted that once the right-wingers were shoehorned into the Commons, most would vote for Portillo to succeed Hague. But by the time of the leadership contest, many had lost faith in Portillo's new brand of 'inclusive' politics (which only fully emerged in October 2000, after most of the selection contests had taken place) and ended up supporting Duncan Smith, who was no more than a faint blip on the political radar at the time of the selection contests. The drugs fiasco had disposed of Widdecombe, the only other right-wing threat.

Agonisingly for the Portillo camp, had the Tories fared only slightly better in the general election, there would have been so many Eurosceptics on the back benches that Duncan Smith and Portillo would probably both have beaten Kenneth Clarke to reach the final round.

As an exercise in getting Eurosceptics onto the Tory benches, the dirty tricks campaign was a great success. As an excercise in making Portillo party leader, it was a catastrophic failure.

In the final vote, Portillo was beaten by one.

12 The Race Card

'*Everyone has to know that I will decide and I will act quickly.*
This is the moment when I approach the bomb and you are
alone and you have to go in and defuse it. Everything depends
on which coloured wire you choose – and if it's the wrong one,
it could be all over for us.'
William Hague, 30 April 2001

William Hague's warning to the 'Leader's Meeting' of senior Shadow Ministers and advisers on Monday 30 April 2001, five weeks before polling day, was apocalyptic: the race time bomb ticking under the Tory party was primed to go off. The party had spent much of the previous two months embroiled in a damaging dispute over its attitude towards race. It had all started in March, when Hague made a speech claiming Britain would become a 'foreign land' if Blair won a second term. The speech included one of his strongest attacks on Labour's record on asylum and prompted howls of 'racism' from the government side, The row intensified when another Tory Yorkshireman, right-wing MP John Townend, praised Enoch Powell's notorious 'rivers of blood' speech. Finally, the Tories' most prominent black member, Lord Taylor, launched into a series of devastating attacks on his party leader, causing panic at Smith Square.

At the start of Hague's leadership, he had gone to great lengths to show his support for ethnic minorities. It did not always have the desired effect, as he found out at the Notting Hill carnival. And as his style and tactics hardened, the latter half of his leadership was better known for a series of controversial initiatives and speeches on asylum.

It reached a new peak when Hague addressed his party's spring conference in Harrogate in March – his last speech to a major Tory gathering before the election, a final opportunity to show what he stood for.

British voters could 'tell that something is going badly wrong when desperate people hide in the undercarriage of high speed trains to get through the Channel Tunnel,' he said. 'We will clear up Labour's asylum mess. We will welcome genuine refugees but we will be a safe haven, not a soft touch. That is not bigotry, it is common sense.'

The speech achieved the rare distinction of being criticised both by left-wing commentator Paul Routledge and by *Sun* political editor Trevor Kavanagh.

'This is Third Reich stuff,' wrote Routledge. 'He [Hague] is pandering to the basest instincts of voters – including racial hatred – in a desperate bid to reverse his failing political fortunes. He wants to turn us into a nation of Alf Garnetts, glowering across the English Channel at Johnny Foreigner.'[1]

Kavanagh wrote: 'Hague took a gamble with his speech about England becoming a foreign land. Either that, or he has abandoned all hope of winning the election. The Tories need a sound policy on immigration – and it doesn't include locking up thousands of families, attractive as that may seem.'[2]

And there were disapproving voices closer to home. Michael Portillo and Francis Maude were both appalled, not so much by Hague's words as by the way journalists were encouraged to interpret the term 'foreign land' as an attack on Europe. The tonal nuances urged on Hague by Portillo and Maude to soften the party's image on race spun out of control in the media stampede.

It was partly to insulate himself against claims of racism that, ten days after his Harrogate speech, Hague, along with Tony Blair and Charles Kennedy, attended a ceremony to sign a pledge sponsored by the Commission for Racial Equality not to play the race card in the election campaign. CRE chairman Gurbux Singh led the attack on Hague's 'foreign land' speech, claiming it hindered the fight against racial discrimination. Hague had little enthusiasm for the CRE document – not because he is a racist, which he is not, but because he regarded it as gesture politics. But he had no choice. Refusal to sign would have been seized on by his enemies as further evidence of Tory 'racism'. His outspoken speeches about 'foreign lands' and attacks on Macpherson had to be balanced by visible evidence that he believed in a multi-ethnic society.

The CRE declaration went by barely noticed. It was another, very different declaration that catapulted the issue onto the front pages and stretched Hague's nerves of steel to the limit.

Veteran Yorkshire East Tory MP John Townend had made little impact in more than two decades in Parliament. In spite of sitting on the Tory benches for every one of eighteen years unbroken Conservative rule, he had never once served as a minister: the nearest he came to holding high office was the giddy heights of chairman of the Tory backbench finance committee. Townend's views on race were one of the few things that got him noticed. He once told Muslims protesting about Salman Rushdie's *The Satanic Verses* to 'go back from whence they came'. And plans to let Hong Kong Chinese settle in the UK meant that 'England as we know it will be lost for ever. They could create another China in England, just as immigrants have created another Pakistan in Bradford.'

But he left his most controversial comment of all until last. On 28 March a speech made by Townend earlier in the month to his local Tory associ-ation in Bridlington found its way into the *Daily Mirror*. 'Our homogenous Anglo-Saxon society has been seriously undermined by the massive immigration – particularly Commonwealth immigration – that has taken place since the war,' he said: 'Illegal immigrants have got a new ploy. They call themselves asylum seekers. In my view the only way to deal with is to send them back quickly. Many come from violent societies and inevitably crime is already beginning to rise in the areas where they are.'3

Labour cited the comments as proof that the Tories were racists, and called on Hague to expel Townend from the party. Hague called Townend's remarks 'wholly unacceptable', but he was not helped by the defiant MP's boastful claim that his speech 'went down a bomb in my constituency.'4

Conservative problems deepened when it emerged that Michael Ancram had sent a memo to Tory Parliamentary candidates on 26 March warning them 'to avoid using language which is likely to generate racial or religious hatred.' The memo was sent in response to queries from candidates asking if they should sign the CRE pledge. Ancram fudged the issue, merely reminding them that Hague had signed on behalf of all candidates. Instead he offered general advice on not using racist language – and left it to individuals to decide whether or not to sign the CRE document.

The Ancram memo was leaked to the *Independent* on 17 April and looked like a tacit acknowledgement that some Tories might be racists. Why tell them not to use racist language if some of them weren't racists? By not giving them clear advice, some would sign and some would not, and those who declined would be called racists. As Ancram struggled to cope with the backlash, a separate row broke out over the Commission for Racial Equality's initiative. Despite having obtained the support of the three party leaders, the CRE wrote to all MPs, asking them to sign up individually.

On 20 April it was revealed that three Conservative MPs had refused to sign. One of the three Tory refuseniks was Townend, who accused the CRE of 'blackmail'. Fellow right-wingers James Cran and Eric Forth also wrote to the CRE saying they would not sign up. But the anger was not limited to Tory right-wingers. Leading Tory liberal Nicholas Soames said the CRE could 'go to hell' and called the declaration a 'loathsome offensive document, a corpse of an idea which is trying to drag racism into the general election.'

Hague found himself in an impossible position. If he tried to force his MPs to sign, he would be faced with a mass revolt; if he didn't, he would be accused of being soft on racism.

It was this critical moment that Portillo entered the controversy with a theatrical flourish.

Asked during a trip to Cardiff on 20 April whether he had signed the CRE document, Portillo replied confidently: 'No. I don't think we should be drawn into committing ourselves to sign up to every apparently well intentioned document. I went into public life to speak for myself and I will use my own language and my own words. MPs are bedevilled by early day motions, questionnaires, pledge forms and everything else from pressure groups and they mainly arrive in the form of "When did you stop beating your wife?" questions.'

The initial reaction in Central Office on hearing of Portillo's intervention was a mixture of shock, confusion and fear. When an aide rushed in to Hague's room and announced, 'Portillo has refused the CRE pledge', Hague shot a worried glance and raised his eyebrow quizzically. He had every right to be suspicious of Portillo's motives. Hague's fate was teetering on a knife edge on one of the most sensitive of issues – and his most senior Shadow Cabinet colleague had gone out on a limb in a way that, regardless of his intentions, would be seen by some as an act of defiance. And he hadn't even had the courtesy to notify Hague in advance.

The wry response of the urbane George Osborne summed up the feelings of many in Smith Square. 'What a magnificent operator that man is,' he drawled, half in horror, half in awe of Portillo's chutzpah.5

On the one hand, Portillo had stolen a march on Hague by standing up to the CRE. On the other, it was hard to accuse him of disloyalty: he had got his leader off the hook.

Portillo had an advantage over Hague in standing up to the race relations thought police. It was one thing to pin a charge of xenophobia on asylum-bashing Yorkshireman Hague, quite another to pin it on a man whose father fought Franco and fled to Britain to avoid death. Thus Central Office could not challenge Portillo's motives for not signing.

Now the CRE found itself in the firing line, accused by leading members of the ethnic community of whipping up racial tensions. Gurbux Singh, former chief executive of left-wing Haringey Council, was criticised for 'naming and shaming' Tory MPs, and the Conservatives were convinced they were victims of a political stunt. Several CRE members had close Labour links, such as Singh and executive member Shahid Malik, a member of Labour's ruling National Executive Committee.

But Townend would not shut up. He claimed Labour wanted the British to become a 'mongrel race' and on 26 April wrote to the CRE informing them that they should be abolished, adding: 'The concept of a multicultural, multi-ethnic, multilingual society is a mistake and will inevitably cause great problems.'

The content and the timing of his remarks could not have been worse, coinciding as they did with a trip by Hague to Bradford which had been intended to reassure ethnic minorities that he was on their side.

But one member of the ethnic minorities was far from reassured.

Few people have as much first-hand experience of Tory racism as Lord Taylor of Warwick. A former special adviser to Margaret Thatcher's government, Taylor was awarded a peerage by John Major following the disgraceful treatment he endured when standing as Tory Parliamentary candidate in true blue Cheltenham in 1992. Some members of the local Tory association tried to stop him being selected, and one called him 'a bloody nigger'. Now, just as the Tories hoped the worst of the race row was over, their most prominent male black member delivered a vitriolic personal attack on Hague for failing to expel Townend.

'The leader of the Conservative Party prides himself on his judo and fourteen pints a day macho image,' said Taylor. 'Now is Mr Hague's chance to demonstrate real macho leadership by withdrawing the whip from Mr Townend and booting him out of the Conservative Party.'[6] Each time he spoke, Taylor condemned Hague in stronger terms. He claimed the leader was 'pathetic' and said he was 'frightened' of his right-wingers.

No one could deny Taylor the right to feel passionately about the issue, but Hague could not allow any party member to treat him in such an insulting manner. Even more alarming, Taylor hinted he was on the brink of defecting to Labour.

Acting on Hague's orders, James Arbuthnot told Taylor that he would be expelled unless he ceased his attacks on the leader.[7] But instead of pulling back, Taylor went even further: 'If John Townend is still in the party at the start of the election, my position may well be untenable,' he wrote on the morning of the crisis 'Leader's Meeting'.[8]

Emergency discussions among Hague's team over how to deal with the Townend–Taylor stand-off resulted in the Leader's Meeting at Central Office starting an hour late on Monday 30 April. Hague knew he had to put an end to the row which had dragged on for a month, and his task was made all the more difficult by Taylor's refusal to take his calls. Hague wanted to talk to him personally, to tell him to stop abusing him, stop being disloyal and urge him to stay in the party. But he couldn't get through.

Unbeknown to the Tory leader when the Leader's Meeting convened, Taylor had taken a call from one of those sitting round the table.

Hague came straight to the point: 'We have to deal with this problem here and now and I would like your views on how we do it.'⁹ Tim Collins had devised a high-risk strategy to silence both Taylor and Townend once and for all: Townend was to be ordered to sign a grovelling retraction of his remarks on race, while Taylor would be told sign a prepared statement saying that he would stay loyal to the Conservatives. If either refused, they would be thrown out of the party on the spot.

'My solution is that we front up Townend and say you have got to sign this – the chances are he won't do it and we can sack him,' said Collins. 'Then we tell Taylor he has got to sign up or shut up. If he is planning to move to Labour then we can flush him out. If he's going to stay loyal we can bring him back into the fold.'

Widdecombe said: 'I think this is a brave solution, but it's too brave. I agree with the principle that it deals with both ends of the problem. But we could end up with Townend staying and Taylor going.'

Maude: 'The worst of all possible worlds would be that someone like Townend is allowed to stay in the party. We must do everything we can to keep our only black member of the House of Lords. There is a lot to commend Tim's proposal.'

Norman: 'We must get the tone right and be seen as an inclusive party.'

John Whittingdale warned of the dangers of expelling Townend: 'We must recognise the fact that quite a large number of people in the party feel that Townend has a right to speak out. There is huge potential for a right-wing backlash if we expel him.'

Others were worried that Taylor was being manipulated by Labour. Seb Coe had got a message to Taylor on Sunday and offered him a meeting with Hague, but Taylor had turned it down.

'I believe this whole thing may be being scripted from somewhere else,' said Ancram, referring to suggestions that Taylor was being secretly coached by Labour in advance of a spectacular defection. Blair's press secretary Alastair Campbell, a past master in pulling off spectacular defections, gleefully added to Tory paranoia, saying he knew nothing about any defection by Taylor, but 'could not be expected to know what everyone in the party was doing.'

Tom Strathclyde said that he had tried to reach Taylor, but could only get through to Lady Taylor. After waiting until everyone else had spoken, Portillo rocked back in his chair, formed a temple with his hands, looked at the ceiling and announced gravely: 'I spoke to John yesterday and I am in no doubt he is on a journey, a personal journey, and that he is completely sincere.'

Taylor was undergoing 'a deep emotional passage', Portillo said, using language similar to that which he had used to describe his own 'journey'. He added: 'This is one of the moments when we have to define ourselves as a party and decide what we are about and what we believe in.'[10] It was a clear message to Hague that regardless of Taylor's insults and loyalty, Portillo would stand by him.

Maude: 'I agree with Michael. This is a defining moment. It is about reaching out to people regardless of their ethnic background.'

Maude and Willetts wanted Townend thrown out of the party without further ado. Widdecombe supported the Collins plan: Taylor and Townend must be treated equally firmly.

Hague said: 'I have listened to the views of the meeting.' But he was not ready to make a decision and called a meeting of the 'inner Strategy Group' – Maude, Portillo, Widdecombe and himself.

It was then that Hague delivered his warning.

'Everyone has to know that I will decide and I will act quickly. This is the moment when I approach the bomb and you are alone and you have to go in and defuse it. Everything depends on which coloured wire you choose – and if it's the wrong one, it could be all over for us.'

Hague returned to his office to set about defusing the situation. He spoke to Townend at 1.20 p.m. and delivered the ultimatum, telling the MP: 'I cannot tolerate the statements you have made on the subject of race. If you do not retract them, I will have no option but to withdraw the whip. This is not negotiable.'[11]

Townend said he wanted to discuss it with his wife. Half an hour later he called back and told Hague he agreed. Hague was amazed. He had fully expected Townend to refuse, and instead got the grovelling apology he had asked for.

'I entirely accept that racism has no place in the Conservative Party and am very sorry that ill chosen words by me may have given a different impression,' declared a contrite Townend. Whether he genuinely regretted his actions is another matter.

Some Conservative sources say Hague was disappointed when Townend ate humble pie. 'William was hoping to be able to throw him out: it would have made him look very strong,' said one aide.[12] Others dispute this view, referring to Hague's habit of avoiding confrontation wherever possible.

Either way, one half of the bomb had been defused, and Hague had to hope that Townend's climbdown would be sufficient to persuade Taylor to do likewise. But Hague's team could not track down the elusive peer. Strathclyde made frantic attempts to contact Taylor all day, to no avail, and when Hague made a press statement on the steps of Central Office about Townend's retraction, he did not know whether Taylor would back down. The stress was clearly visible on the Conservative leader's drawn face.

'We mean business about being an inclusive party that has no truck with racism. And we mean business about being a disciplined party determined to win the election.'

But he was being equally tough with Taylor. 'I cannot allow people in receipt of the Conservative whip in the House of Lords to agonise publicly about whether they support the party. I hope he will stay in the party, but I do think he has to make clear now that he will do so.'

The first that Central Office knew of Taylor's response was when staff heard him interviewed on television moments after Hague's statement. Taylor maintained his fierce criticism of Hague, describing his actions as 'too little, too late'. But crucially he said that he had 'no problem' signing a loyalty pledge in the form of an open letter from Conservative candidates from ethnic minorities declaring the Tories were 'open and tolerant'.

The following day Strathclyde had lunch with Taylor and won assurances from him that he would keep to his word and not rush off to Campbell and join Labour. Taylor said: 'I have achieved my goal of getting the Conservative Party to clearly state its commitment to a vision of Britain where racial intolerance and bigotry are totally unacceptable.'[13]

He didn't actually sign the loyalty pledge, but said he 'concurred' with it. Grudging or not, both Taylor and Townend remained in the Tory party.

Hague had picked the right coloured wires.

13   Body Language

*'Body language is very important. We have to look like victory.
We must praise each other, talk about each other. We must look
as though we are going to be the next government.'*
William Hague to the Shadow Cabinet, 25 April 2001

It was while discussing arrangements for a visit to David
Hull's Turn Cole Farm in Southminster, Essex, during the foot-and-
mouth crisis in April 2001 that the idea came to Hague.

'How would you feel if Michael came along too?' he asked his
Parliamentary Private Secretary John Whittingdale.

Whittingdale was in a good position to judge. He not only knew farmer
Hull, whose farm was in his constituency, but he also knew Michael
Portillo extremely well and, like Hague, Whittingdale knew that
something had to be done to stop the sudden spate of reports alleging
plots, divisions and post-election coups.

Whittingdale's main concern was that local farmers might resent a tour
of the area designed for Hague to see the havoc wreaked by foot-and-
mouth hijacked for a political stunt. But Hague was adamant. With Blair
expected to announce the general election at any time, he could not afford
to start the campaign proper at war – or being perceived to be at war –
with his Shadow Chancellor.

And so the two of them stood in the muddy yard of Mr Hull's farm on
19 April and swore allegiance to each other in one of the more surreal
episodes of the election.

'Every member of the Shadow Cabinet, quite rightly, is behind William
Hague,' said Portillo, to the sound of farmyard noises. 'William knows he
has complete loyalty. There's no doubt about that in any of our minds –
not William's, mine or anyone else's.'

Hague chimed in: 'I absolutely agree with every word Michael has just said. I have the complete loyalty of the Shadow Cabinet. They are loyal to each other and they are loyal to me. We are not going to be sidetracked by media reports based on nonsense, from the job of putting forward our policies on the foot-and-mouth crisis that we are here to put forward today.'

Not surprisingly, the farmyard farce did little to end rumours of mudslinging between their own rival flocks. The latest spate of reported plots and counter-plots was more intensive than anything they had been through before: the occasional hand grenade had turned into carpet bombing.

It had started on Good Friday with a report that Portillo would challenge Hague after the election even if Hague won,[1] and was followed up on Saturday by a claim that Kenneth Clarke was working in cahoots with Michael Portillo. The basis of this allegation was that Clarke had reportedly persuaded the former Tory MEP, pro-EU campaigner John Stevens, to cancel plans to stand against Portillo in Kensington in the election.[2] Stevens was said to have claimed that Clarke's action was evidence that a left–right alliance between Portillo and Clarke to make Portillo leader was on the cards. This was followed by a report on Sunday stating that Clarke had said privately that Portillo would be a 'better leader' than Hague.[3]

The situation now descended into soap opera.

Monday's press featured Clarke's denial that he had intervened to help Portillo in Kensington.[4] On Tuesday, Maude was said to be preparing to act as the 'hitman' who would 'take out' Hague after the election, paving the way for Portillo to take over.[5] On the same day, leading right-wing commentator Janet Daley issued a cry from the heart that was shared by an increasing number of despairing Tories:

> Does the Conservative Party have a death wish? Or does it just contain some of the most unconscionably self-seeking individuals in modern political history? You may have heard about the latest eruption of internecine eye-gouging. The Shadow Chancellor, Michael Portillo (who else?), has allegedly been endorsed as next

leader of the party by Kenneth Clarke (who else?) in open expectation of the ousting of William Hague after the election – whatever its result.[6]

Furious at being labelled Portillo's 'hitman', Maude prepared a vitriolic press release in order to condemn the report, but it was never released. Hague intervened to stop it when he learned of its contents. Along with insisting the 'hitman' story was untrue, the release went on to claim that the reports were part of a dirty tricks plot against him. 'This has all been caused by those who promote their own at the expense of others,' the never-released press release stated. The coded message was clear: Maude was accusing enemies such as Platell and Coe of smearing him. His complaint about 'those who promote their own at the expense of others' harked back to his resignation threat the previous December over claims that Platell was responsible for spreading 'poison' about him.

When the Shadow Cabinet met on 25 April, Hague's exasperation was evident.

'It is very frustrating when stories build up out of nothing,' he told his colleagues. 'I seriously believe they don't come from the Shadow Cabinet and that we are loyal to each other.' Shadow Ministers shifted in their seats, waiting to see if he was going to point the finger of blame. Then, choosing his language carefully, he homed in on Portillo. They were the only people present who had experienced first hand the Cabinet treachery that ripped Major's administration to pieces.

'A lot of us around this table have worked in bodies like this which were deeply disloyal. I am certain that this body is not like that.'

It was Major who, in an off the cuff remark picked up by a rogue TV microphone, referred to the 'bastards' in his Cabinet. Portillo, who opposed Major's stance on Europe, was widely believed to have been one of them. Hague was in the Major loyalist camp.

It was as though Hague was trying to convince himself, as much as them, that what he was saying was true. He carried on: 'The best thing we can do to tackle it is to battle through with our own agenda. That is what we should be focusing on this week. And our agenda this week is the economy.'

And then, departing from his normal cool, managerial self, Hague issued a restrained but heartfelt plea to put all the rifts, divisions, defeatist talk and noises off behind them and to stick together in the difficult times that lay ahead. 'Body language is very important. We have to look like victory. We must praise each other, talk about each other. We must look as though we are going to be the next government,' he said.

When he finished, there was a brief silence. No politician's body language is more expressive than Michael Portillo's. He sits in meetings, mostly silent, detached. He unclenched his fingers, lowered his eyes to the level of the others present and began by thanking Hague warmly for his public declaration of trust in him at the farmyard six days earlier. 'I would like to thank you, William, for the many things you have done for me in the past ten days.'

Hague nodded in appreciation. But Portillo had not finished, and continued: 'I have to say, we were slow to respond. One of the lessons is that we have to be quick on the uptake. It is very important that we are in touch with colleagues' – and he stressed the word 'colleagues'.

It was his way of telling Hague to sideline Platell and Coe, whom Portillo deeply mistrusted, and who were 'staff' – or 'functionaries' not worthy of the status of 'colleagues'. Portillo delivered his own homily to the Shadow Cabinet: 'In future we have to speak to each other more and respond more quickly once we have decided what action to take.'

Ulster spokesman Andrew Mackay said: 'I agree with William. It is our party workers who are worst affected by stories like this.'

Transport spokesman Bernard Jenkin said: 'William, I believe I speak on behalf of the entire Shadow Cabinet when I say that you have behaved with great dignity.'

Archie Norman said Labour had been spreading false rumours that he was about to leave politics and become chairman of Railtrack. The Tories must be on permanent guard for such Labour dirty tricks.

Michael Portillo's reluctance to do battle with Gordon Brown had been a source of frustration to Hague for most of the past year.

The tension surfaced at the end of April in one of the 'Leader's Meetings' that took on greater importance once the election was under way: they were brought forward forty-five minutes to 8.15 a.m. during the campaign, and would last about one hour. During the election the only addition to the 'Leader's Meeting' was Ffion, who since she spent the entire campaign at her husband's side needed to know what was happening. She would sit at the side, back from the table and said no more than she said on the election trail.

The plan on the Tory 'grid' for the last week in April centred on a series of speeches and newspaper articles on economic policy, and coincided with reports that morning that a global economic downturn was on the cards and that Britain was not ready to cope with its effects. Brown had insisted the UK could weather any downturn, but commentators were sceptical.

Portillo was pencilled in by Central Office aides to do radio and television broadcasts on the subject, but his staff indicated he did not want to go ahead. It was not the first time he had shown reticence in speaking on the subject: Portillo believed the economy was so strong that there was little point in his trying to take on Brown directly. His staff would say to Central Office: 'Michael's view is that if he can get through the election without having to debate the economy with Brown it will be a good thing.' Widdecombe believed that Portillo, like Maude, was intimidated by Brown.[7] This illustrated another fundamental difference between Hague and Portillo. Featherweight Hague's instinct was to leap in, jabbing away the moment his opponent's guard dropped. Cruiserweight Portillo preferred to lean back on the ropes and shadow box. True, he had landed three knock-out blows since becoming Shadow Chancellor, but Hague's followers felt that they were all against his own side: the minimum wage, Bank of England independence, and the tax guarantee. Hague had showed him how to score points, frequently leaving Blair with a bloody nose in their despatch box tussles, but Brown's ample chin was unbruised.

Some Tories think Portillo's non-confrontational style was an overreaction to the swashbuckling 'Who Dares Wins' speech he made as Defence Secretary to the 1995 party conference – the most disastrous speech he ever made. Afterwards he was so contrite that he called in senior military officers at the Ministry of Defence and apologised for its aggressive tone.

The moment Hague saw the reports of a possible downturn in the economy, he asked Portillo to take the gloves off and go for Labour. Encouraged by Andrew Lansley, Hague decided to accuse Labour of holding a 'cut and run' election. For four years the Tories had been forced to stand on the sidelines seething with impotent rage as Brown and Blair audaciously ripped the mantle of economic competence from the Tories and wore it with dazzling style. Now all of a sudden, a rip had appeared in the hem. Hague wanted Portillo to grab the thread and pull it with all his might. Who could say how it might unravel?

'It was a golden opportunity for us,' said a Tory strategist. 'The economy had gone reasonably well since 1997, but now, with the election on us, there were the first signs that there could be problems down the line. William and Andrew [Lansley] wanted Michael to argue that Labour wanted to get the election out of the way because they knew things were looking gloomy.'8

Hague met Portillo privately and asked him to carry out the attack. Portillo refused, telling him: 'I will not do it, William.'

When Hague asked him why, he replied: 'Because no one will believe it.'

It was a blatant challenge to Hague's authority, but the leader was powerless to force Portillo to obey him. He would have refused, and Hague could hardly dismiss him in the middle of an election.

Hague was not the only person who noticed Portillo's shyness. In a briefing to reporters ten days before polling day, Alastair Campbell had said that it was 'extraordinary' that the Conservatives had 'not called a single press conference on the economy'.

The Tories knew they were almost certainly heading for defeat – and a major defeat – and would discuss it privately. But most regarded such talk as sacrilege in an open meeting, when there was only one item on the agenda: victory. Portillo said in Hague's absence at one meeting: 'We have to be careful about what we are saying because after the election and we have lost, we have to carry on' – which led to a senior Shadow Minister lodging a complaint with Hague. It was against this background, and with the 'farmyard covenant' still fresh in all their minds, that the 'Leader's Meeting' at the end of April gathered. Portillo and Hague were absent.

The Tory media team gave a run down of the morning's press. The main story was the global downturn. Strathclyde chipped in as breezily as ever: 'This is a good story for us. We have to hit them very hard. Oliver [Letwin] was on the *Today* programme and I thought he was excellent.' (Letwin's main contribution to the campaign would come later, and would attract rather more critical comment.)

Ancram was in an awkward position. Unlike Strathclyde, he knew of Portillo's change of heart because Portillo had told him in advance of the meeting that he did not, after all, want to run hard with the economy that day. 'Yes,' said Ancram awkwardly, 'but it's very important that front benchers know they are not to go on these shows until it has been authorised by Central Office.' (This was his way of referring to Portillo's objection to challenging Labour on the economy on that day.)

'I have had a conversation with the Shadow Chancellor and his advice is that this story is so bad for the Government and the heat is really on them and that we should just let them take the hit and not put up the Shadow Chancellor or his people for interviews,' said Ancram.

One voice around the table blurted out in disbelief: 'What heat?'

Ancram: 'The heat of the story.'

Others waded in, disputing that the Government was under any pressure.

Ancram: 'The Shadow Chancellor's instructions are that we should not put anyone up and we should go on letting the Government take the heat.'

Widdecombe scoffed in derision, and an exasperated Duncan Smith said: 'This is not the way to proceed. This issue is going very well for the Government. We should be in there knocking the hell out of them.'

Ancram struggled to maintain the line Portillo had dictated to him. 'I'm sorry, but the Shadow Chancellor has given clear instructions.' He shuffled the papers in front of him with the palms of his hands, willing the meeting to move on to another less tricky issue. 'Er, well then, let's move on, shall we, let's move on . . .', he said briskly, looking to Lansley to rescue him. 'What's our main story today, Andrew?'

Lansley looked around nervously before answering: 'Actually chairman, today we were planning to talk about . . .' – he paused – 'the economy.'

'Yes . . . right,' said Ancram, moving on quickly to Arbuthnot: 'What's going on in the House today?'

Arbuthnot: 'Erm, we're debating the economy, chairman – at our request.'

By now, Ancram was searching for a lifeline. He turned to broadcasting press officer Andrew Scadding. 'Let's look ahead, then, what are we doing this week on the radio and TV?'

'It's a bit of a problem, chairman,' said an embarrassed Scadding. 'We were planning to go on the economy.'

Strathclyde couldn't take any more. 'This is completely ridiculous, chairman. The economy is the only story in town and we can't talk about it.' Widdecombe melodramatically banged her head on the table.

Platell seized the chance to attack Portillo. 'Can someone please explain this to me? The only story in town is the economy and we are giving the Government a completely free ride on it. It's running well for them. You are telling me that the Shadow Chancellor has said we shouldn't talk about a story that is going well for us? God help us if that is what it is going to be like in the election.'

Widdecombe: 'I agree. Have we taken leave our senses? We should be in there fighting, not running away.' Tim Yeo, Duncan Smith and Strathclyde supported her.

Ancram was resigned to defeat. 'I'll take this view to the Shadow Chancellor,' he said dejectedly, and later in the day Portillo changed his mind and agreed to go on the attack – in public.

Weeks later, during the campaign, Hague and Portillo clashed again over the same issue when the Conservative leader wanted to hold a press conference to attack Labour over the economy. 'I don't think it is appropriate or necessary for me to be there,' Portillo told Hague.

'Well I do,' said Hague.

Portillo duly appeared.

14 They're off!

'If Tony Blair does not bloody well announce this election soon, I'll go out and do it.'
William Hague in Central Office, 8 May 2001

There was a reverential silence as Tory officials downed tools, their eyes glued to the banks of televisions in the 'war room'.

At any moment, Tony Blair was to announce formally that, with the worst of the foot-and-mouth crisis over, the 2001 general election would take place on 7 June. His manner of announcing the election was in defiance of all tradition. Prime Ministers usually announce elections from a better known political stage, the Commons despatch box, after a short drive to Buckingham Palace to seek the Queen's permission to dissolve Parliament. But from the first State Opening of Parliament under Blair's regime in 1997, when he shamelessly upstaged her arrival at Parliament in a horse-drawn carriage by going on a walkabout with Cherie from Number 10 to the Palace of Westminster, he had shown he was no respecter of protocol.

Blair decided to announce the 2001 election in a slightly less formal and more televisual setting than the mushy pea-green leather benches of the House of Commons. After driving to the Palace in his Daimler at 1 p.m. on Tuesday 8 May to inform the Queen of his election plans, Blair drove straight past Big Ben, over Westminster Bridge and on to St Saviour's and St Olave's comprehensive school in Southwark, south London.

William Hague was irritated when Downing Street announced that there would be a delay between the Prime Minister's visit to the Palace and the formal announcement at the school later in the afternoon. 'If Tony Blair does not bloody well announce this election soon, I'll go out and do it,' he joked.[1]

As they waited for Blair to arrive at the school, a pall of gloom descended over Central Office. Blair, king of the photo opportunity, had pulled it off again. St Olave's was a multi-ethnic, inner city Church of England state school with a reputation for excellence. There was something for everyone. There were few settings likely to make a middle-aged male politician look more attractive than being surrounded by 600 teenage girls in school uniforms, screaming with excitement when he took his jacket off. (Michael Portillo would have approved.)

Performing a more than passable impression of his Vicar of St Albion caricature in *Private Eye*, Blair stood in the school hall, framed by stained glass windows and a cross behind him, and promised to help the pupils make the most of their 'God given talent': 'I say to you today: we must reach a time, in our time, where the only rightful place for every man, woman and child in Britain is where their talents take them.'

By contrast, Hague was to launch his own campaign on a soap box in Watford outside a town-centre night club called Destiny. There wasn't a screaming teenage schoolgirl in sight, just a few bored OAPs. 'We were all thinking, damn him, Blair has pulled off another sensational coup. It's going to be fantastic and we'll look dowdy and dull in comparison,' said one Conservative strategist.

But as Blair stood up alongside the headmistress, hymn book in hand, and started singing with the girls, a woman helper in the corner of the 'war room' started giggling. Heads turned, wondering what she was laughing at. She was staring at the television. They realised what she was laughing at. Then someone else laughed. Gradually, it spread round the room, until the whole room was rocking with mirth.

It was ridiculous. The whole event was utterly ridiculous. How could the super-slick Millbank machine get it so wrong? Labour's panzer division was stuck in the mud. Within hours, the Tory hoots of derision were echoed by a more powerful chorus. None of the pupils who heard Blair's clarion call to re-elect Labour were even old enough to vote. And some of their parents were none too pleased at their children being used as props in a political stunt.

The following day's papers blew a collective raspberry at Blair's election launch. Quentin Letts of the *Daily Mail* said:

This was the tackiest, tinniest political event I have (yet) been to. His speech was delivered like an American telly-evangelical sermon and concluded with an echo of the Parable of the Talents. This guy really does defy satire sometimes. 'We're on our way to heaven,' sang the girls of the choir. From the wings, Alastair Campbell watched them with jaw twitching, eyes narrowed, a Doberman guard dog alert for Tory fifth columnists. It was little short of disgusting that such admirable young people should be so greasily manipulated for political ends.[2]

In fact, a group of young Tory activists had tried to wreck the event, posing as ordinary members of the public and heckling Blair as he arrived. They needn't have bothered. Blair did a better job inside.

Hague's plan to stand on a soap box in Watford, portraying him as a man of the people, ready to meet real people in real streets, while 'phoney Tony' put himself on a pedestal at carefully choreographed events, suddenly looked like a master stroke. The Tory leader looked natural, not naff. He was copying the underdog tactics used by another unfashionable conservative, George W. Bush, against another liberal, Al Gore. And it seemed to have worked.

When the Tory 'Leader's Meeting' convened at 8.15 a.m. the following morning, there was an air of bewildered jubilation. They couldn't believe they had got off to such a good start – and Labour to such a bad one. But Francis Maude was not so sure. 'I have to say that when I watched the TV news last night I thought Blair was quite impressive,' he said. 'He got the mood right for the three seconds that most viewers would have seen. That's what's so clever about him.'

Hague shot him an icy glare. Platell, sensing her leader's irritation, leapt in. Blair's performance may have looked good on television, she said, but the chorus of criticism from Fleet Street could be more significant: when the opening night of the Millennium Dome proved a resounding flop and was panned by Fleet Street, that press reaction killed the whole project. 'The same could happen here and I think it will. Everybody is saying Blair made a terrible mistake.'

James Arbuthnot commented sarcastically: 'After four years of arrogance from Blair, we are going to be subjected to four weeks of humility.'

'Mock humility, James, mock humility,' he was chided by Strathclyde.

There were more cheers in the 'war room' when, later in the day, the BBC TV News described the opening day's exchanges as a David against Goliath victory for the Conservatives.

Hague's first serious election event, the launch of the party manifesto *Time For Common Sense*, on 10 May, was a masterpiece of compromise between the party's rival wings of 'mods' and 'rockers'. The £8 billion worth of tax cuts was a reminder to the 'rockers' of the glory days when lowering taxes was Thatcher's trump card over and again. But in deference to the 'mods', the amount was less than some would have liked and the small print revealed it would be spread out over three years. Portillo's final approval for a 6p per litre cut in petrol duty looked like a victory for the 'rockers' – but it was nine months after Hague had pleaded with him to do it during the fuel blockade. The reintroduction of the married couple's allowance was another nod to the 'rockers' – but there were no headline grabbing cuts in income tax rates.

Hague, the law and order 'rocker', promised to recruit an extra 3,000 police, force criminals to serve longer jail sentences and speed up the system for sending home bogus asylum seekers. But Hague the 'mod' showed his commitment to the public services by promising maximum waiting times for cancer and heart patients and accepting rising spending on state schools and the NHS. Hague the anti-EU 'rocker' pledged to rule out joining the euro for the lifetime of the next Parliament and stop Brussels gaining more power over the UK. But Hague the 'mod' stressed his overall package was aimed at 'mainstream Britain' – code language to Portillo. that he had taken a step back from the right towards the centre.

The launch won favourable reviews from those who normally panned the Tories. The *Independent* said:

> An unexpectedly slick Conservative Party has been first out of the traps. William Hague has dominated the opening skirmishes of the campaign, and yesterday's early manifesto launch keeps up the pace. What is more the document itself is impressive – although that judgement is partly the product of rather low expectations. It sets out a relatively coherent programme, with a couple of populist twists intended to impress car drivers. This is a manifesto that deserves to be taken seriously.[3]

'Don't worry, Oliver, you have my full support.'

Portillo's vote of confidence in Shadow Chief Secretary to the Treasury Oliver Letwin was meant to cheer him up. It was just as well that Letwin didn't hear what Portillo said when he put the phone down: 'The man is an idiot. He is incapable of talking to the press and sticking to a line.'[4]

The exchange came during one of the most farcical episodes of the election campaign: the strange case of Oliver Letwin and the missing £20 billion.

It had started four days earlier when a frowning Hague cast his eyes round the room at the 8.15 a.m. 'Leader's Meeting' on 14 May. He drew his colleagues' attention to an article in the *Financial Times* claiming that the Tories were planning to offer not £8 billion worth of tax cuts, but £20 billion. The implication was clear: there would have to be swingeing reductions in public spending to pay for the tax cuts.

'According to the *FT*, the source was a member of the Shadow Cabinet,' said Hague, casting an accusing look around the room. It was an invitation for the culprit to come clean, though the Conservative leader was far from certain he – or she – would do so. No one did.

A silence of several seconds ensued. It was broken by Michael Portillo. 'Far be it from me to name the member of the Shadow Cabinet responsible for the briefing,' he said, with a half smile. 'All I can say is that he is both a member of the Shadow Cabinet and a member of the Treasury team, and he is not present at this meeting.'

The Shadow Chief Secretary is the only departmental number two who is a member of the Shadow Cabinet. And he does not attend the Leader's Meeting. Portillo didn't need to read out the name of the offender. By now, they all knew: it was Oliver Letwin.

The Tories' flying start to the election campaign had crash landed. Labour seized on the *FT* report, claiming it upheld their claims that the Tories were still determined to wipe out the welfare state.

Letwin had only been given the post of Shadow Chief Secretary at the last minute. Portillo wanted right-wing MP John Bercow to do the job, but Hague was nervous about allowing Portillo to cram leading supporters into the Treasury team. (Another suggestion, former Michael Heseltine aide Richard Ottaway, was ruled out because Hague was equally nervous of allowing Portillo to build links with Heseltine.)

Portillo's productivity increased noticeably after the arrival of energetic Letwin, who churned out reams of figures and ideas that his boss was only too pleased to use.

It was Letwin's naiveté, not his industry, that landed him in trouble. He had a genius for numbers, but it required only a fraction of such brain-power to work out the source of the *FT* story. A flick of a computer switch by staff at Labour's Millbank headquarters showed Letwin was already on record as having raised the prospect of cutting spending by £20 billion.

Hague was advised by his aides that the best way to defuse the row was to arrange an interview with a sympathetic newspaper to clear up the confusion. Once Letwin had given his side of the story and put his comments in context, the media would march on to the next story. To be accused of offering big tax cuts was not such a damaging smear.

'We had editors on the phone every twenty minutes asking if they could interview Oliver,' recalled a Central Office official. Hague agreed it was the right thing to do – but Portillo blocked it.

There is no doubt that Letwin had gaffed. The Tory manifesto was clear: it proposed £8 billion worth of cuts. But Portillo was more anxious than his leader. Unlike Portillo, Hague still had an inherent faith in the power of tax cuts. If Letwin had erred, at least he had erred on the right side.

Portillo said the only way to make the story go away was to make Letwin go away. And so he was sent into hiding in the wilds of his West Country constituency, where he obeyed Portillo's orders and keep his mouth shut. This only made things worse. The row overshadowed a speech in Cardiff by Hague in which he challenged Blair to rule out tax increases in a Labour second term. Maude fled from a Tory press conference at Central Office after nine minutes when he was besieged with questions about fugitive Letwin: he claimed that he had an important campaign meeting, but was later tracked down having a pub lunch with Conservative activists at The Cricketers in his Horsham constituency.

Meanwhile, in the depths of West Dorset, Letwin was corralled by a reporter and promptly denied the *FT* story. It was another bad move. The *FT* was livid at its integrity being called into question and threatened to run a much fuller version of what Letwin had said to them off the record about the Tories' tax plans.

Hague's aides told Portillo's press officer Malcolm Gooderham that the Shadow Chancellor must speak to the *FT* to sort out the mess. The row could not be allowed to go on wrecking the entire Tory campaign. Gooderham replied: 'Michael will go militant over this and will take it right to the end to defend Oliver.' Portillo wanted Letwin to denounce the *FT* in public, but Hague's advisers told him he could not talk to a newspaper – and certainly not the august *Financial Times* – in such a manner.

After four days of mayhem, Portillo relented and told Letwin to phone the *FT*, at which point Letwin proceeded to go from one extreme to the other, effectively standing up their original version and making fools of Portillo and Hague who had disputed it.

'The story as written in the *FT* is a perfectly accurate report of comments made by me,' said Letwin, while maintaining that the £20 billion was an 'aspiration' not a commitment.[5] It was at this moment that Portillo calmly reassured his deputy over the phone that he had his full support. But the moment he put the receiver down he fumed at Letwin's pathological inability to 'talk to the press and stick to a line'. It was a brutal but fair assessment. For all his brilliance, Letwin was easy meat for the vultures of Grub Street. No more was heard from him for the rest of the campaign. But Hague knew Letwin's name was likely to come up when he was interviewed by John Humphrys on the *Today* programme on 17 May while the row was still dragging on.

The afternoon before the interview, Portillo walked into Amanda Platell's office in Smith Square. It was the first time he had ever entered her room, and sat on a chair opposite her.

Portillo was worried about Hague's interview the next morning.

'What do you think Humphrys will ask him?' he asked.

'Three main things: William's leadership, whether you are after his job, and tax. The rest don't matter.'

Wincing at her Antipodean bluntness, Portillo suggested a long list of other issues he believed would feature.

'Nah,' grunted Platell: 'It will be the three I said.'[6]

In spite of their many bitter rows since Portillo had returned to the Shadow Cabinet, the Arctic freeze in relations between them had thawed by a degree or two during the election campaign, at least to the extent that they now talked to each other instead of glowering across the table, trying to stare each other out in playground power games. They had a grudging mutual respect and were fascinated by each other.

Hague got to hear of Portillo's visits to Platell's office during the election and teased her: 'I hear your new friend Michael has been along to see you.'

On the evening before the Humphrys interview, Platell and Wood joined the 'Gang of Four' and had a long discussion about what subjects were likely to come up. Portillo asked Wood how he thought Humphrys would approach it, and Wood told Hague: 'Humphrys gave Blair a hard time so you can bet he's going to try and murder you. It will be the toughest fifteen minutes of the campaign and you have to know that. You can't win the interview. The best you can hope for is a nil–nil draw. One mistake and we're buggered. You mustn't give a bloody inch.'

Portillo expressed horror at Wood's blunt manner. 'You can't talk like that in front of William. It's not just William who's on there tomorrow, it's all of us,' he said protectively, his voice rising: 'You have no idea what it's like to do these things.'

Hague, well used to the earthy dialect of his two ex-Fleet Street advisers, looked at Platell and Wood and raised his right eyebrow, nonplussed. Like Alastair Campbell, renowned for his uncompromising and often profane frankness with Tony Blair, Platell and Wood had been hired to be honest with Hague, brutally so if necessary. It seemed none of Portillo's advisers ever spoke to him in such terms.

The intensity of the previous two years, not least the clashes with Portillo and Maude and their own spin doctors, had brought Hague closer to Platell and Wood than he was with any member of the Shadow Cabinet. A few days before the election, standing in his suite at the Mandarin Oriental surrounded by his 'closed door set' of Ffion, Coe, Platell and

Wood, waiting for Portillo and Maude to arrive, a resigned Hague turned to them and said: 'You know, I sometimes think that you are the only people worth anything in this party.'

Portillo seemed more anxious than Hague about the Humphrys interview – in particular how the leader was going to deal with the Letwin isue. The following morning at the BBC studios, while Hague was waiting in the 'green room' where guests are entertained, Platell, received a phone call. It was Portillo.

'Tell William that if Humphrys presses him on Letwin, and it's difficult, he can give him up,' he told her.7 Told of Portillo's advice moments before he confronted Humphrys, Hague said nothing. He couldn't believe a Shadow Cabinet Minister would, in effect, suggest disowning another Shadow Cabinet Minister in a radio interview. Hague was more concerned about what Humphrys might ask him about Portillo than about Letwin and, as he expected, Humphrys tried to drive a wedge between him and the Shadow Chancellor, asking him five times if Portillo would make a good leader of the party.

'There are very, very many people in the Conservative Party who one day will make great leaders of the party. There is no vacancy,' said Hague.

Humphrys: 'Do you include Michael Portillo in that?'

Hague: 'I am sure a great many people would. There is no vacancy.' And so Humphrys' interrogation went on – to no great avail. Hague brushed aside his questions about Letwin.

The Letwin incident not only inflamed tensions between Hague and Portillo. It also prompted Maude to write a memo to Ancram on 14 May complaining about the way the entire campaign was being run by Hague's team. He claimed that other Shadow Ministers 'felt remote' from the campaign – by now a familiar refrain from many shadow ministers – and was scathing in his criticism of the handling of the media, remarks that were directed at his enemy Platell. He also protested about the way Portillo had been treated at the launch of the party's London manifesto, when the Shadow Chancellor was so angry that he walked out, leaving Shadow Minister for London Bernard Jenkin bitterly upset.

The Maude memo said:

There needs to be someone senior and authoritative in charge of each day's campaigning organisation – preferably throughout, but at any rate, ensuring continuity through the preparation period and through the execution. The role involves co-ordination, ensuring everyone necessary is across the issues and the current plan; ensuring that the right papers are being prepared, and that there is editorial and message consistency across the piece; ensuring that any spokesman doing media has the right briefing material; ensuring that when a last minute change occurs, as happened both at 10 p.m. last night and again literally the last minute this morning, there is a single person who makes it all happen. [This was a reference to the Letwin row.] Lots of people who needed to know did not know until quite late yesterday that we were doing a press conference on fuel duty at all; even this morning senior people in the war room did not know that we were planning to do a broader tax attack with Michael involved.

There needs to be some rather more focused and senior commitment to major events away from CCO [Conservative Central Office] involving senior Shadow Cabinet members. Michael had a difficult time at the London launch on Friday because no one had really gripped what was happening. No one is really gripping what we do with my response to the Lib Dem manifesto in Plymouth tomorrow. It needs press office and presentational attention to what kind of event it is to be and how it is to be managed; it needs senior CRD [Conservative Research Department] attention to what is the campaigning message; again it needs a single person who is charged with pulling it all together. There are loads of briefing papers around; it is never very clear what is their status; what is just internal and what will be, or indeed has been handed out. Other Shadow Cabinet members feel somewhat remote from the campaign. It would be helpful for some effort to be made to brief them on what we are planning to do over the coming week, let them know of major changes, inform them of what is our top line campaigning message, and generally download their impressions, views and ideas.

The campaign was a week old, and the commanders of the 'war room' were already questioning Hague's direction.

15 The Mummy Returns

'I don't wish to have what they call a multicultural society. I hate these phrases. Multicultural society! A multicultural society will never be a united society.'
Margaret Thatcher, 22 May 2001

The first sign of trouble over Margaret Thatcher's entry into the election campaign emerged on Saturday 19 May when Central Office learned of an interview she had given to a national newspaper, to coincide with her starring role alongside Hague at an election rally in Plymouth, an event planned for months but known only to a tiny handful of senior Conservatives.

Who could forget the first occasion they appeared together at a party gathering, when as a sixteen-year-old he had addressed the 1977 Conservative conference in Blackpool and urged Margaret Thatcher to 'roll back the frontiers of the state'? Her last minute decision to back him against Kenneth Clarke in the 1997 leadership contest was crucial to Hague's victory, but she was not always so impressed with him once he had got the job. Nor he with her.

Hague felt badly let down when she virtually hijacked the 1999 Tory conference, using it as a platform to defend General Pinochet – not the kind of issue likely to reconnect the Conservatives with ordinary voters.

She was said to refer to him in private as 'Wee Willie'[1] and to have criticised him for not taking a sufficiently firm line on the euro. But they had smoothed over any differences before the election and Hague believed Thatcher could be a powerful ally in persuading reluctant Tories to go out and vote, a tactic that was ever more important as hope of defeating

Labour faded and he concentrated on preventing a collapse among the party's core supporters.

Thatcher's office had agreed to send an advance copy of her Plymouth speech to Central Office, but there was another potential hazard to be dealt with first: an interview with the *Daily Mail* due to appear on the morning of the speech. By the weekend, Hague had found out what was in the interview and broke the news to the 'Gang of Four' at the Mandarin Oriental on Sunday night. 'We all know that Margaret Thatcher will be appearing on Tuesday in Plymouth, but she is also doing an interview with the *Daily Mail* in which she says she does not believe in a multicultural society.'[2]

It was hardly on a par with Enoch Powell's 'rivers of blood'. But it is impossible to overstate Tory sensitivity to the race issue. Three weeks earlier, Hague had come close to losing his nerve in trying to control the furore over Tory MP John Townend's remarks about immigration 'undermining homogenous Anglo-Saxon society' and about Britain's 'mongrel society'.

In her interview, Thatcher was equally forthright: 'I want a society of opportunity for all, irrespective of colour or ethnic background. But I don't wish to have what they call a multicultural society. I hate these phrases. Multicultural society! A multicultural society will never be a united society.'[3]

If the unknown Townend could spark a major race controversy with a few ill chosen words about race, how much worse would it be when Thatcher made similar remarks in a major election speech – and with Hague standing at her side as she delivered them? Equally relevant was the fact that black Conservative peer Lord Taylor, who had forced Hague to make Townend apologise for his comments, had stressed the importance of believing in a 'multi-racial, multicultural society' – the very concept Thatcher now scorned.

But Hague's concern was as nothing compared to that of another member of the 'Gang of Four'.

Embracing multiculturalism had become one of the totems of Michael Portillo's metamorphosis from the 'Who Dares Wins' Portillo of old to what one wag called the 'Who Hugs Wins' new Portillo. The man who rushed to Thatcher's door on the night she resigned, begging her to stay had travelled a long way since then, mostly in the opposite direction. The arch Thatcherite, whom she once saw as her son and heir, was now, in the eyes of some and perhaps even of Thatcher herself, an anti-Thatcherite. The Iron Lady had little empathy with touchy-feely politics, and since Portillo's return to politics as Kensington MP, there were reports that she was bewildered by the changes in him.

The parting of the ways was symbolised by his acrimonious exit in November 2000 from the 'No Turning Back' dining group of MPs, made up of full strength Thatcherite 'ultras'.

Her loss of faith in him was matched by his loss of faith in her. He was appalled by her attack on the multicultural society. When he was told her comments in the newspaper interview he was adamant that she must be stopped. There was another worry. What if she repeated her comment about a multicultural society – or 'MCS', as Conservative officials referred to it in shorthand as the phrase was bandied about non-stop for three days – in the Plymouth speech? Hague would be tarred with the same racist brush.

Portillo told Hague he had three options: 1. Get the phrase removed from the *Mail* interview. 2. Cancel her appearance in Plymouth. 3. Hague must make it clear at the rally that he disagreed with her.

Option 1 was not practical: the interview had taken place and inter-viewer Simon Heffer was hardly likely to agree to remove the offending words.

Option 2 was fraught with danger: the press was bound to find out that her appearance had been cancelled and there would be an even bigger fuss.

Option 3 was equally risky: if Hague disowned Thatcher the moment she had finished speaking in Plymouth, it would cause pandemonium.

'Portillo wanted William to appear on stage after Thatcher had finished, hold out his arm towards her and say something like, "Margaret, you are a wonderful person, but I have to disagree with what you say about multi-culturalism . . ."', said a Conservative source.4 'Can you imagine what might have happened? The audience might have booed him.'

The 'Gang of Four' meeting on Sunday broke up without reaching a decision. John Whittingdale's loyalties were torn in three directions. He had been Thatcher's political adviser in Number 10, one of Portillo's most loyal supporters, and was now Hague's right-hand man. It was his job to keep relations smooth between Hague and Portillo and between Hague and Thatcher.

On this occasion Whittingdale was in no doubt about with whom he should side. He told Hague that scrapping Thatcher's appearance would be a disaster. Nick Wood agreed and told Hague: 'If we cancel Thatcher's speech, we might as well pack up and go home.' By Monday lunchtime, rumours that her speech was to be stopped reached Thatcher's office. She was said to be 'angry and deeply hurt'.[5]

Portillo was not alone in his concern. Hague was worried too, and considered politely asking Thatcher not to attend, before dismissing the idea. He was not convinced her remarks would cause such a fuss, and it was too late to go back on his decision. There was another factor. It had been his decision to invite her. He had kept Portillo and Maude in the dark because he knew, as with some of his speeches, that if he told them in advance they would object. If he cancelled Thatcher's appearance, it would be a humiliating personal rebuff for him.

Portillo conceded that it was too late to cancel Thatcher's speech, but insisted she was disowned. As rumours of Portillo's plan spread among senior Tories on the Monday, Hague faced a revolt. One Shadow Minister told him: 'If you disown Thatcher, I will not be able to continue campaigning for you. It's madness.'

Whittingdale told him he must go ahead with the rally as planned – and hope for the best. Platell spent most of Monday trying to contact Hague, who, unusually, was not taking her calls, most of which were intercepted by Coe, who told her Hague was busy. After lunch she told Coe: 'You had better tell William I need to speak to him – now!' She was supported by Tim Collins, who sent a pager message to Coe: 'For God's sake, Seb, if we aren't careful we are going to lose the election today.'[6]

Eventually Hague returned Platell's call. She told him: 'I have come too far to desert you now, William, and if you stick to this decision I will stand by you without a flicker of dissent. But I am telling you that if you don't change your decision, we are finished.'

Feelings were still running high as Hague and Portillo met at the Mandarin Oriental that night. Portillo was adamant: the moment Thatcher's interview appeared in the *Daily Mail* – now only hours away – there would be uproar, and the Tories would be plunged into another race war. He was supported by Maude, but old campaigner Ancram urged caution on Hague. 'We should cool it,' he said. 'The interview doesn't look as bad as all that to me. Denouncing her will be a huge story.'[7]

Portillo restated his case for slapping down Thatcher. Hague said, 'Right, thank you, Michael' – and decided to ignore his advice. But another more immediate problem had to be faced. In eight hours' time Portillo and Lansley were due to appear at the Tories' Tuesday morning press conference at Central Office. Thatcher's comments about race in the *Daily Mail* would be on the streets by then and were almost certain to come up, said Portillo. Someone must be ready to deal with it.

But Portillo did not want to do it himself. He suggested that Lansley, who unlike Portillo still considered himself to be a Thatcherite, should do it. 'Andrew will have to be the one who deals with it, because if I do it, it will be a bigger story,' said Portillo. Lansley agreed. They would make it clear that Thatcher spoke for herself, and not the whole party, but only if the issue was raised.

As Portillo and Maude left the Mandarin Oriental, they bumped into Platell and Wood waiting anxiously in the hotel lobby downstairs. Portillo and Maude told them the press conference was going ahead. Wood and Platell assumed it meant the plan for Lansley to disown Thatcher at the following morning's press conference was going ahead. The two Shadow Ministers walked past without further explanation. Wood and Platell rushed to Hague's room and banged so hard on the door that it nearly came off its hinges.

'The speech is going ahead as planned,' said Hague.

'And the press conference?' said Platell.

'If it comes up, Andrew will find a form of words to deal with it.'

Thatcher's comments on a multicultural society would not be challenged. Her speech would go ahead without any disclaimer by Hague. The *Daily Mail* interview appeared, including the 'multicultural society' phrase that had got the Tories into such a lather, and they waited for the thunderbolt to strike at their morning press conference.

But not a single journalist raised it. Even the eagle-eyed young predators at Millbank, forever on the lookout for 'Tory gaffes', missed a trick for once. Tory officials sat, hearts in their mouths, as the press conference droned on. As Portillo and Lansley shuffled their papers, ready to depart, the Tories sighed with relief: miraculously, no one had mentioned Thatcher – until almost the very last question.

Watching Tory aides nearly fainted. The race bomb that Hague had defused three weeks ago was about to be detonated. The hairs on Lansley's neck stood up. But just as he was about to rehearse his carefully thought out answer to the question: 'What do you think about Lady Thatcher's claim that there is no such thing as a multicultural society?' He had to change gear again. The question had nothing to do with a multicultural society. The reporter wanted a response to her claim that Britain should 'never' give up its sovereignty to the EU.

The next hurdle was Plymouth. Thatcher was in vintage form, perhaps sensing that at the age of seventy-five, this may be the last general election where she would appear on the hustings. Shortly before lunchtime, Central Office received a copy of her speech. Hague's officials scanned it at 100 m.p.h., looking for any reference to MCS. They were mightily relieved to see that she did not once refer to a multicultural society or race.

When she entered the stage, she shrugged off a supporting hand from Maude, (who unbeknown to her, had supported Portillo's attempt to silence her) determined to show she did not need anyone to prop her up. She joked that although the visit was supposed to have been a secret, she had seen a billboard on her way to Plymouth Pavilions advertising the film *The Mummy Returns*. 'So I knew you were expecting me after all.'

The joke wasn't in the advance copies of her speech sent to Central Office. Tory advisers shuffled their feet nervously. What else had she left out? But she kept to the printed text for the rest of the speech – except for five words. When she got to the section on Europe, she could not resist going further than the prepared text, and accused Blair of being prepared to steamroller Britain into the euro, adding off the cuff with Churchillian defiance: 'I would never be prepared.'

She had broken her word to stick to Hague's policy of ruling out the single currency for the next Parliament only. But it was not going to cause riots in the streets.

Hague joined her on stage and paid warm tribute to her achievements. They both got standing ovations.

16   Jekyll and Hyde

'You messed up. It's always the same. All Central Office thinks about is William Hague. They don't think of others.'
Michael Portillo on 29 May 2001.

Michael Portillo is one of the most mercurial figures on the political stage. Friends talk of his elegant charm, warmth and attentiveness and unbreakable loyalty, but there is another side to this deeply emotional Latin.

Some of his friends believe he went through a form of emotional breakdown when he lost his Commons seat in 1997 and subsequently admitted to homosexual experiences in the past.

As recently as the winter of 2000 some of his confidants thought he was so disillusioned with politics that he would turn away from it completely and find another, less confrontational life. The dark side of his personality was illustrated by an extraordinary incident during the 2001 general election campaign when Portillo went to Brighton on 29 May.

It was a re-run of a similar event the previous week further along the south coast at Plymouth – with one major difference. The former Prime Minister topping the bill in Brighton was John Major, not Margaret Thatcher: Hague and Portillo were his support act.

Hague was not in the best of spirits. Earlier in the day he had endured the ordeal of a more than usually hostile interview by Jeremy Paxman in the conservatory of Brighton's Grand Hotel for that night's *Newsnight* programme on BBC2. Paxman repeatedly taunted him over the policy changes forced on him by Portillo, and riled Hague by challenging Ffion's role in the election. Hague gave a series of limp replies about working out all policies together with Portillo. It was one of his poorest performances in the election. With polling day less than a week away, he was struggling to keep his morale up.

By contrast, Portillo had seemed almost demob happy, cracking one of the best jokes of the campaign at the Tories' morning press conference earlier in the day. Asked if he was frightened by the prospect of a landslide, he replied that he wasn't expecting one, but 'if we get one it's fine by me.' His reply to a question about Thatcher bordered on the flippant: 'We will always be immensely proud of her record but she did stop leading the party eleven years ago.' He did not bear the demeanour of a man whose shoulders were sagging with the burden of impending defeat.

Portillo opened the Brighton rally in style with a generous tribute to John Major (the man who once bracketed him as one of the Cabinet 'bastards'), and displayed his full range of charm and good humour, cracking jokes like a professional warm-up man. But things started to go wrong after the rally when Portillo was to take part in a photo call on the staircase of The Grand Hotel, together with Major, his wife Norma, William Hague and Ffion. Portillo, who was on his own, was left bobbing around at the back trying to get into the picture. The scene was famously captured on Amanda Platell's video diaries programme broadcast after the election, in which she joked about Portillo saying to himself: 'Does my quiff look good in this?'

After the photo call, Hague, Major and Portillo and their entourages were each due to be picked up by cars at the front entrance of the hotel, from where they would depart in convoy for Roedean school, where helicopters were waiting to whisk them back to Battersea helipad in London. As soon as the three men had emerged from the hotel, Hague and Major, who unlike Portillo each have an official car and bodyguards, got straight in and were driven off. Portillo was to be picked up by a car driven by a local Tory official, but just as the Hague and Major cars drove away, police ordered the entire convoy – including Portillo's car – to depart, for security reasons. (Understandably, The Grand takes politicians' security more seriously than most.) Portillo had not had time to get in his car, and stood seething on the steps of The Grand while his driver went round the block, returning a couple of minutes late to collect him.

The delay was so minor that his car arrived at Roedean only minutes after Hague's helicopter had departed, and in the event Portillo's helicopter reached London less than five minutes after Hague's. But that was no comfort to Portillo, who aimed his anger at Susie Black, a young Tory official who had worked as a secretary in the office of Sir Robin Janvrin, the Queen's Private Secretary.

'You messed up. It's always the same,' he told the trembling girl. 'All Central Office thinks about is William Hague. They don't think of others.'[1] In fact, it was no one's fault, and Susie protested: 'I don't know what has happened.' But Portillo, accompanied by his aide, ex-Central Office staffer Kevin Culwick, fired back: 'I'll tell you what has happened: you weren't properly prepared, that's what happened.' He continued to complain as they sat in the car on the way to a helipad at nearby Roedean.

Half an hour later, he was still criticising Susie in the helicopter – even after, close to tears, she had apologised to him: 'I am very sorry Mr Portillo, I don't know what went wrong. It wasn't my fault.'

'I'll tell you what went wrong – you didn't plan it properly,' he repeated. Eventually he realised how rude he had been and made a grovelling apology. 'I am so sorry, I have been very rude, haven't I?' The embarrassed young woman told him there was no need to say sorry. But Portillo, full of remorse for his behaviour, said: 'No, I insist, I was very, very rude to you. It was unforgivable.'

A passer-by who witnessed the outburst at The Grand said: 'He was incredibly angry and I really don't know why. It was completely uncalled for.' One of Susie's colleagues said: 'She is an absolutely super girl, the most efficient PA you could ever find. She is brilliant and it is inconceivable that she would have made a mess of arrangements.'

Susie was comforted by friends when she arrived back in London that night. 'She was shaking with nerves and said he had been truly awful to her,' said one. 'She just couldn't understand why he had done it. She was very red faced. I think the shock of it had made her come out in a rash.' According to one source, Ms Black told friends: 'No one has ever spoken to me like that before. It's so wrong.'[2]

A local Tory official said: 'I have never in my life known a man speak to a woman like that. Will someone please tell me that he won't get away with this kind of behaviour?'[3]

Another aide who had been in Brighton, Shana Hole, adviser to James Arbuthnot and one of the most experienced political aides in Westminster, observed to friends: 'It reminds me of a saying: "God pays late, but he pays well".'[4]

A Central Office insider said: 'I can only assume that Michael was jealous because William has an official car and bodyguards, and was miffed at having to make do with an ordinary car from a local volunteer. On top of that, they had gone without him. It rubbed salt into his wounds.'[5]

The next day word of the row spread around Central Office, where there were calls for Portillo to be asked to explain his conduct. But with polling day six days away, a news blackout was ordered to protect him.

Portillo's temperament was frequently in evidence in his rocky relationship with the equally volatile Amanda Platell. The pair spent most of their seventeen months working together in Hague's team circling each other warily, like a matador and a bull, searching out the opponent's strengths and weaknesses, rarely coming into direct contact, but clashing when they did. They had more in common than pouting, red lips. Forceful, emotional, headstrong and intuitive, both were outsiders, alien to the starched Home Counties culture of Smith Square. Portillo believed Platell wanted to destroy him because she saw him as a threat to Hague. Platell believed Portillo wanted to destroy her as a first step to destroying Hague.

One of their most strange encounters came on 25 January 2000, the day Peter Mandelson was sacked from the Cabinet for the second time – on this occasion, over allegations that he had intevened to help one of the millionaire Indian-born Hinduja brothers obtain a British passport.

Mandelson was in a better position than most to understand what Portillo had gone through when he admitted to homosexual experiences in his student days, since he himself had suffered taunts about his private life and was 'outed' by *Times* journalist Matthew Parris on the BBC2 programme *Newsnight* in October 1998. In December 2000, a week after reports that Portillo was on the verge of giving up politics because of attacks from his own party, Mandelson took the unusual step of praising his call for greater tolerance by Conservatives, lauding Portillo's 'emphasis on social inclusiveness in his own party'. Whether it was the hand of friendship from a kindred spirit or a cynical attempt to exploit Tory divisions is hard to say.

Conversely, Platell had good reason to loathe Mandelson. It was her exposé of Mandelson's gay partner when she was editor of the *Sunday Express* in 1998 that led to her dismissal. Shortly after Mandelson's resignation was announced, Platell was leaving Hague's Commons office and passed the Shadow Chancellor's room. The door was open and she peered inside. Portillo was alone, working at his desk. They had barely exchanged a word since the serious of explosive rows when Portillo and Maude had accused her of leaking details of the No Turning Back dinner. Platell knocked on the door.

'Come in.'

Platell entered the room and saw a bespectacled Portillo sitting behind his desk sticking yellow Post-its on a sheaf of documents. After several seconds, he looked over the rim of his glasses at her, then returned to his documents. He said nothing. She walked across, sat down at the desk directly in front of him, and said: 'I thought I would come and ask you if there is anything I can do to help.'

Portillo, without looking up: 'No.'

Platell: 'There must be something I could do to help. Any problems you may be having with particular newspapers, that sort of thing, I might be able to help. It's my job.'

Portillo: 'Amanda, leave it.'

Platell: 'Michael, this doesn't seem to be a very sensible way to go on. We have an election coming up and the fact is that I'm going to be there right through it. We can't achieve very much if you won't even talk to me.'

Portillo: 'I don't wish to.'

Platell: 'What? You're not going to speak to me? Not for ever?'

Portillo: 'Forever may not be very long.'

She left.

They had an equally bizarre confrontation two months later at Princess Diana's favourite restaurant, Le Caprice in London's St James district.

Platell spotted Portillo dining with *Times* editor Peter Stothard, the day that an article appeared in that paper by Michael Gove which said:

> It is not hard to find Conservative MPs, advisers, and apparatchiks who have reason to criticise her. And it is not hard to imagine why she would have put backs up in the Tory party. Prejudiced as some may be, Platell's background, gender and personality cannot account for the number and depth of voices ranged against her. Listening to them, one builds up a picture of a woman who is not without talent or charm, but who is out of her depth in a front line political role.[6]

Having spotted Portillo and Stothard dining *à deux* in Le Caprice, Platell bowled right up to them. She pulled up a seat and said 'Michael, Peter – what a surprise to find you here together, today of all days,' she purred menacingly.

Stothard: 'How, er . . . nice to see you.'

Platell: 'I hope you don't mind me saying so, but there's one thing that has been nagging me all day long. It's really bugging me.'

Stothard: 'What's that?'

'You just have to tell me what shade of lipstick you gave me today.'

The colour photograph of Platell on the paper's front page appeared to show her wearing a puce coloured lipstick, not her normal choice.

With that, the killer bimbo from Fleet Street flounced out.

Platell was not alone in her suspicion of Portillo and Maude. In the summer of 2000, she dined with Sir Archie Hamilton, chairman of the Conservative backbench 1922 Committee. Platell told him there were some 'bad people' in the party.

Hamilton: 'Who?'

Platell: 'People like Portillo and Maude. They are doing terrible things to William.'

Hamilton: 'I know.'

Platell: 'But no one is dealing with it. It just goes on.'

Hamilton: 'There's nothing I can do. People have to do what they believe to be right.'

Platell: 'Which people?'

Hamilton: 'People like you.'

Platell: 'Let me get this straight. Are you telling me to deal with Portillo and Maude? This is serious.'

Hamilton: 'I'm telling you that you must do what you believe to be right.'

Nearly a year later, immediately after the election defeat, Platell had a chat with Hamilton in Central Office. He conceded: 'William should have sacked Portillo and Maude. You can't run a party without shedding some blood.'

Platell took his remarks as confirmation that other senior party figures believed Portillo and Maude were disloyal to Hague. But she felt no one else was prepared to do anything about it.

Maude was equally certain that Platell was the villain. 'She did untold damage to the Conservative Party,' he said.

Another feisty female servant of the Tory party, Anne Jenkin, wife and secretary of Tory MP Bernard Jenkin, sees Portillo very differently from Platell. Mrs Jenkin was so convinced that Portillo was the Tories' saviour that she risked a marital fallout by campaigning against her husband in the 2001 leadership contest: Bernard was Iain Duncan Smith's campaign manager.

'I have known Michael for more than twenty years,' said Mrs Jenkin. 'He is one of the most charming and considerate men I have ever known. All these stories about his haughtiness and arrogance simply aren't true.'[7] She cites the example of Portillo's former secretary, Clemency Ames, who had worked for him for thirteen years but suddenly found herself unemployed, along with her boss, when he unexpectedly lost his Commons seat in 1997. 'The morning after his defeat, when his world had collapsed, he spent much of it phoning round trying to find another job for Clemency,' said Mrs Jenkin. Portillo's former ally, Aldershot Tory MP Gerald Howarth, took her on.

Anne's husband Bernard Jenkin is an example of how Portillo's friends have changed over the years along with his changing political views. Once one of his most devoted supporters and a close family friend, Jenkin found himself elbowed out of the Portillo coterie after his Commons comeback in 1999. It is not clear why. Despite being a traditional right-winger, Jenkin is not one of the Tory 'bigots' Portillo came to despise. He was among those who freely admitted to having taken drugs in the past and has progressive views on homosexuality not so different from Portillo's.

Like Susie Black, Jenkin experienced Portillo's less charming side during the 2001 general election. As Tory spokesman on London, he was deeply upset when Portillo inexplicably blew a fuse during the launch of the party's policies for the capital, held under the London Eye on 11 May. Portillo, the party's most senior London MP, was invited to the launch, largely to promote additional media interest. The Tories wanted the focus to be on their ideas for solving the capital's transport problems, but the media had other ideas.

Reporters had little interest in London or transport or Jenkin, but perked up when Portillo homed into view. Instead of asking him about London and transport, they assailed him with questions about a new row over Labour claims that there was a 'black hole' in Conservative tax plans. The confusion had been compounded by Shadow Social Security spokesman David Willetts who, in a radio interview that morning, had foolishly brushed off a challenge about Hague's pledge to cut £8 billion off taxes with the casual aside: 'Let us settle for £7 billion.'

Portillo refused to answer reporters' questions about tax. 'I do not do uncontrolled situations,' he said, marching off towards Westminster Bridge before the event was over, leaving a stranded bag-carrier running round asking: 'Where's Michael?'

Jenkin was very upset. 'I'm being accused of messing up the manifesto launch. Michael phoned up and said it was chaotic and how dare I involve him in such an event.'[8] One official said: 'It was unfair to blame Bernard. He did a good job and could hardly be expected to know about the tax row. That was down to Central Office.'[9]

Former Brigg and Cleethorpes Tory MP Michael Brown was one of Portillo's closest friends in the early 1980s. 'We hit it off straight away,' says Brown, who knocked on doors for Portillo during the 1984 by-election in Southgate (now Enfield Southgate) and organised two holidays in the

West Indies – one in 1991 at a five-star hotel in Anguilla, the other the following year at a villa in Barbados – for Portillo's closest friends. The group included Portillo and wife Carolyn; Brown and his friend, black Tory activist Derek Laud; John and Cilla Whittingdale; and two other couples, both friends of the Portillos. Brown has happy memories of the holidays. 'Michael and Carolyn were wonderful company and utterly devoted to each other.'[10]

In 1994, when Brown was in trouble and needed Portillo most, his former friend – now a Cabinet Minister tipped to become Prime Minister – was nowhere to be seen. Brown had to resign as a Government whip over allegations about his private life, and Tory friends rallied round as Fleet Street tried to hunt him down. Fellow Conservative MP David Davis hid Brown in his Yorkshire home until the fuss died down. 'Lots of people phoned me and offered to help and wrote to me, but I didn't hear a word from Michael,' said Brown. 'I was pretty miffed. I had the tabloids at the door and nowhere to go until David bailed me out.'

It was not until some time later, when Brown ran into Portillo at the Commons, that Portillo spoke to him about the matter. 'He said to me, "How did you cope with doorstepping?"' said Brown. (Doorstepping is the term given to the practice of reporters camping outside a victim's house for hours, days or even weeks, until they get an interview.) 'I thought what an odd thing it was to say. It was not until much later that it occurred to me why he had said it. He was thinking of the day when it would happen to him. There was a ticking time bomb under him.'

By coincidence, when in the summer of 1999 the furore over Portillo's gay past erupted, Brown was on holiday at a villa near Florence with friends from Portillo's circle including Stephen Sherbourne, Margaret Thatcher's former political secretary at Number 10. Brown received a frantic call from his office at the *Independent* newspaper demanding an exclusive on Portillo and gays.

Brown was torn between his employer and his friend. Sherbourne who campaigned for Portillo in the 2001 leadership contest, took Brown to one side and told him: 'The only thing you can do to help Michael is to do nothing. He will never forget.'

Brown put loyalty to his friend first and refused to put pen to paper, risking his job in the process.

'There are two Michael Portillos,' said Brown. 'There is Michael Portillo the private person, the most charming and polite company you could wish for. And there is Michael Portillo the leader in waiting, who is far from easy to deal with and tends to be arrogant.'

Another friend who felt let down by Portillo is businessman Greville Howard, who lent him his Georgian home in Lord North Street in 1995 so that he could challenge John Major for the Conservative leadership, only for Portillo to change his mind. Howard supported Iain Duncan Smith in the 2001 contest and let him use the house. 'He [Portillo] let us install the telephone lines, then bottled out and we had to pick up the mess. He says he is not responsible for his supporters, but if he can't control them, he's not suitable to be leader.'[11]

Portillo displayed both sides of his Jekyll and Hyde character at a Conservative Way Forward dinner in March 2000 at London's Grosvenor Square Marriott Hotel. After making one of his early 'inclusive' speeches (which had watching CWF chairman and No Turning Back group host Eric Forth and his pal David Davis spitting into their Brown Windsor soup), Portillo was engaged in conversation by a political admirer.

'Don't you think it is important for the party to say never to the euro?' ventured the fan politely – only to be taken aback when Portillo exploded: 'We have got to win the fucking election before we can do anything!' He immediately realised his mistake and apologised profusely to the stranger, whom he had never met before. 'What I meant is there is no point in us doing anything about the euro at the moment,' said Portillo, adding enigmatically: 'Keep the faith.'

The fan joked: 'Whether he meant keep the faith with him or the party, I don't know.'

Portillo's ability to be as extravagantly penitent as he is petulant, was demonstrated at a dinner party with friends, when he suddenly launched into a tirade of abuse after the wife of a senior political commentator had innocently asked about an item in the press which referred to him. Three weeks later, she received a magnificent bouquet of flowers and couldn't work out who they were from. It was Portillo.

Portillo's critics maintain that the most potent manifestation of his dark side is the band of fanatics who have attached themselves to him over the years. Friends counter, with some justification, that Portillo cannot be held responsible for the excesses of the zealots who support him any more than a football club can be responsible for the excesses of the hooligans that support it.

The most notorious example came when the Shadow Chancellor's chief spokesman Malcolm Gooderham was accused of sabotage against Hague. Gooderham was appointed to the job after Portillo's first choice Robbie Gibb was vetoed by Hague, because Platell and Coe said he couldn't be trusted.

During the 2001 general election campaign, *Daily Mirror* political reporter Paul Gilfeather secretly tape recorded a conversation with Gooderham, in which Portillo's spokesman appeared to encourage the paper to publish video shots of protesters wearing Hague lookalike masks following the Tory leader. Gooderham, a former television researcher, was quoted as telling Gilfeather: 'There's very funny TV footage of Hague being pursued by Labour activists wearing rubber masks. They'd be worth finding – especially the scene where one of the protesters attempts to shake hands with Hague.'[12]

This was a fortnight after Portillo had stood side by side with Hague in an Essex farmyard declaring his 'complete loyalty' to the party leader. Portillo phoned Hague and told him that Gooderham, recruited by Portillo when Hague refused to let Robbie Gibb do the same job, had been 'entrapped' by the *Mirror*. Hague did not believe it. Platell and Coe told him Gooderham should be fired. Portillo refused.

For everyone who describes Portillo the Mr Hyde, there is another who will describe Portillo the Dr Jekyll. And there are many who are familiar with both.

17 Landslide

'People looked at the Tory party with their tongues hanging out. All in all, we looked like a thoroughly unpleasant bunch.'

Nicholas Soames, 11 June 2001

The Tories had had plenty of time to contemplate the prospect of a second landslide defeat. It had been widely expected from 19 June 1997, the day Hague was elected leader.

Throughout all the political scandals, controversies and crises that had hit New Labour in the intervening four years, one factor had, for all but a frenzied fortnight during the fuel blockade, remained constant: Blair's landslide-proportioned lead in the opinion polls. William Hague had tried every form of political resuscitation known to man, but the 'dead patient' – Portillo's lethally accurate term for his party's continued 'flatlining' at a life-threatening 30 per cent – had stubbornly refused to revive.

On Thursday 31 May 2001, D-Day minus seven, Hague effectively threw in the towel. The only question was not which side would win, but the margin of victory. Using an interview with BBC TV, Hague urged voters not to be harsh on him. Don't let Labour get another landslide, he pleaded. He wasn't merely looking to salvage his pride, but his leadership too. If he could cut into Labour's majority, he might just live to fight another day. Maude, Portillo and Norman had been convinced that this was the limit of Hague's ambition, not just for the last week of the campaign but for the last year.

Like so many of Hague's most important decisions, the 'stop the landslide' strategy was not even discussed at the 'Leader's Meeting' or by the 'Gang of Four'. Hague and Portillo both knew the implications of a heavy defeat: Hague would resign and Portillo would stand for – and probably win – the leadership. Hague's main aim now was not to win: it was to hang onto his job.

The BBC interview was followed up on Sunday with a Tory poster featuring a photograph of a smug looking Blair in a bubble with a large hand wielding a pin under the slogan 'Go On, Burst His Bubble'. The poster was planned in February with Tory advertising agency 'Yellow M' as a last-ditch attempt to turn what New Labour image-makers regarded as Blair's greatest asset, his face, into a handicap. The Tories had tried it in 1997, producing the infamous 'demon eyes' poster to try and make Blair seem sinister. Now they portrayed him as cocky. Both achieved the same result: a Labour landslide.

Early in 2001, Coe and Platell approached Hague to advise him to prepare a 'landslide strategy' – just in case the worst came to the worst. Few members of the Shadow Cabinet would have dared to be so frank.

The idea behind the 'landslide strategy' was to repeat the 'Queensland effect'. In 1995 in Queensland, Australia, National Party leader Rob Borbidge scored a shock victory over the Labour Party, which had been way ahead in the polls, by campaigning on the message that the ruling party was 'arrogant and took voters for granted'. A leaked Millbank memo, believed to have been written by Michael Stephenson, a former Australian Labour Party official who had joined Blair's 2001 election team, warned of the danger of Hague trying to ape the 'Queensland effect': 'Before the election, 75 per cent of Labour voters said they thought Labour would win easily. [The National Party] tapped into a mood of cynicism about politics. They ran a negative campaign based on the message that Labour took voters for granted,' read the Millbank memo.[1]

Hague was not the first person to raise the issue in public. That distinction went to Alastair Campbell, who to the irritation of many in his own party called a press briefing on 28 May to brag that Blair would increase his majority from 179 to 241, prompting newspaper headlines of 'Labour: It's In The Bag'. This made a nonsense of Labour's persistent pleas to its supporters to guard against complacency.

But Hague knew Campbell was right – his own party's private research had been feeding him with the same gloomy statistics for six months. The

Tories had paid a six-figure sum for a highly sophisticated computerised telephone polling system which accurately predicted the result to within twelve seats. Its findings were so sensitive that only three people knew of them: Hague, Coe, and Tory director of field operations Stephen Gilbert, who was in charge of the system.

The call centre, on the third floor of Central Office, could process and analyse as many as 2,000 calls a night. Each evening a different key seat would be targeted, and the system was so advanced that it could even target particular wards of key constituencies. The operators did not even have to think for themselves. The computer would automatically dial the voter. The elector's name – and the questions to be asked – would flash up on the screen. All the operator had to do was to read them out and record the answers. And it had another significant advantage over the age old door-to-door canvassing method. People are more inclined to tell the truth over the phone than to someones's face. The same voter who assured the doorstep canvasser that they would vote for their party said the opposite when called the same evening by the computer controlled operator.

The party's candidates out on the stump, most of whom said Hague was doing better than the polls suggested, proved to be hopelessly wrong. Iain Duncan Smith, who spent the entire campaign on the road, kept reporting back that things were far from bleak 'out in the country'. London spokesman Bernard Jenkin told Hague that the party would 'do well' in the capital, a forecast that proved to be way off the mark.

Hague knew the truth all along, because Gilbert had been telling him for months that Labour was heading for a majority of over 150, and in the last few weeks of the campaign the figure came even closer to the final result. As the landslide loomed, paranoia inside Central Office reached a frenzy. Hague was tipped off that a report from the party's area campaign directors suggesting that Hague himself was the biggest liability on the doorstep would be leaked to the press. The Conservative leader personally issued orders to print only one copy – to make it easier to catch the culprit if it was leaked. The ploy worked.

It was not until Hague prepared for an interview with BBC political editor Andrew Marr on Wednesday 31 May that Platell and Coe raised the subject of a landslide strategy during the campaign itself. Hague listened, but did not respond. When Platell briefed Marr, she suggested he raise the subject, though did not say how Hague would respond. She couldn't, because she didn't know.

When Marr spoke to Hague before the interview, he told him he planned to raise the issue. Hague conferred privately with Coe, who told him he thought he should tackle it. When the interview took place, Hague was ready for the landslide question. 'I think it would be very dangerous,' he replied. 'Obviously we are working on making sure there is no landslide. What we have seen in the last four years is an extraordinarily arrogant attitude.'

His comment received prominent press coverage, but curiously was barely mentioned at that day's Leader's Meeting. When an official referred to Hague's remarks, the Conservative leader shrugged his shoulders and said: 'I know it wasn't planned, but there we are.' No one challenged him. What was the point? He was falling down the rock face trying to grab hold of a ledge.

The following day Tony Blair expressed incredulity. 'We have the extraordinary spectacle of a Conservative Party and a Conservative leader either urging people not to vote or to vote Conservative to reduce the so-called Labour majority in an election that hasn't even happened. That is precisely what they want to do, to sneak in by the back door.'

The decision to turn the 'Burst His Bubble' poster into the 'Landslide Strategy' was also taken on the spur of the moment. The poster had been planned months ago as part of a final attack on Blair. But Hague's advisers decided that since he had now raised the landslide issue, they might as well adapt the poster to its last gasp message.

Officials briefed the press that the aim of the poster was to 'wipe the smile off Tony's face', an idea they had stolen from chief Blair-baiter, *Sun* columnist Richard Littlejohn, who frequently incited readers to 'wipe the smile off the grinning Jackanape's face.'

The Tories' inexorable march to defeat was not without its lighter moments. In spite of all the bickering and tensions between the senior players, there was a strong *esprit de corps* in Central Office which lasted right up to the moment that the polling stations closed at 10 p.m. on Thursday 7 June.

Spirits were never higher than on 16 May, when a series of public relations catastrophes stopped the Labour juggernaut in its tracks. Blair was assailed at a hospital in Birmingham by Sharron Storer, whose partner Keith Sedgwick was a cancer patient. The Prime Minister was rudely silenced as she brushed aside his apology for delays in her partner's treatment, berating him: 'You're not very sorry, because if you were, you'd do something about it.'

On the same day Jack Straw was heckled at a police conference, but the ordeals of Prime Minister and Home Secretary paled into insignificance compared with the 'Prescott Punch' when Deputy Prime Minister John Prescott brawled with farmworker Craig Evans, who had thrown an egg at him during a visit to Rhyl in North Wales. When the first pictures were broadcast, Portillo was sitting in the war room eating a banana (he gets through several a day), watching one of the many television sets fixed head-high to the walls. His eyes would flit from one screen to another, as though admiring his image from each angle. When he saw the Prescott punch, Portillo jumped to his feet and starting leaping around the room, whooping with joy, banana in hand. Hague, when told of the incident, wryly observed: 'It's not my policy to hit voters during an election.'

There was another comic interlude when the Conservatives joined in the fun at the expense of Tory turncoat Shaun Woodward. Wife of super-market heiress Camilla Sainsbury and master of a country mansion in Oxfordshire, Woodward had never lived down having once boasted that 'even my butler has a butler'. When, on the eve of the election, Blair para-chuted him in to the rugby league and whippets safe Labour seat of St Helens South, it was a natural target for his former allies. To embarrass Woodward, the Tories sent up to St Helens half a dozen young volunteers dressed as butlers. On the morning of their departure, they lined up on parade in the Central Office boardroom for the 8.15 a.m. Leader's Meeting. When the noble Lord Strathclyde arrived late and rubbed his eyes in disbelief, Hague's deputy private secretary, chirpy Tina Stowell said: 'Tom thinks he's walked into his front room.'

Hague retained his sense of humour right to the end. On the final Sunday of the campaign he appeared on the BBC Television programme *Breakfast With Frost*. An earlier guest on the same programme was impressionist Rory Bremner, who poked fun at Hague's oft-repeated slogan, 'In Europe But Not Run By Europe' by reworking it to 'William Hague: in trouble, but not run by trouble'. Hague, waiting a few feet away in the 'green room' chuckled: 'You never said a word more true.'

There was more laughter when Hague and his advisers discussed the Labour poster showing Hague with Thatcher's hair. It was supposed to frighten voters, but former Thatcher aide John Whittingdale told him it had backfired. 'They can send as many posters to my constituency as they like: my people love it,' he said.

Boris Johnson, Tory candidate for Henley and editor of the *Spectator*, found himself on the end of some vintage Platell vitriol after he had inter-viewed Sir Edward Heath for the 10 May edition of his magazine. Heath, who was retiring from the Commons, described Hague as a 'laughing stock' – a scoop for Boris the hack, but scandalous treachery by Boris the hack politician. Platell learned of the interview at 10.30 p.m. on 9 May when it appeared in the first edition of the *Daily Telegraph*. She phoned Johnson, who was asleep at home.

Platell: 'What the hell do you think you are doing?'

Johnson: 'You have woken me up. The children are asleep.'

Platell: 'Go to a phone in a quiet room.'

Johnson: 'I'll call back.'

Platell: 'Stay on the line. I want the answer to three questions: Did you interview Heath knowing that he has frequently criticised William and has rarely done anything else? Does Heath call William a laughing stock? Did your magazine punt the "laughing stock" to the rest of Fleet Street?'

Johnson: 'Er . . .'

Platell let rip: 'You are a complete disgrace. You have kept the whole of Central Office up. Do you realise the damage you have done to people who have devoted years of their lives working for the party? Your position as editor of the *Spectator* is completely incompatible with being a candidate for this party.' With that, she hung up.

Ffion Hague was by her husband's side for almost every minute of the campaign. She was criticised by some for refusing to say anything more expansive than 'I am enjoying the campaign greatly' or 'I am here to support William', but most commentators praised the discreet, dignified, loyal and elegant way she conducted herself. Ffion, a city 'headhunter' by profession, had frequently been urged by Tory aides to play a bigger role as the Tories' 'first lady', but she refused. Like Portillo's wife Carolyn, coincidentally also a 'headhunter', she objected to being treated as an appendage of her husband.

Tory advisers saw Ffion as a way of providing Hague with a much needed injection of glamour, but Ffion argued that the moment she did one interview she would be regarded as fair game: one word out of place and she would get the same treatment meted out to the Duke of Edinburgh. By and large, the Trappist approach had worked for Cherie Blair. Although Cherie had a higher public profile, largely due to her prominence as a lawyer, she did not give interviews to newspapers and magazines, though her husband's public relations were so slick that unlike Hague, he hardly needed any help from his wife.

Ffion's resistance to being dragged into the limelight was observed by filmmaker Charlotte Metcalfe, who made a fly-on-the-wall documentary for Channel 4 entitled *Just William . . . and Ffion*, broadcast in September 2000.

> Unlike William, Ffion is thin skinned, shy and sensitive. She was excruciatingly uncomfortable whenever I turned the camera on her and continued to insist the film was about her husband and not about her. She was easy to offend. We were due to film a scene of her dressing to go to the Blue Ball and our assistant producer telephoned Ffion's office to confirm the address. Within a few hours I received an angry e-mail from Central Office requesting that I dealt with Ffion in person. Meanwhile, Ffion left me a frosty message saying we had caused unwelcome confusion at her office and would no longer be able to film that evening. A shopping sequence I was due to film with her was cancelled as she could not see why it was necessary.[2]

Hague's wife had good reason to be wary. Platell's ill-conceived attempt to promote her with the 'Save The Pound' pendant had backfired, and when the two women sat down in private together to produce 'Project Hague', a list of ideas to improve her husband's image, it was maliciously leaked by an enemy in Central Office.

Cynics in Smith Square said the thinking behind encouraging Ffion to be more prominent was similar to the logic they claimed was behind the appointment of Coe and Platell as his two most senior and visible personal aides. With an Olympian on one side of him, a brunette in the background and a blonde on his arm, some of the surrounding glamour must rub off on the funny looking bald bloke in the middle.

Hague's strategy in the four-week election campaign was a like a tape-recorded version of the party's struggles over the previous year – with the fast forward button pressed down. Portillo, Maude and Norman had constantly urged him to tone down his approach on the issues he felt had worked best for him and with which he felt most comfortable: Europe, asylum and tax. But Hague spent most of the first half of the campaign concentrating on precisely those three issues, prompting sharp disagreements with the trio, occasionally supported by the fourth 'mod' in the Strategy Group, manifesto author David Willetts.

The tension was exacerbated by Hague's decision, kept secret from the other three men, to allow Lady Thatcher to get involved in the campaign. She too banged the jungle drums on Europe.

For more than a year, Hague had planned to make the 'Save The Pound' pledge his clarion call in the last stages of the election. Portillo and his allies argued against him, but the Conservative leader, supported by Lansley and Collins, would not back down. After claiming that the polls showed Hague's tactics weren't working, Hague's Tory foes ganged up on him to insist that he change tack, claiming that Tory candidates were complaining that voters wanted to hear less about Europe and more about the party's plans for health and education. The criticism of Hague's decision to make the election a referendum on the single currency was later echoed by Dominic Cummings, campaign director of Business For Sterling, the leading anti-euro organisation. 'The British people and British business long ago decided that they would not cast their vote on the basis of their hostility to the euro and the election has not changed their minds,' said Mr Cummings.3

There is little doubt that the style and content of Hague's campaign changed in the last ten days of the campaign.

On 18 May, it was a bullish Hague who put asylum at the heart of his election message in a provocative visit to Dover accompanied by Ann Widdecombe. Their aim was to draw attention to the ever growing queues of asylum seekers trying to get into Britain. Hague said Britain was the 'asylum capital of Europe' and blamed the Government for the death of fifty-eight Chinese illegal immigrants who had suffocated in a lorry in Dover the previous year. He promised a new law to ensure that any asylum seeker who had come to Britain via a 'safe' country such as France could be detained and sent back immediately, and received enthusiastic support from Widdecombe, who said the Conservatives would introduce a 'meet the plane' scheme whereby immigration officers would target suspect aircraft from countries such as India.

Hague's concern not to offend Portillo, who deplored the leader's approach to the subject, was embarrassingly obvious. He stressed how Portillo's Spanish father Luis was the type of immigrant who would still be let in.

Two days before the Dover visit, a Conservative election television broadcast used shock tactics to attack Labour's law and order record. In one of the most violent party political films ever shown on British TV, three gangsters were shown being let out of prison before they have served their full sentence, only to commit terrible crimes – which are portrayed in gory detail.

But it was not only Labour who criticised Hague for using such provocative tactics. The 'mods' in the Shadow Cabinet were annoyed too and complained. And on 1 June, Hague struck a different tone. He used a visit to Bradford, which has one of the largest ethnic communities in Britain, as a showcase for his pro-ethnic credentials. His appearance did not have the *élan* of Portillo's jacketless walkabout in Brick Lane, but Hague had the same message to deliver: 'inclusivity' – Portillo's favourite buzz word.

The Little Englander Hague of Dover had become the One Nation Hague of Bradford. 'It has never mattered to me whether people are Muslim, Christian, Hindu, Sikh, Jewish, white, black or Asian,' he said. 'As far as I am concerned, we are all as British as each other. The Conservative commitment to One Nation means that we will govern for all the people of Britain.'

He unveiled new initiatives to improve state schools and the NHS; plans to improve inner cities by demolishing run down tower blocks; more power to enable charities and private companies to transform failing schools; and installing police desks in local shops.

Hague made a speech far removed from his 'foreign land' speech in nearby mainly white Harrogate a few weeks earlier. 'I believe in a Britain where intolerance, bigotry and racism are rooted out and replaced by a genuine openness, genuine inclusivity and genuine tolerance,' he said. 'I want a society that can celebrate its diversity and pluralism.' It could have been scripted by Portillo.

He was not only seeking to clasp ethnic minorities to his bosom; he wanted non-Tory Eurosceptics to join his 'Save The Pound' crusade: 'There are many decent, patriotic people who are not natural Conservatives, but who are just as concerned as we are about preserving our self-government,' said Hague. 'I am appealing to those people.'

He denied any change of tactics. 'We will continue to campaign very strongly on the euro over the remaining days of the campaign, but we will also continue to bring out the whole lot of issues that we have campaigned on – tax, crime, education and health.'

It was absurd to imagine that years of deep unpopularity were going to be changed by a few warm words in the final moments of the campaign, and the tactics preoccupying most senior Tories had nothing to do with the general election, but with the leadership election which they all knew would commence the moment the vote had been counted.

As Hague braced himself for the defeat, he gave the clearest possible hint that he knew he would not be in the job much longer. Interviewed on *Breakfast With Frost* on Sunday 3 June, he said he would 'take the blame' for any failure. 'I take my responsibility for whatever the outcome,' he said, knowing full well that within five days he would be resigning as leader. In his last election speech on the eve of polling day he made a final appeal to the 'decent, down-to-earth' people – farmers, teachers, police, doctors, and small businessmen who had returned Margaret Thatcher to Downing Street three times in a row – to do the same for him.

Hague's bedraggled forces of Conservatism were soundly beaten. The Tories won only one more seat than in 1997, and Tony Blair was swept back into Downing Street. Hague was true to his word: the moment the landslide was clear, he fell on his sword and made no attempt to shift the blame.

There is little question that his inability to convince people he was a credible alternative Prime Minister to Tony Blair was the single biggest reason for his failure to mount a stronger election challenge. As Iain Duncan Smith pointed out in the subsequent leadership contest, Hague never recovered from fatal errors in his first few months as leader: in particular, his ill-judged response to the death of Princess Diana, and that baseball cap. But this did not mean that there weren't plenty of others he could blame for making things worse.

His four years as leader were defined by a continuous behind-the-scenes struggle over the direction of the party, a struggle which intensified when Portillo joined the Shadow Cabinet in February 2000. The likelihood of the two men forming a successful partnership was never great. Few political egos are as immense as that of Portillo, a man who walks into a room and knows, indeed expects, that heads will turn. And they do. No one had ever called William Hague a man of destiny.

Indeed, he would not have dreamed of standing for the leadership had not Portillo lost his seat in 1997, because they both knew that Portillo would have won. Hague would have happily served as his Shadow Chancellor – and would have made a better job of it than Portillo did for Hague. Even when Portillo was missing from the leadership line-up, Hague only stood at the last minute. A few hours after sealing with a toast of champagne his promise to run as deputy to Michael Howard, Hague changed his mind after Alan Duncan talked him into it. One of Hague's most loyal allies said: 'William has no ego. The only reason he stood in

1997 was because he thought he had a better chance of stopping Ken Clarke than had Michael Howard.'

The view of many Conservatives towards Hague's leadership credentials are reflected by the entry in former Tory MP Gyles Brandreth's diary for 4 March 1997, when Hague's name was first mentioned as an outside bet to replace Major.

Brandreth, no enemy of Hague's, wrote of tea room talk: 'Hague – "please, you can't be serious!"'4 Three months later, with Portillo removed from the equation, it did get serious. Hague was leader.

Even Margaret Thatcher had never been wholly enthusiastic about him. Her support for him in the 1997 leadership contest was belated in the extreme, and in her view he had still to improve on his performance in front of her at the 1977 party conference. It was only when John Whittingdale phoned to tell her that John Redwood had teamed up with Clarke for the last round of the 1997 contest against Hague, giving pro-European Clarke a good chance of victory, that Thatcher swung her handbag for him. 'Right, I'm coming down,' she said, and within fifteen minutes was touring the Tory tables in the Commons tea room. 'I'm for Hague. What about you? He's excellent, isn't he?'5

Perhaps it is not so surprising that a man who had devoted his entire life to politics, and yet only weeks away from his election as leader did not see the position as his by right, did not have a clear view as to what to do when he got there. Hague, for ever the schoolboy in short trousers, tried to be a grown up politician. He knew he had to widen the Tories' – and his own – woefully narrow base, but it needed more than baseball caps, cocktails at the Notting Hill carnival and a botched attempt to break the umbilical cord with Thatcherism. And when people reacted by throwing his HAGUE baseball cap in the water flume and tipping the daquiri over his head, he went back to mummy.

If people would not accept Hague Lite, a progressive, modern, outward looking Tory leader; he would offer them Classic Hague, bashing asylum seekers, Brussels bureaucrats and criminals. It was the same formula that had won him an ovation in Blackpool nearly a quarter of a century ago, and, combined with the dazzling debating skills that Blair could never match and a revamped publicity machine, it won him another ovation from party activists and supporters in Fleet Street. But the applause from Portillo, Maude and Norman inside the Shadow Cabinet, and Clarke, Heseltine and Patten outside it, was less than deafening. They believed that simply because he had failed to make a success of a new agenda for the Tories, that was no excuse for taking them back to the past. Nor were they prepared to give up without a fight.

Hague struggled constantly to restrain the power of Portillo. He invited him to sit at his top table, while purging the Portillistas from his HQ, thinking this would contain him. It did not. Portillo's political commandos continued their guerrilla tactics from the bush. And once camped inside the general's tent, Portillo found other dissident officers ready and willing to join the mutiny. Hague retreated into a bunker, with his Praetorian Guard of Coe, Platell, Wood, Collins and Lansley. It was similar to the tiny cell that had engineered Blair's New Labour revolution: Blair, Campbell, Mandelson, pollster Philip Gould and Anji Hunter. They too had had to harness the awesome power of their party's frustrated egotistical man of destiny: Gordon Brown.

But unlike 'Team Blair', 'Team Hague' failed badly.

Eighteen years of Conservative rule which had seen Britain transformed from a country mired in debt, union tyranny and inefficiency to the dawn of low unemployment, low inflation and economic dynamism was remembered chiefly for the chaos of Black Wednesday, sleaze, anti-Europe fanaticism and vicious infighting.

In addition, Labour had finally found its JFK. Hague started out trying to be a Tory Blair. But it was Blair without the smile, the hair, the guitar and four kids, a man designed for the televisual age of politics. It was a hopeless task.

It would have taken a giant political figure to overcome all that, and William Hague was no giant. His quick wit and palpable decency were never going to be enough to compensate for his lack of glamour, his party's baggage and the constant drip of poison.

Hague may feel that if only he had received more support from some of those around him, he might not have gone down in history as the first

Tory leader in nearly a century not to become Prime Minister. Another dozen or so seats could have been enough for him to survive.

Portillo may feel that if only Hague had listened to him, the Tories would not have suffered such a fate. But it is highly unlikely that any strategy, any policy, any soundbite or any image makeover – or any other Tory leader – would have made much difference.

Four days after the general election, Nicholas Soames, whose grandfather Winston Churchill had suffered a landslide defeat in 1945, said: 'People looked at the Tory party with their tongues hanging out. All in all, we looked like a thoroughly unpleasant bunch.'[6]

18 Anyone but Portillo

'No one likes me. Matthew Parris can't stand me, the Sun *hates me, I seem to unite people against me in antagonism.'*
Michael Portillo, May 2001.

Ann Widdecombe could hardly contain her glee. Michael Portillo had just been knocked out of the Tory leadership contest by one vote. As she was leaving the Commons, Widdecombe espied one of her Shadow Cabinet colleagues who, despite his long-standing dislike of Portillo, had backed him because he thought he was going to win. 'You sold your soul for a mess of potage,' Widdecombe told him. He ignored her and traipsed off into the night.

On the same night two men sat inside 10 Barton Street, Westminster, the four-storey Georgian house with its own chapel that was the campaign headquarters of the Portillo team. One was inconsolable, completely shattered by the defeat; the other seemed merely disappointed.

Francis Maude, Portillo's campaign manager, took the defeat much worse than the candidate himself.

'I'm sorry, I didn't deliver it for you,' said Maude.

'It's all right. Don't blame yourself,' shrugged Portillo.

Portillo acted more like a man who had had a burden lifted from his shoulders than one who was broken. For some time, doubts had been growing in his mind as to whether he still wanted to be leader. It came as a shock to his devoted band of followers who could not believe that at the very moment when the crown was his for the taking, he no longer had the will to seize it.

Early in May, shortly before Parliament was dissolved for the general election campaign, one of Portillo's closest friends said to him: 'We are going to get thrashed in the election and William will go. Are you going to stand? This is your moment: you know that, don't you? The hand of destiny is going to touch you on the shoulder.' Portillo laughed, recognising the ironic reference to Blair's remark after the Good Friday Agreement in Ulster, and repeated the full quote: 'This is not a time for soundbites. I feel the hand of history on my shoulder.'

But his expression was more sombre as he expressed his deeper feelings. 'No one likes me. Matthew Parris can't stand me, the *Sun* hates me. I seem to unite people against me in antagonism.'[1] *Times* columnist Parris had sharpened his quill on Portillo, but there were few MPs whose egos had not been pricked by such arrows. Hague had had to live with the *Sun*'s dead parrot. Redwood was saddled with Parris's cruel 'Vulcan' taunt.

'I don't know . . . Perhaps we need someone completely fresh, someone with no baggage, someone like James Mawdsley,' mused Portillo. Mawdsley, a former public schoolboy, had spent fourteen months in a Burmese jail protesting about the abuse of human rights. On his release, he made no secret of his Conservative sympathies and said he would like to help them return to power. His image as a brave, young, principled political activist is as far as you could get from the image of the Tories as the party of sleaze, old age, self-interest and self-hate. Portillo recognised that it was only someone such as Mawdsley, who had not the remotest link with the Conservatives' past, who could provide them with a future. His remark bore testimony to all the doubts that swirled around in his head on his 'journey'. While those around him became more convinced he should be leader, he himself grew less so.

When Portillo flew to Morocco hours after Hague's defeat, most assumed that confirmation that he would stand as leader was a formality. His friends had no such faith. Maude called a fellow member of the Shadow Cabinet and said: 'We have got to get hold of Michael and convince him to stand.'

Maude, Archie Norman, Nicholas Soames and Stephen Dorrell all phoned Portillo in Morocco, urging him to put his name forward. Dorrell told him: 'You must become leader or else we might as well all pack up and go home. Only you realise the scale of what needs to be done, and only you are positioned to draw support from the left and right of the party.'

Portillo was still uncertain. He wanted to consult one more friend before deciding. When he arrived back in Britain on Sunday afternoon, he went straight to Chadacre House, near Bury St Edmunds in Suffolk, home of millionaire property dealer David Hart. This surprised some of his friends and was another indication of Portillo's refusal to compromise. The exotic and unconventional Hart is a shadowy right-wing figure on the fringe of politics, who had been credited with undermining the NUM in the miners' strike and played a role in Portillo's SAS speech: the sort of figure of whom some politicians would be wary, certainly on the eve of a leadership contest. If Portillo's visit had been known at the time of the contest, it would have only served to reinforce the worries of those who questioned his judgment. They would have feared that a Portillo victory would mean the likes of Hart being closer to power than they should ever be. But Portillo valued Hart as a loyal and trusted friend.

Portillo's loyalty to those who have supported him is one of the keys to his character. 'He is not Anglo-Saxon, he is Castilian,' said one of his closest confidants: 'He feels a passionate loyalty to those who have loved and supported him. If they have been prepared to serve him, then he will always stand by them.' One Tory MP described how, shortly after Portillo arrived at the Commons, he went to hear him address a fringe meeting at his first Tory conference as an MP, and became an admirer. More than fifteen years later Portillo told the MP: 'I will never forget the way you walked to the last hotel on the promenade to hear me speak.' The MP had no idea Portillo even knew he had attended the function. But such loyalty could also be blind.

When Portillo returned to London after meeting Hart, his mind was made up.

The following day, standing in his office beneath a giant portrait of Charles James Fox, Portillo told his campaign team: 'I want to run this almost like a general election campaign. I want to communicate to the party what sort of leader I want to be, and to the country what sort of

Conservative Party I want to lead. There will be no negative campaigning and no obfuscation.'

Although bookmakers had made him strong favourite, there was one way to guarantee victory: by doing a deal with Kenneth Clarke. Speculation about a Portillo–Clarke deal had been circulating for months – and denied by both sides. But less than a week after the election the two men met in secret with the specific aim of exploring the possibility of an agreement to stand on a combined ticket. Clarke once said that John Major had 'stumbled on a pretty good combination' when he and Portillo worked together as Chancellor and Treasury Chief Secretary in 1993.

The meeting in Clarke's House of Commons room was brokered by Stephen Dorrell, who for years had been a close ally of the former Chancellor. Clarke sat in his room waiting for Portillo to arrive. But any chance of an agreement being reached between the two was ended the moment Portillo opened the door.

Clarke had expected him to come alone so they could discuss the highly sensitive matter of the precise terms of the agreement, and in particular which of the two would be leader. But Portillo was not alone. Clarke's irritation at seeing Portillo's campaign manager Francis Maude in tow was nothing to his astonishment and annoyance at seeing Dorrell lined up against him. Until that point, Clarke had believed Dorrell was acting as a neutral intermediary.

He made his displeasure known. 'Ken told them he had been working on the assumption that Stephen was acting as a go-between, not as a member of the Portillo team,' said a source. 'If Dorrell hadn't been there and Michael had gone on his own, there is a high probability that the two of them would have agreed on a deal. Ken likes to deal directly with people, Portillo turning up with a delegation was a mistake.'

In deciding when to announce his candidacy, Portillo was imprisoned by his past. If he dithered, it would provoke comparisons to his fatal delay in 1995. So the Portillo camp decided to make a virtue of their jump start and mount what was, in effect, a coup. They wanted to build up such a head of steam that Portillo would win by acclamation, without the inconvenience of having to count any votes. They already had the support of nearly half the Shadow Cabinet including Maude, Norman, Tim Yeo, David Willetts, Oliver Letwin and Andrew Mackay. Others, sensing that Portillo was heading for a runaway victory, jumped on the bandwagon before they got left behind. The day after Hague's defeat, Shadow Health Secretary Liam Fox, who had clashed repeatedly with Portillo, was asked by a colleague who he would support and replied: 'It's anyone but Portillo.'

A couple of days later, when Fox had declared for Portillo and the same colleague asked him about his *volte face*, he said: 'It's the numbers.' But the Portillo camp's determination to bulldoze its way to victory backfired. Tory MPs were phoned and told: 'It's all over. Michael is obviously going to win. If you don't support him now, you are finished.' In to achieve a quick kill, Portillo made yet more enemies.

Party chairman Michael Ancram entered the contest precisely because of his dislike of Portillo and the tactics used by his supporters: Portillo had phoned Ancram personally to apologise after some overenthusiastic Portillistas started referring to Ancram as 'an old duffer' to try and undermine his campaign (though Ancram himself didn't bother to apologise for having derided Portillo's 'stardust' politics).

David Davis, Chairman of the Commons Public Accounts Committee and another enemy of Portillo, launched his own campaign, though mainly as a way of putting down a marker for a future leadership contest. Davis' campaign was manned by right-wing MPs like Eric Forth who a year or so earlier would have been prepared to lay down and die for Portillo. Now they too had enlisted with the 'anyone but Portillo' brigade.

By contrast, Iain Duncan Smith's campaign set off at a snail's pace. His failure to persuade more than one member of the Shadow Cabinet, Bernard Jenkin, to support him, prompted hoots of derision. How could he possibly be taken seriously as a leadership contender if only one of those who had sat around the Shadow Cabinet table with him and knew his strengths and weaknesses had enough confidence in him to support him? Duncan Smith was undaunted. Unlike Portillo, whose campaign got off to a flying start and nosedived, Duncan Smith spent the first two weeks taxiing on the runway and checking the engine. Kenneth Clarke, meanwhile, jetted off to Vietnam on a week-long mission not for the Tory party but for British American Tobacco, of which he was deputy chairman, leaving his supporters at home frantically ringing round to see if he could muster enough support for one last bid to become leader. When he got back they told him that he could do it.

Under a new and Byzantine system of electing a new leader, a series of ballots of MPs took place to whittle down the field and produce a straight choice of two members, from which pair the 320,000-odd party members in the country would make the final decision. This led to a long drawn out and rancorous contest which stretched over the entire summer. The result was scheduled to be announced on 12 September but was delayed twenty-four hours as a mark of respect to those killed in the devastating terrorist attacks on the USA.

In the first ballot of MPs on 10 July, Michael Portillo led with 49 votes, ten ahead of Duncan Smith on 39 and Clarke on 36. But that ballot had to be re-run two days later as the two backmarkers, Michael Ancram and David Davis, were tied on 21 (a possible outcome which the new rules had not anticipated). Victory appeared tantalisingly close for Portillo, but he knew otherwise. He told his team: 'You keep telling me I am going to win, but I just can't see where the votes are coming from. I talk to these people but I don't get the impression they are going to vote for me.'[2]

'These people' were the MPs Portillo was trying to woo. At a meeting of the Tory 1922 Committee, one of Duncan Smith's leading supporters, right-wing MP Julian Brazier, asked Portillo what he would do about Section 28, the law that bans the promotion of homosexuality in schools. It was a trap. The Duncan Smith camp knew that Portillo was sympathetic to Labour's view that it should be abolished, and Portillo fell headlong in, by indicating he may reconsider the party's position on the issue. It played right into his enemies' hands, allowing them to start scare stories about Portillo and his 'obsession' with side issues like gays.

The Shadow Chancellor was not assisted by his friend and former Cabinet ally Peter Lilley, who chose this moment to publish a pamphlet calling for the legalisation of cannabis. The past connection between them led some to assume, quite wrongly, that Lilley must be giving voice to

Portillo's true feelings on drugs. Portillo scored another own goal when he addressed the Parliamentary Press Gallery on 12 July, the day of the second ballot of MPs. Asked whether, in view of his comments about the laws on cannabis, he was in favour of legalising Ecstasy, he said he hadn't thought about it and sat down. He was asked if he was in favour of gay marriages. He didn't know. Yorkshire Post political editor Brendan Carlin asked him: 'Are you still on a journey, or are you just refuelling?' A senior member of Duncan Smith's team in the audience said later: 'That was the moment when we knew Portillo had blown it. He seemed to be treating the whole thing with contempt and people were making fun of him.'

The frustration spilled over in a crisis meeting of Portillo's advisers back in his Barton Street headquarters. David Lidington said: 'When people think of Portillo, all they think about is Section 28 and drugs.' Fellow Tory MP Richard Spring said: 'For God's sake, these issues are completely peripheral, we have got to close it down.' They never did.

Portillo and the men running his campaign, Maude and Norman, had spent most of the previous eighteen months criticising the way Hague had run the Tory party. Now they were in charge of their own campaign and had a free hand over tactics and strategy – and they made a hash of it.

Nor was it only MPs who were proving resistant to Portillo's charms. From the moment he announced his leadership challenge, his campaign team were receiving hostile feedback when they returned to their constituencies each weekend. Several found themselves under attack from senior local party members, some of whom threatened to resign if he became leader.

'They would say Portillo was devious or slimy or that they didn't trust him and didn't like what he and his people had done to William,' said one MP. 'In some cases, what they really meant was that they didn't like him because they thought he was gay, but the dislike was very deep.'[3] Ann Widdecombe's post-election jibe about 'the little band of backbiters' around Portillo proved as lethal to his leadership hopes as her equally wounding 'something of the night' description of Michael Howard had to his leadership hopes in 1997. Thanet North MP Roger Gale told a colleague: 'I'm doing everything I can to stop Portillo because I can't stand him. I think he's dreadful and my association think he's dreadful too.'4 There were complaints that Portillo was 'detached'. Some MPs who had asked to see him to help them make up their minds were still waiting for a meeting after he had been knocked out in the third ballot.

The second ballot of MPs on 12 July, when Portillo's vote went up by just one while Duncan Smith and Clarke each increased theirs by three, was ominous for Portillo; he had lost momentum. He had five days to win over a handful of the thirty-five MPs who had voted for Ancram and Davis, who had now dropped out, enough to get him through to the ballot of party members.

But an act of wild recklessness, by those far more desperate to make him leader than Portillo was himself, sealed his fate. Margaret Thatcher's last-minute backing had helped Hague become leader. Now Portillo's supporters invoked her name in an attempt to wrest enough votes away from his fast-gaining right-wing rival Iain Duncan Smith. Forty-eight hours before the third ballot of MPs, the *Sunday Telegraph*, one of Portillo's strongest allies in Fleet Street, declared that Lady Thatcher supported Portillo over Duncan Smith. The paper reported that she had told her friends: 'I don't think Iain's got sufficient experience. I think Michael is the best candidate. He's the man with the charisma, with the Cabinet level experience, and he has been very loyal to me. She thinks Iain's a good man. But she believes he does not have the experience. Remember, she is at bottom a great political realist who recognises that depth and experience must be the deciding factors.'5

The report came as a surprise to most who knew Thatcher. It was well known that she believed Portillo had 'lost his way' since his conversion to 'touchy-feely' Conservatism, which was anathema to her. If anything, she was closer to Duncan Smith, who was still proud to call himself a Thatcherite, and she had been deeply hurt during the election campaign when she discovered that Portillo had urged Hague to disown her at the election rally in Plymouth because of remarks she had made about a multicultural society. From the moment Hague resigned, she decided not to support any leadership candidate, unless and until it came down to a straight fight between Clarke and a right-winger. In that event, Thatcher would support the right-winger – which is precisely what she did when she endorsed Iain Duncan Smith in August.

Instead of scuppering the Duncan Smith bid, the *Sunday Telegraph* report hammered the last nail into Portillo's coffin. It is not clear how the information had reached the paper. Some believed the story originated from her having wished Portillo well and thanked him for his loyalty when he announced his candidacy, but this was before Duncan Smith threw his hat into the ring and was not meant to be an endorsement. Others believed it came from remarks by Thatcher's former Downing Street adviser Charles Powell at a BBC party in the Atrium restaurant at Westminster in June – remarks that had reached *Sunday Telegraph* deputy editor Matthew D'Ancona, one of Portillo's most fervent media admirers, via Francis Maude.

Thatcher was furious when she heard of the *Sunday Telegraph* report and took the highly unusual step of issuing a statement to denounce it. 'I do not hold the views it attributes to me and I am not backing Michael Portillo against Iain Duncan Smith,' she insisted. One of her advisers said: 'I have never seen her so cross since she left Downing Street.' It was a curious replay of a remarkably similar episode involving Portillo and the *Sunday Telegraph* in 1995, shortly before John Major, fed up with rumours of a leadership threat, resigned and challenged his critics to put up or shut up. 'Late in April,' according to Kenneth Clarke's biographer, Andy McSmith, 'anonymous Portillo supporters briefed the *Sunday Telegraph* that their man had the backing of 100 Tory MPs and was capable of pushing Kenneth Clarke into third place.'[6]

Even more extraordinarily, the claim made during the 2001 leadership contest that Portillo had the support of 100 Tory MPs had been made in 1995: his campaign team were using the same tactics that had failed him in the past.

Portillo suffered another blow when Amanda Platell's video diaries, a secretly filmed account of the election campaign, were broadcast on Channel 4 television on the same Sunday. The film was a blatant breach of trust by Platell and its timing was clearly designed to inflict maximum damage to Portillo's chances. But her allegation that he and his supporters had briefed against Hague reinforced what Widdecombe had said a month earlier, and what others had been saying for years.

Tory MP Alan Duncan, a member of Portillo's campaign team, said: 'Michael's campaign was very badly run. It had to be crafted carefully to appeal first to MPs, then to party members and then to the public. It had to be a phased process. Instead it was an in-your-face campaign from day one. Lilley's intervention was crass and the activities of one or two of his spin doctors was appalling. Electing Michael was always going to be a risk and the party was not prepared to take the risk. He gives some of them the shivers, there is no getting away from it.'

Portillo's diffident conduct during the campaign convinced his friends that he had lost the burning desire to be leader. 'He knew there was a well of hatred towards him, not just from people in his own party but from the public too,' said a Shadow Minister. 'He wanted to change the Tory party, but he knew he could only do that if people were prepared to accept him as he was. He was not prepared to lie about himself or his views. If people accepted him and made him leader, then he would have a mandate to change the party. If they didn't want him, he was equally content to walk away. Unlike many leaders who are prepared to do anything and say anything to win power, Michael wouldn't do it. He didn't want it badly enough to dissemble. It had to be on his terms or not at all.'

At the height of the leadership contest, Portillo was sitting on a plane returning from a day trip to Brussels where he had met Tory Euro MPs. His advisers were busily studying list of MPs names and strategies, plotting how to woo the extra few votes that could make him leader. Back in London, a storm was raging over claims that Portillo had not declared £20,000 paid to him for speaking engagements years ago. Portillo was high in the clouds in another world. He pulled out a large map from his hold-all and spread it across his lap. It was a plan of 'Albertopolis', an ambitious project to link the museums in his Kensington constituency via a network of underground tunnels. He described with pride how he had discussed it with Labour peer and film maker David Puttnam. It seemed so much more rewarding than becoming leader of Her Majesty's Opposition.

His defeat in the third ballot on 17 July, when he finished third, one vote behind Duncan Smith, was a personal tragedy.

Michael Portillo was the natural leader of the Conservative Party: young, brilliant and charismatic, and the one person capable of uniting left and right.

For a decade, his supporters had been plotting to make him leader. His first abortive attempt in 1995 was soiled not so much by Portillo's self doubt as by the premature installation of phone lines by his over-eager backers. He would have won the 1997 leadership contest but for having lost his seat in the election. But while the Prince across the water sailed off on a voyage of self-discovery, the Portillistas stayed at home, devising his passage back to power. They lined up the ripest of plum seats for him in Westminster, before switching to Kensington and Chelsea when Alan Clark died. Elsewhere they beavered away in the Tory backwaters, helping right-wing candidates get selected in safe and target seats so that when they got to the Commons, Portillo's army would be there to lift him into the throne.

The question is: did Portillo know what was going on? There are those who say he knew exactly what some of his fanatical allies were doing on his behalf: witness his challenges to Hague's authority in the Shadow Cabinet and his fierce loyalty to those closest to him who were threatened. Others say he knew nothing, and that it was a by-product of his character. Portillo was more like a cult figure than a political leader, and attracted not political supporters, but cult followers who tend to act in extreme ways. At times, Portillo himself seemed oblivious to the effect he had on others. Shortly before the last decisive ballot of MPs, he mused to a colleague. 'I wonder who William will vote for? Do you know, I think he will vote for me.' He was wrong. Hague voted for Duncan Smith, and had decided to do so long before. Hague's solitary vote would have been enough to save him.

All politicians make enemies. Successful politicians make more enemies than most. But few have made as many as Michael Portillo. For every Portillista who would walk through fire for him, there were two more Tories who would rather see him burn than see him and his 'backbiters' run the party – and the country.

And when the full extent of his transformation became clear, he made yet more enemies. Some of the very people who had kept his flag flying while he was in exile deserted the cause when he returned. Portillo was trying to reach out, but it seemed to some like a leap in the dark. The man who had pioneered the poll tax now wanted to help the poor and oppressed – and the oppressed gay and ethnic minorities. They were not heavily represented in the ranks of the Conservative Party, where the decision on the new leader would be made.

Then some of his former followers looked up and saw another right-wing Conservative. He too had shown a individual streak, but he fought his own battles. He was not surrounded by a band of guerrillas who spent their lives sticking knives into the backs of his rivals. He had none of Portillo's bravura, but he had none of his baggage. He had not served in government, but he had served his country. He was calm, not quixotic. He seemed normal. His views, appearance and prejudices reflected those of his party. Nor did he change his political philosophy every time he went to the wardrobe. The Tory party knew little about Iain Duncan Smith.

It knew too much about Michael Portillo.

19 'Smithy'

'I will campaign on the things that really matter to people, the things that affect them most in their daily lives, obsess them — these are the things that must obsess us.'

Iain Duncan Smith, 13 September 2001

Coming from someone who claims to disapprove of politics by soundbites, it tripped off the tongue very neatly. 'My concern would be if we launch off on pashmina politics, where we wind up adopting the fad just about to go out of fashion.' Iain Duncan Smith's commentary on the Blairite posturings of his right-wing rival Michael Portillo was one of the more memorable observations of the 2001 leadership contest. It encapsulated not just the doubts harboured by many Conservative supporters about Portillo's new brand of politics, with its emphasis on gays and ethnic minorities. It also belittled Portillo personally: his fixation with political fashion, his expensive suits and ever changing hairstyle. If any male politician had the nerve to wear a pashmina, it is Portillo.

The term was coined by Duncan Smith's campaign manager Bernard Jenkin. He was attending a sports day at his son's private school when one of the mothers shouted: 'Where's my pashmina?' They've gone out of fashion already, Jenkin chuckled to himself . . . exactly like Michael Portillo's politics. The description invited people to compare and contrast Portillo with solid, father of four, ex-Scots Guards Captain Iain Duncan Smith. It is easier to imagine him leading a bayonet charge against Indian mutineers in the days of the Raj than wearing an Indian silk scarf. Advertising mogul Maurice Saatchi complimented Jenkin on the pashmina soundbite: 'I wish I'd thought of that.'

With Portillo out of the way, Duncan Smith turned his fire on his one remaining rival Kenneth Clarke, a former Home Secretary, Chancellor,

Health secretary and Education secretary who had been a leading figure in both the Thatcher and the Major governments and made Duncan Smith look like a beginner. Well known for his general bonhomie and love of beer, cigars and jazz, Clarke was highly popular with the public – but unlike Duncan Smith had pro-European views which put him at odds with the majority in his party.

It was Duncan Smith's hostility to Clarke that had made him defect from his former mentor John Redwood during the 1997 leadership contest. Duncan Smith had run Redwood's campaign, but when Redwood teamed up with Clarke in a desperate attempt to defeat Hague, Duncan Smith was appalled and voted for Redwood's enemy Hague. Redwood might be able to work for a man who wanted to abolish the pound, but Duncan Smith could not.

Iain Duncan Smith had arrived in the House of Commons in the final bitter years of the Conservatives' eighteen-year rule under Thatcher and Major. After succeeding Norman Tebbit in Chingford in the 1992 general election, he immediately joined Tory rebels fighting Major over the Maastricht Treaty which created the European Union and paved the way for the abolition of the pound and the transference of more powers from Westminster to Brussels.

Duncan Smith soon made his mark. Gyles Brandreth's diary entry for 21 May 1992 records his 'alarmingly good maiden speech'. Inevitably, the subject was Europe. 'Another anti, broke the rules, did twenty minutes and certainly didn't avoid controversy, but it was undeniably powerful stuff. I do envy these people who feel so passionately about it and seem to have such a firm grasp of detail,' wrote Brandreth. Nine months later, Duncan Smith's growing reputation as a rebel led ambitious contemporaries to shun him. Brandreth's entry on 22 February 1993 describes how a group of Tory MPs met to set up a group of 'thoughtful' members from the 1992 intake:

> We're now six: . . . Stephen [Milligan] wanted to include Iain Duncan Smith ('He's completely wrong on Europe, but he's very bright and he's going a long way'), but David [Willetts] was wary of having a known rebel in our number.[1]

In those days Duncan Smith spent almost as much time at 17 Great College Street, Westminster, headquarters of the Eurosceptic MPs, as he did in the Commons. Initially he was a peripheral figure, watching as Tory MP Bill Cash plotted the next attempt to wreck the Maastricht agreement. Duncan Smith's earnest style led some to joke that he was like Julian in Enid Blyton's Famous Five, but his army leadership skills and quick grasp of complex parliamentary procedures quickly catapulted him to the status of ringleader. These qualities also earned him several invitations for tea at the Belgravia home of Margaret Thatcher, who was beginning to believe that Tebbit's forecast that Duncan Smith was the party's saviour may not have been as exaggerated as she had first thought.

But while Thatcher was impressed by Duncan Smith's bravery, John Major was appalled by his treachery. Duncan Smith was careful not to join the 'Whipless Ones', the eight Tory MPs led by Teresa Gorman who were thrown out of the party for constantly defying the Government, being shrewd enough to realise that such a move could disqualify him for ever from becoming leader of the party. But he stopped only just short. In sixty-two votes on the Maastricht Treaty Bill between November 1992 and May 1993, Duncan Smith voted with the Government just four times, abstaining forty-seven times and voting with Labour eleven times. The Government tried to buy him by offering him the junior post of Private Parliamentary Secretary, a glorified bag carrier. They wanted him to work for deputy Chief Whip Greg Knight, which would have entailed his spying on the very group of Euro-rebels to which he belonged. He rejected the offer. Asked how Major's whips had tried to bully him, Duncan Smith replied: 'They said, "Look in the mirror and you will see your career behind you".' He looked the other way.

Duncan Smith has frequently said that Europe was the reason he came into politics, and it is the subject about which Kenneth Clarke feels most passionately. Clarke is as determined to ensure Britain joins the euro and works more closely with Brussels as Duncan Smith is determined to protect the pound and keep Brussels at arm's length. He has not ruled out leaving the EU altogether.

During the leadership battle Clarke made repeated attacks on Duncan

Smith's Europhobia: 'If we are perceived as obsessed by Europe we will get nowhere.' Clarke dismissed Duncan Smith's challenge, saying most people didn't take him seriously. 'The two people who I suspect they regard as the Prime Minister candidates, who could take on Tony Blair and look like potential Prime Ministers, are Michael Portillo and myself,' he said before the final ballot of MPs.

When he found himself up against Duncan Smith in the final phase of the leadership election, the insults flew thick and fast. Clarke called Duncan Smith's supporters 'headbangers' and said their man was a 'hanger and flogger'. The last statement was undeniable: Duncan Smith had voted in favour of capital punishment and caning. The Clarke camp knew that Duncan Smith's anti-European views gave him a big head start. But they were quietly confident that Clarke's greater experience and popular appeal would tell as the campaign progressed. They believed there was a good chance that Duncan Smith might make mistakes. But their faith in Clarke's reputation as a big hitter proved misplaced when, in their only full-scale television confrontation, Duncan Smith was the more coherent and impressive performer in a BBC2 *Newsnight* debate, while Clarke appeared tetchy.

Duncan Smith duly won Thatcher's endorsement, and she coupled praise for his fight against the Maastricht Treaty with a scathing attack on Clarke. 'It would have been reassuring to hear from Ken Clarke about some mistakes which led the party to the greatest defeat in its history. After all, he – not Iain Duncan Smith – was one of those who made them. Indeed, I simply do not understand how Ken could lead today's Conservative Party to anything other than disaster. He is at odds with the majority of its members on too many issues.'[2]

Her words stung both Major and Clarke into action. Twenty-four hours later Major pointedly refused to say he would be loyal to Duncan Smith if he became leader, and rounded on Thatcher for 'encouraging new young Conservative MPs' like Duncan Smith to undermine his administration. 'During the last Parliament, Iain was one of a number of colleagues who voted night after night with the Labour Party in the Labour lobby with the purpose of defeating the Conservative Government.'

Clarke called Duncan Smith the candidate of the 'hard right': 'Nothing is more likely to turn away young voters from the Conservative Party than the idea that we are going for the kind of agenda that Mrs Thatcher seems determined to force on us now.'

It was the cue for the Tory grandees to weigh in, mainly on Clarke's behalf. 'Those of us who were part of the last government remember very well the divisions created by the Eurosceptics, and Iain Duncan Smith was at the forefront of that divisive process,' said Michael Heseltine. Douglas Hurd, Foreign Secretary when Duncan Smith was trying to sabotage the Maastricht Treaty, was uncharacteristically bellicose. 'Iain Duncan Smith made his reputation by following his own convictions, certainly, but by undermining, in concert with the Labour Party, what we were trying to do in Europe. He can't really call on any automatic loyalty against that background.'

Major was still scarred by Duncan Smith's disloyalty. But Clarke's disloyalty to Hague over Europe, when he appeared with Tony Blair on a pro-euro platform in the autumn of 1999, was much fresher in the minds of the Tory party's predominantly Eurosceptic members.

No sooner had Major and Thatcher left the battleground than Duncan Smith's entire campaign was nearly derailed by an obscure 79-year-old Welsh Tory activist.

The first that Duncan Smith knew about the racist connections of Edgar Griffin, one of the vice presidents of his campaign, was when his spin doctor Mike Penning received a phone call on the afternoon of Thursday 23 August. Was it true, asked the reporter, that Griffin, vice chairman of Montgomeryshire Conservative Association, was also father of British National Party leader Nick Griffin and had admitted he sympathised with the BNP's policies? Remarkably, Edgar Griffin's wife Jean had stood as a BNP candidate against Duncan Smith in his Chingford constituency at the 2001 general election.

Within thirty-five minutes Griffin was expelled from the Duncan Smith team, but the affair did not deter Tory enemies from seizing on the incident. 'Iain's problem is that however nicely he says it, his message attracts precisely these sorts of people,' said Steve Norris.

Duncan Smith tried to repair the damage a few days later, telling Asian leaders in Acton, west London, that he had always been 'unwaveringly opposed to the evil of racism'. Conscious that he was being painted as a right-wing extremist, he turned towards the centre. 'I am by instinct, a One Nation Tory,' he said. 'By that I do not mean what that enduring Conservative phrase is sometimes taken to mean: dousing our social problems with public money alone and burying our identity in a federal Europe. I mean something that is neither left nor right nor centre: bringing people together.'

The right-wing background of a large section of Duncan Smith's leading supporters alarmed some of his Conservative opponents. Nicholas Soames referred to them as 'swivel eyed *****'. Many, like Bill Cash, share Duncan Smith's obsession with Europe, and they include more than a smattering of ex-servicemen, including Penning and Julian Brazier. Several, like Romford MP Andrew Rosindell, have had links with the far-right Monday Club. 'Mr Duncan Smith is not merely to the right of Mr Hague,' wrote one pundit, 'he is miles to the right of him. His dedicated admirers among Tory MPs are the sort of individuals who, if they had not somehow been propelled into political life, would be deemed as being among the worst examples of the failure of care in the community.'[3]

Duncan Smith brushed aside the right-wing label. 'Whenever I'm asked about this so called concept of right wing and left wing I just don't understand it.' But he demonstrated his eagerness to break with the past when, only a week after she had endorsed him, he politely asked Thatcher not to attend the party conference in Blackpool to prevent her overshadowing his coronation. She agreed. He took another left turn in a newspaper interview when the thorny issues of Section 28 and drugs were raised. This time there was a distinctly silky feel to the man who barely six weeks earlier had mocked Portillo's 'pashmina politics': 'We have become identified with what we dislike and hate, rather than the things we like. Section 28, I accept, has about it a totem which is about saying to a group in the community: "We actually rather dislike you." That is a problem and a party like ours has to think how to resolve that.'

The Tory drugs policy was up for grabs too. 'I think we have to look at all this.'4

It must have brought a smile to Portillo's face. He had tried to stop Thatcher getting involved in the election campaign and floated the idea of changing the law on drugs and Section 28 - and was pilloried by the very people who now backed Duncan Smith.

There were some who were less than convinced by Duncan Smith's liberal leaning. Hywel Williams, former aide to John Redwood, claimed Duncan Smith was responsible for attempts to smear Hague as gay during the 1997 leadership campaign. Williams said Duncan Smith referred to Hague's team as 'the bachelor boys' and claimed Redwood had been forced to rebuke him. Duncan Smith's spokesman has dismissed the claim as 'fiction'.

Inspite of his victory, Duncan Smith's critics have no intention of giving up the fight for the heart of the party. Three weeks after Portillo's defeat, Francis Maude and Archie Norman announced plans for a new Conservative policy forum whose aim will be to change the way the party 'thinks, sounds and behaves'. The group will be separate from Conservative headquarters but 'firmly rooted' within the party. 'We need to change the way we think, the way we sound and the way we behave,' said Maude. 'Patch and repair will not do it. We need a new tone of voice, less partisan, more measured and more appreciative of the good things about our country.' Maude said the Tories risk coming third in the next election because no one seemed ready to make the kind of changes necessary to win back public support. The forum's backers reads like a roll call of the Portillo campaign team: Tim Yeo, Andrew Mackay, Nicholas Soames, Nick Gibb, Damian Green and Julie Kirkbride. Maude denied it was an attempt to keep Portillo's leadership hopes alive or to destabilise the new leader, but it is hard to see it not becoming a focal point for the Portillistas.

Further signs of dissent came from Steve Norris, who refused to promise to stay in the Tory party if Duncan Smith won. Put to him that it was his democratic duty to accept the result, he replied: 'Goodness, no. My democratic right is to look across all the parties and see which of them

most reflects the views I hold.' The possibility of more high-profile defections – following in the footsteps of former Tory MPs Peter Thurnham,
Peter Temple-Morris, Alan Howarth and Shaun Woodward who switched
to Labour; and Emma Nicholson, who joined the Liberal Democrats –
will give Duncan Smith nightmares.

The Tory party was not alone in being uncertain about its future. The
Eurosceptic *Daily Mail* backed pro-European Clarke. The Labour-
supporting *Sun* threw its weight behind 'Smithy', as it christened Duncan
Smith – the same nickname given to his war hero father. (Tory MPs refer
to him as 'IDS'.

He has been called 'Hague Mark II' or 'Hague without the jokes'. But
week by week, as the leadership campaign progressed, his family history
emerged, adding more than a few flashes of colour to his grey image.

Duncan Smith is one-eighth Japanese on his mother's side, following
the marriage in 1880 of his Irish great-grandfather Leonard 'Leo' Shaw, a
steamship captain for the King of Siam, to Ellen Oshley, daughter of a
Japanese artist who came from an ancient samurai family. The couple had
eight children and lived just outside the forbidden city of old Peking. Leo
was a distant relative of the playwright Bernard Shaw. One of the couple's
daughters, Cecilia, Duncan Smith's grandmother, was sent to convent
school in Shanghai and later worked as a governess in Fuzhou, where she
met her husband, Melton Summers, who had come to China to improve
the postal system. Duncan Smith's mother Pamela sailed to England in
1928, where she became a ballet dancer. His father, Group Captain Wilfred
'Smithy' Duncan Smith was one of the RAF's most decorated heroes in
the Second World War. The Spitfire ace brought down nineteen enemy
aircraft and was awarded a DSO and bar and the DFC and two bars.
'Smithy' senior and Pamela met in Italy towards the end of the war when
she was on tour with the Anglo–Polish ballet company and fell in love
when they bumped into each other at a pub in London a year later.

Duncan Smith had a traditional officer's son's education, attending
HMS Conway School in North Wales, where the emphasis was on discipline and sport rather than intellectual skills. He shone on the rugby field,
where he played alongside Clive Woodward, who went on to coach the

England rugby team and remains a friend. Duncan Smith left HMS Conway with eight 'O' levels and three 'A' levels and spent a year studying in Perugia, where he continued his parents' love affair with Italy but seems to have spent most of it playing rugby and having a good time. He returned to Britain to go to Sandhurst and was commissioned into the Scots Guards in 1975 before being posted to Ulster during one of its most violent periods, then became ADC to Major-General Sir John Acland when Acland was appointed commander of the Commonwealth Monitoring Forces in Rhodesia/Zimbabwe during the transition from white to black rule. 'We got on extremely well. He is pleasant. He has got a sense of humour. He is a genuine patriot. He has got high personal standards and he was an excellent ADC,' said Acland.[5]

Duncan Smith never saw full army combat, and left the service a year before the Scots Guards were sent to the Falklands, where they were involved in some of the heaviest fighting including the battle to gain Mount Tumbledown. It is a matter of conjecture what effect it would have had on his political career had he delayed his departure from the army by another twelve months and had the chance to emulate his father's wartime heroics. A Falklands hero Tory leader versus an electric guitar playing Labour leader – a PR man's dream.

But while Duncan Smith's former comrades were being shot at in the Falklands, he was a sales and marketing manager with GEC Marconi. In 1988 he joined a building company, Bellwinch. Within months the firm was hit by the recession and Duncan Smith spent a short – and salutary – period out of work before joining *Jane's Defence Weekly* and *Jane's Fighting Ships* as a marketing director.

In 1982 he married Betsey, daughter of the fifth Baron of Cottesloe, a former Lord Lieutenant of Buckinghamshire and retired naval commander whose hobbies are listed in Who's Who as 'steam railways, Sherlock Holmes and shooting'. For most of Duncan's Smith's nine years as an MP, Betsey has juggled coping with the couple's four young children and working as her husband's secretary. It was only after a long discussion with her that he committed himself to the leadership contest.

'I've no intention of using my family as a vehicle for my own ambitions.

I don't want to suck my children into politics, it's too brutal, too horrible. Blair overuses them. He uses them almost more than anyone I have ever known. The idea that they appear on the steps when you go on holiday, devalues the process. Blair's people use it to promote him. I hope I never do that.'[6]

But he is well aware of more immediate problems. 'The character of your leadership is set in the first three or four months. That's the lesson we learned from William. He never recovered from that baseball cap and his response to the death of Diana. It's the next three or four months that count. If the wrong colours are applied to my slate, they will be there for ever. I have to be able to show in the first few months that my strengths are the dominant features, so that people will say, "That bloke looks as though he knows where he's going."'[7]

At 5.15 p.m. on Thursday 13 September 2001, Sir Michael Spicer, chairman of the 1922 Committee, announced the final result of the leadership contest:

Iain Duncan Smith 155,933 votes
Kenneth Clarke 100,864 votes

Appendix 1

Chronology

1997

19 June   William Hague elected Tory leader.

1998

6 October   The *Sun* calls Hague a 'Dead Parrot'.

1999

24 March   Amanda Platell appointed Head of Media.

20 April   Peter Lilley's 'Thatcherism U-turn' speech.

6 May   Tories make modest gains in town hall elections.

13 June   Tories make big gains in European Parliament elections.

15 June   Peter Lilley, Michael Howard, Norman Fowler and Gillian Shephard out in Shadow Cabinet reshuffle.

9 September Portillo admits to gay experiences in student days.

4 October   Tories launch 'tax guarantee' in 'Common Sense Revolution' at party conference in Blackpool.

14 October   Maude threatens to resign over 'Save The Pound' launch.

20 November Jeffrey Archer quits as Tory candidate for London mayor.

26 November Michael Portillo elected MP for Kensington and Chelsea.

18 December Shaun Woodward defects to Labour.

2000

January   Disheartened Hague considers resigning.

1 February   Portillo appointed Shadow Chancellor. Archie Norman appointed Shadow Environment spokesman. John Redwood, John Maples sacked.

3 February   Portillo U-turn on Tory opposition to minimum wage and Bank of England independence.

3–8 February Hague refuses to let Portillo employ Robbie Gibb as spin doctor.

	Portillo and Francis Maude threaten to resign unless Hague sacks Platell and Coe. Platell and Coe threaten to resign if Gibb works for Portillo.
15 February	First 'Save The Pound' tour.
18 April	Hague's first major speech on asylum.
26 April	Hague demands more leeway for self-protection for householders after Norfolk farmer Tony Martin's jail sentence for killing burglar.
4 May	Tories gain seats in town hall elections, lose Romsey by-election to Liberal Democrats. Ken Livingstone becomes mayor of London.
14 May	Downing Street memo reveals Blair demands more 'killer facts' to stop Hague winning Commons clashes.
19 May	*Daily Telegraph* hails 'Superman' Hague.
6 June	Hague's first speech attacking 'liberal elite'.
6 July	Portillo threatens to resign unless Hague scraps tax guarantee.
8 August	Hague's 'fourteen pints' boast.
30 August	Hague scraps tax guarantee.
14 September	Fuel blockade. Army called in.
17 September	Tories lead Labour in opinion polls for first time in eight years.
18 September	Portillo ambushed by Shadow Cabinet over cut in petrol tax.
3 October	Portillo reaches out to ethnic minorities and gays in party conference speech.
4 October	Ann Widdecombe announces £100 on-the-spot fines for anyone caught with cannabis.
8 October	Seven Shadow Cabinet Ministers admit taking drugs in the past.
24 October	Portillo and Maude denounced at 'No Turning Back' dining group of MPs.
31 October	Portillo and Maude resign from NTB group.
12 November	Portillo and Maude threaten to resign over leak of NTB dinner row.
29 November	Press report claims fed-up Portillo does not want to be Tory leader.
14 December	Hague attacks Macpherson Report on racism in police and launches fresh attack on 'liberal elite'.
15 December	Portillo tells Hague: 'I am a liberal. And I am a member of the elite.'
17 December	Maude attacks 'poison' in Tory party. Threatens to resign.

2001

4 March	Hague says Blair victory will turn Britain into a 'foreign land'.
28 March	Tory MP John Townend says immigrants have 'undermined Anglo-Saxon society'.
13 April	Reports of a Portillo plot to oust Hague after election.
19 April	Portillo and Hague loyalty pledge in Essex farmyard.
20 April	Portillo refuses to sign Commission for Racial Equality anti-racist pledge.
27 April	Black Tory peer Lord Taylor attacks Hague for not expelling Townend from party.
1 May	Hague forces Townend and Taylor to back down over race row.
8 May	Blair announces election at St Olave's school, south London.
10 May	Tory manifesto launched.
14 May	Shadow Chief Secretary Oliver Letwin's '£20 billion tax cuts' gaffe.
22 May	Margaret Thatcher speech in Plymouth.
29 May	Hague, Portillo and John Major attend Brighton rally.
31 May	Hague warns of Labour landslide.
7 June	Labour wins second election landslide.
8 June	Hague announces he is to stand down as soon as new leader elected.
13 June	Portillo launches leadership bid.
19 June	Duncan Smith launches leadership bid.
10 July	Result of first ballot of MPs: Portillo 49, Duncan Smith 39, Clarke 36, Ancram 21, Davis 21.
12 July	Result of re-run of first ballot of MPs: Portillo 50, Duncan Smith 42, Clarke 39, Davis 18, Ancram 17. Davis and Ancram drop out.
15 July	Margaret Thatcher denies press report claiming she backs Portillo. Amanda Platell accuses Portillo of disloyalty to Hague in TV 'video diary'.
17 July	Result of second ballot of MPs: Clarke 59, Duncan Smith 54, Portillo 53. Portillo, in last place by one vote, drops out. Clarke and Duncan Smith go forward to the ballot of party members.
13 September	Result of ballot of party members: Duncan Smith 155,933 votes, Clarke 100,864 votes, on a turnout of 79 per cent of the membership. Iain Duncan Smith becomes new leader of the Conservative Party.

Appendix 2

The Key Meetings

Strategy Group

Venue: ground floor boardroom at Central Office

Meetings: 10 a.m. Monday (Strategy Group did not meet during general
                    election campaign)

Role: in-depth discussion about what the Tory party stood for

Members: *From February 2000:*

                    William Hague *Leader of the Opposition*

                    Michael Portillo *Shadow Chancellor*

                    Francis Maude *Shadow Foreign Secretary*

                    Ann Widdecombe *Shadow Home Secretary*

                    Michael Ancram *Conservative Party chairman*

                    Archie Norman *Shadow Secretary for the Department of Environment,
                    Transport and the Regions*

                    Andrew Lansley *Shadow Cabinet Office Minister*

                    James Arbuthnot *Chief Whip*

                    Tom Strathclyde *Shadow Leader of the House of Lords*

                    Tim Collins *Conservative Party vice chairman*

                    Rick Nye *Director of Research*

                    Sebastian Coe *Hague's Private Secretary*

                    Added from January 2001:

                    Iain Duncan Smith *Shadow Defence Secretary*

                    David Willetts *Shadow Social Security Secretary* (for manifesto
                    discussions)

Leader's Meeting

Venue: ground floor boardroom at Central Office

Meetings: Monday to Thursday 9 a.m. (8.15 a.m. during general election
                    campaign)

Role: daily review of events

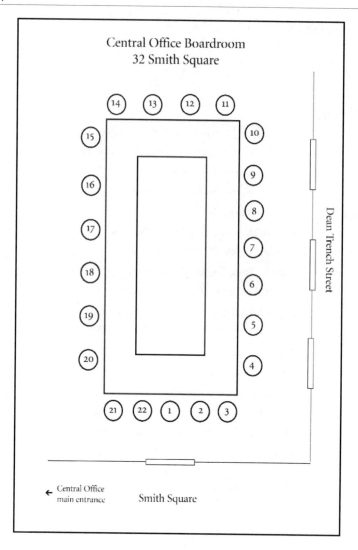

Central Office Boardroom
32 Smith Square

Dean Trench Street

Central Office
main entrance

Smith Square

Members:

1. William Hague

2. Michael Ancram

3. Tina Stowell *Hague's Deputy Private Secretary*

4. Danny Finkelstein *Director of Policy*

5. Archie Norman

6. Andrew Lansley

7. Stephen Gilbert *Director of Field Operations*

8. David Prior *Chief Executive*

9. Tom Strathclyde

10. Nick Gleave *Assistant to Sebastian Coe*

11. Ann Widdecombe

12. Michael Portillo

13. James Arbuthnot

14. Tim Collins

15. Andrew Scadding *Deputy Head of Media (broadcasting)*

16. Rick Nye

17. Amanda Platell *Head of Media*

18. Nick Wood *Deputy Head of Media*

19. Francis Maude

20. George Osborne *Political Secretary*

21. John Whittingdale *Hague's Parliamentary Private Secretary*

22. Sebastian Coe

(during election, Ffion Hague also attended)

'Gang of Four'

Venue:	Hague and Ffion's suite at London's Mandarin Oriental Hotel
Meetings:	every evening except Saturday during general election campaign at 9 p.m.
Role:	key decision-making body of campaign
Members:	William Hague
	Michael Portillo
	Francis Maude
	Michael Ancram
	Andrew Lansley
	(Sebastian Coe also present)

Appendix 3

William Hague's Shadow Cabinet, February 2000

Leader of the Opposition: The Rt Hon William Hague MP

Shadow Secretary of State for Foreign and Commonwealth Affairs: The Rt Hon Francis Maude MP

Shadow Chancellor of the Exchequer: The Rt Hon Michael Portillo MP

Party Chairman: The Rt Hon Michael Ancram QC MP

Shadow Secretary of State for Home Affairs: The Rt Hon Ann Widdecombe MP

Shadow Secretary of State for Trade and Industry: The Rt Hon David Heathcoat-Amory MP

Shadow Secretary of State for Defence: Iain Duncan Smith Esq MP

Shadow Leader of the House of Lords: The Rt Hon The Lord Strathclyde

Shadow Secretary of State for Northern Ireland: The Rt Hon Andrew Mackay MP

Shadow Secretary of State for Health: Dr Liam Fox MP

Shadow Secretary of State for Social Security: David Willetts Esq MP

Shadow Secretary of State for Culture, Media and Sport: Peter Ainsworth Esq MP

Shadow Secretary of State for International Development: Gary Streeter Esq MP

Shadow Minister of Agriculture, Fisheries and Food: Tim Yeo Esq MP

Shadow Leader of the House of Commons and Constitutional Affairs: Mrs Angela Browning MP

Shadow Secretary of State for Education and Employment: Mrs Theresa May MP

Shadow Minister for the Cabinet Office and Policy Renewal: Andrew Lansley Esq CBE MP

Shadow Minister for Transport: The Hon Bernard Jenkin MP

Shadow Chief Secretary to the Treasury: Oliver Letwin Esq MP

Opposition Chief Whip (Commons): The Rt Hon James Arbuthnot MP

Opposition Cheif Whip (Lords): The Lord Henley

Shadow Attorney General: Edward Garnier Esq QC MP

Iain Duncan Smith's Shadow Cabinet, September 2001

Leader of the Opposition: The Rt Hon Iain Duncan Smith MP

Deputy Leader and Shadow Foreign Secretary: The Rt Hon Michael Ancram QC MP

Shadow Chancellor of the Exchequer: The Rt Hon Michael Howard QC MP

Party Chairman: The Rt Hon David Davis MP

Shadow Secretary of State for Home Affairs: Oliver Letwin Esq MP

Shadow Leader of the House of Lords: The Rt Hon The Lord Strathclyde

Shadow Secretary of State for Defence: The Hon Bernard Jenkin MP

Shadow Secretary of State for Work and Pensions: David Willetts Esq MP

Shadow Secretary of State for Health: Dr Liam Fox MP

Shadow Secretary of State for Environment, Food and Rural Affairs: Peter Ainsworth Esq MP

Shadow Leader of the House of Commons: The Rt Hon Eric Forth MP

Shadow Secretary of State for Culture, Media and Sport: Tim Yeo Esq MP

Shadow Secretary of State for Local Government and the Regions: Mrs Theresa May MP

Shadow Secretary of State for Northern Ireland: Quentin Davies Esq MP

Shadow Secretary of State for Trade and Industry: John Whittingdale Esq OBE MP

Shadow Secretary of State for Education and Skills: Damian Green Esq MP

Shadow Chief Secretary to the Treasury: John Bercow Esq MP

Shadow Secretary of State for Scotland: Mrs Jacqui Lait MP

Shadow Secretary of State for Wales: Nigel Evans Esq MP

Shadow Secretary of State for International Development: Mrs Caroline Spelman MP

Shadow Minister for Transport: Eric Pickles Esq MP

Opposition Chief Whip (Commons): The Rt Hon David Maclean MP

Opposition Chief Whip (Lords): The Rt Hon The Lord Cope of Berkeley

Shadow Attorney General: William Cash Esq MP

Shadow Minister for Work: James Clappison Esq MP

Notes

1: 'Where was Jeb Bush when I needed him?'

1. Private information.
2. Private information.
3. *Daily Telegraph*, 13 June 2001.

2: The Spaniard's Return

1. Private information.
2. Private information.
3. Private information.
4. Private information.
5. Private information.
6. Private information.
7. Private information.
8. Private information.
9. *Today*, BBC Radio 4, 10 February 2000.
10. *Sunday Times*, 6 February 2000.
11. Hywel Williams, *Guilty Men* (Aurum Press, 1998), p. 205
12. Private information.
13. *The Times*, 15 February 2000.
14. Private information.
15. Private information.
16. Private information.
17. Private information.
18. Private information.
19. Private information.
20. Private information.
21. *Observer*, 23 January 2000.

3: Taxing Times

1. Peter Riddell, *The Times*, 7 October 2000.

2. Private information.
3. *Guardian*, 4 February 2000.
4. Private information.
5. Private information.
6. Private information.
7. *The Times*, 10 February 2000.
8. Private information.
9. Private information.
10. Private information.
11. Private information.
12. Private information.
13. Private information.
14. Private information.
15. Private information.
16. Private information.
17. Private information.
18. *Daily Telegraph*, 11 July 2000.
19. *The Times*, 30 August 2000.
20. Private information.
21. *Daily Telegraph*, 6 October 2000.

4: Two Tribes

1. Private information.
2. Private information.
3. Private information.
4. Private information.
5. Private information.
6. Private information.
7. Jo-Anne Nadler, *William Hague: In His Own Right* (Politico's, 2000), p. 31.
8. *Daily Telegraph*, 10 February 2000.
9. Private information.

10. *Breakfast With Frost*, BBC Television, 15 August 2001.

11. *Sun*, 6 October 1998.

12. *Sun*, 6 April 2000.

13. Private information.

14. Private information.

15. Private information.

16. *Sunday Times*, 6 February 2000.

17. *The Times*, 17 February 2000.

18. Private information.

19. Private information.

20. Private information.

21. Private information.

22. *The Times*, 26 June 2000

23. Interview with author.

24. Interview with author.

25. Private information.

5: Back from the Brink

1. Private information.

2. *Mail On Sunday*, 2 April 2000.

3. *The Times*, 15 October 1999.

4. Private information.

5. Private information.

6. Private information.

7. *The Times*, 10 October 1997.

8. *Sunday Telegraph*, 30 April 2000.

9. Interview with Mary Riddell, *Daily Mail*, 4 May 2000.

10. Interview with author.

11. Private information.

12. Private information.

13. Private information.

14. Private information.

15. Private information.

16. Andrew Rawnsley, *Servants of the People* (Hamish Hamilton, 2000), p. 370.

17. *Daily Telegraph* editorial, 19 May 2000.

18. *Mail On Sunday*, 14 May 2000.

19. *Sun*, 20 July 2000.

6: Fuel on the Flames

1. Private information.

2. *The Times*, 25 August 2000.

3. *News Of The World*, 17 September 2000.

4. Private information.

5. Private information.

6. Private information.

7. Private information.

8. Trevor Kavanagh, *Sun*, 19 September 2000.

9. *Sun*, 21 September 2000.

10. *Hansard*, 10 April 2000.

11. *Sunday Times*, 22 April 2000.

7: Gone to Pot

1. Private information.

2. Interview with author.

3. A. N. Wilson, London *Evening Standard*, 23 August 1999.

4. Nicholas Kochan, *Ann Widdecombe: Right from the Beginning* (Politico's, 2000), p. 288.

5. Interview with author.

6. Private information.

7. Interview with author.

8. Private information.

9. *The Times*, 4 October 2000.

10. *Daily Express*, 4 October 2000.

11. *Today*, BBC Radio 4, 4 October 2000.

12. Private information.

13. *Daily Telegraph*, 7 October 2000.

14. *Guardian*, 6 October 2000.

15. *Observer*, 8 October 2000.

16. *Mail On Sunday*, 8 October 2000.

17. *Mail On Sunday*, 8 October 2000.

18. Interview with author.

19. *Daily Mail*, 9 October 2000.

20. Interview with author.

21. *Observer*, 1 June 2001.

22. Private information.

23. Private information.

8: The Last Supper

1. *The Times*, 28 October 2000.

2. Private information.

3. *Daily Telegraph*, 29 November 2000.

4. Private information.

5. *The Times*, 28 October 2000.

6. Private information.

7. Private information.

8. *The Times*, 7 November 2000.

9. *Sun*, 29 November 2000.

10. Private information.

11. Private information.

12. Private information.

13. Private information.

14. *The World This Weekend*, BBC Radio 4, 17 December 2000.

15. Private information.

16. In *Just William . . . and Ffion*, Channel 4 Television, 1 October 2000

17. Private information.

18. Private information.

19. Private information.

9: The Liberal Elite

1. *Guardian*, 15 December 2000.

2. Interview with Rachel Sylvester, *Daily Telegraph*, 10 June 2000.

3. Private information.

4. Private information.

5. *Daily Mail*, 15 December 2000.

6. *Sunday Telegraph*, 17 December 2000.

10: Jackets or No Jackets?

1. Private information.

2. Private information.

3. Private information.

4. Private information.

5. Interview with author.

6. Private information.

7. Private information.

8. Private information.

9. Private information.

10. Interview with author.

11. Private information.

12. Private information.

13. Private information.

14. Interview with author.

15. Private information.

16. Interview with author.

17. Private information.

18. Private information.

19. Interview with author.

20. Interview with author.

21. Private information.

22. Private information.

23. Private information.

24. Private information.

25. Private information.

11: Dirty Tricks

1. Private information.

2. Interview with author.

3. Interview with author.

4. Interview with author.

5. Private information.

6. Interview with author.

7. James Landale, *The Times*, 25 November 1999.

8. Interview with author.

9. Interview with author.

10. Interview with author.

11. Interview with author.

12. Interview with author.

13. *The Times*, 28 February 2000.

14. *Sunday Times*, 23 June 1996.

15. *The Times*, 11 May 2000.

16. *Guardian*, 14 March 2000.

17. Interview with author.

18. Interview with author.

12: The Race Card

1. *Daily Mirror*, 5 March 2001.

2. *Sun*, 7 March 2001.

3. *Daily Mirror*, 28 March 2001.

4. *The Times*, 28 March 2001.

5. Private information.

6. *The World at One*, BBC Radio 4, 27 April 2001.

7. Private information.

8. *The Times*, 30 April 2001.

9. Private information.

10. Private information.

11. Private information.

12. Private information.

13. *The Times*, 2 May 2001.

13: Body Language

1. *Daily Mail*, 13 April 2001.

2. *The Times*, 14 April 2001.

3. *Sunday Telegraph*, 15 April 2001.

4. *Daily Telegraph*, 16 April 2001.

5. *Daily Express*, 17 April 2001.

6. *Daily Telegraph*, 17 April 2001.

7. Private information.

8. Private information.

14: They're Off!

1. Private information.

2. Quentin Letts, *Daily Mail*, 9 May 2001.

3. *Independent*, 11 May 2001.

4. Private information.

5. *Financial Times*, 17 May 2001.

6. Private information.

7. Private information.

15: The Mummy Returns

1. *Sunday Times*, 3 October 1999.

2. Private information.

3. Interview with Simon Heffer, *Daily Mail*, 22 May 2001.
4. Private information.
5. Private information.
6. Private information.
7. Private information.

16: Jekyll and Hyde

1. Private information.
2. Private information.
3. Private information.
4. Private information.
5. Private information.
6. Michael Gove, *The Times*, 21 March 2001.
7. Interview with author.
8. Private information.
9. Private information.
10. Interview with author.
11. *Daily Telegraph*, 28 June 2001.
12. *Daily Mirror*, 4 May 2001.

17: Landslide

1. *Guardian*, 2 June 2001.
2. *The Times*, 30 September 2000.
3. *Daily Telegraph*, 7 June 2001.
4. Gyles Brandreth, *Breaking the Code* (Weidenfeld and Nicolson, 1999), p. 472.
5. Private information.
6. Private information.

18: Anyone but Portillo

1. Private information.
2. Private information.
3. Private information.
4. Private information.
5. *Sunday Telegraph*, 15 July 2001.
6. Andy McSmith, *Kenneth Clarke: A Political Biography* (Verso, 1995), p. 242.

19: 'Smithy'

1. Gyles Brandreth, *Breaking the Code*, p. 156.
2. *Daily Telegraph*, 21 August 2001.
3. *The Times*, 26 July 2001.
4. *Sunday Telegraph*, 2 September 2001.
5. *The Times*, 24 August 2001.
6. *Mail On Sunday*, 15 July 2001.
7. *Sunday Telegraph*, 2 September 2001.

Index